10/01

THE STORY OF
PUNISHMENT

PATTERSON SMITH REPRINT SERIES IN
CRIMINOLOGY, LAW ENFORCEMENT, AND SOCIAL PROBLEMS

A listing of publications in the SERIES *will be found at rear of volume*

PUBLICATION NO. 112: PATTERSON SMITH REPRINT SERIES IN
CRIMINOLOGY, LAW ENFORCEMENT, AND SOCIAL PROBLEMS

HARRY ELMER BARNES

THE STORY OF
PUNISHMENT

A RECORD OF MAN'S INHUMANITY TO MAN

SECOND EDITION REVISED

MONTCLAIR, N. J.
PATTERSON SMITH
1972

First edition copyright 1930 by The Stratford Company
Revised edition published by special arrangement with
Harry Elmer Barnes
Copyright ©1972 by
Patterson Smith Publishing Corporation
Montclair, New Jersey 07042

Library of Congress Cataloging in Publication Data

Barnes, Harry Elmer, 1889 – 1968.
  The story of punishment.

  (Patterson Smith reprint series in criminology, law enforcement, and social problems. Publication no. 112)
  Reprint of the 1930 ed., with revisions by the author.
  Includes bibliographies.

  1. Punishment.   2. Prisons.   3. Crime and criminals.   I. Title.

HV8497.B3 1972   364.6   74-108229
ISBN 0-87585-112-6

To

CLARENCE S. DARROW
FOREMOST AMERICAN OPPONENT OF
JURISTIC SAVAGERY

Publisher's Note to the Second Edition

Harry Elmer Barnes first published this work in 1930. In 1966, when the book had long been out of print, Dr. Barnes accepted this publisher's invitation to make it again available in the Patterson Smith Reprint Series in Criminology, Law Enforcement, and Social Problems. He readily agreed to make revisions in the work which would bring up to date the material originally covered, and to add a final chapter on developments in penology in the intervening forty years. His death in 1968 occurred after he had reviewed the entire text, made necessary alterations in the original material, and revised the chapter-end bibliographies. He had not, however, been able to complete the projected epilogue or to make all the numerous small adjustments necessary to express his thoughts in the present tense. The reader will therefore wish to bear in mind that although the body of Dr. Barnes's text is here presented in the form in which it was written in 1930, it reflects in its entirety his views up to the day of his death.

Preface

THE present volume is the outgrowth of a request from the publishers for a concise history of punishment for crime. It is an effort to present a clear, brief story of the methods wherewith society has reacted to what it has regarded as anti-social conduct. It should be borne in mind that the work is in no sense designed to be a systematic manual on criminology. Its major theme embraces only one portion of the crime problem, namely, the efforts made to repress criminal behavior. Theoretical aspects of the crime problem are brought into the story only in so far as they are intimately related to the theory and practice of punishment.

The writer has in no sense aimed to produce a book laden with detail or embodying episodes of purely esoteric interest or curious import. Considerations of practical utility related to the task in hand, rather than concern with pedantic exhibitionism, have governed his selection of material and his distribution of space in the volume. Those who desire vast detail on the subject of modern punishments, particularly in England, together with a wealth of bibliographic detail, have at their disposal the highly useful and competent *History of Penal Methods* by Mr. George Ives. Others who may be in search of arresting anecdotes relating to earlier and brutal forms of punishment can discover what they are seeking in the classic works of Mr. Pike and Mr. Andrews.

The space allotted to the different subjects treated has been determined by the writer's estimate of the importance of the material in dealing with the crime problem at the present time. He has not allowed himself to be led into the temptation to devote elaborate space to descriptions of great personal interest and sensational content, in particular the diversified and ingenious methods of corporal punishment utilized by society down to the beginning of the last century. He has,

therefore, devoted much more attention to imprisonment
than to the earlier practices of corporal punishment and transportation. Descriptions of the latter make, perhaps, more
thrilling reading than discussions of the prison system. Yet
the ancient barbarities have now passed away in large part,
whereas we have to deal directly and immediately with the
prison system and its stupid anachronisms. Nevertheless, the
writer believes that all the essential facts in regard to corporal
punishment and transportation have been adequately presented for the purposes of the present work.

In describing some of the more incredibly brutal aspects
of punishment through the ages, the writer has followed the
practice of quoting liberally from standard books on the
various subjects and eras involved. He has done this primarily
to avoid the charge of having himself concocted a lurid story
for the purpose of increasing the circulation of this book. The
record of society's savagery in repressing crime is sufficiently
incredible without the necessity of exaggeration.

As the author conceives it, the chief value of the present
book is not to be found in the record contained therein of
the past mistakes which society has made in dealing with
crime and the criminal. If the book is to have any real and
permanent significance it will only arise from the fact that a
clear statement of the follies of the past may exert some
influence in forwarding the ultimate realization of a rational,
humane and scientific approach to the whole crime problem.

As Professor James Harvey Robinson has suggested, no
other subject is quite so useful as history in undermining the
prestige which attaches to our various forms of sanctified
savagery and intolerance. There can be little doubt that this
statement holds particularly true with respect to the history
of punishment for crime. There is no field where the remedial
psychotherapy of historical insight should be more immediately effective than with respect to society's bungling efforts
to repress crime. If man is capable of learning anything from
history, the lessons of the futility of past and present methods

of punishing crime are clear enough so that they should be obvious to any person not blinded to fact by class or professional myopia.

In short, the author is even more concerned with the influence which books like the present one may exert upon the future of punishment than he is with the degree to which he may have succeeded in clearly portraying the imbecilities of the past.

I am indebted to my friend and former student, Mr. John Edward Ratigan, for a careful reading of the proofs. Professor George Lincoln Burr of Cornell University has been kind enough to criticize the section dealing with torture.

HARRY ELMER BARNES.

New York City,
    January 12, 1930.

Contents

Preface ix

I. Historic Methods of Ascertaining Guilt . . . 1
   I. Theories of Crime and Punishment as a Phase of Intellectual History
   II. Methods of Ascertaining Guilt in Early Society
   III. Torture as a Method of Ascertaining Guilt
   IV. The Third Degree: the Persistence of Torture in Modern Times
   V. Trial by Jury

II. Crime and Punishment in Early Society . . . 38
   I. Law, Custom and Religion in Primitive Society
   II. Crime in Early Society
   III. Punishment of Crime in Primitive Society
   IV. The Mitigation of the Principle of Blood-Feud
   V. The Growth of Public Control of the Adjustment of Private Wrongs
   VI. Summary

III. Methods of Inflicting Corporal Punishment . . 56
   I. Flogging
   II. Mutilation
   III. Branding
   IV. Stocks and Pillory
   V. Other Sundry Punishments

IV. Transportation as a Method of Punishment . . 68
   I. The British Experience with Transportation
   II. Other Experiments with Transportation

V. The Reform of the Criminal Law (1750-1850) 93
   I. The Intellectual Background of the Reform Movement
   II. Beccaria and His Work

xiii

    III. The Reform of the Criminal Law in England

    IV. The Transformation of the Criminal Code in America (1776-1825)

VI. Prisons: Their Rise and Development . . . 113

    I. The Late Origins of Penal Institutions

    II. The Convict Hulks

    III. The Origins of the Prison System in America

        1. General Historical Background of Penal and Juristic Reform

        2. John Howard and the European Origins of Prison Reform

        3. The Pennsylvania System of Prison Discipline as the Model for Imitation by New York State

    IV. The Beginnings of Prison Reform in New York State and the Origins of the Auburn System

    V. The Struggle Between the Auburn and Pennsylvania Systems

    VI. The Origin and Development of the Elmira Reformatory System

VII. The Nature and Evils of Imprisonment . . . 150

    I. Persistence of Corporal Punishment in Conjunction with Imprisonment.

    II. How Prisons Demoralize the Convict Personality

    III. Prison Discipline and Prison Officers

    IV. Punishment and the Public Mind

    V. The Solution

    VI. The Nuisance of the County Jail

VIII. The Progress of Penology 201

    I. The Development of Differentiation in Institutions for the Treatment of the Criminal Classes

    II. Psychiatry and Crime

    III. The Commutation of Sentence for Good Behavior

    IV. The Indeterminate Sentence and Parole

    V. Inmate Self-Government and Social Re-education

    VI. The Development of Prison Labor

    VII. The Sterilization and Segregation of the Feeble-Minded Classes and the Habitual Criminals

CONTENTS

VIII. Probation and the Non-Institutional Care of Delinquents

IX. Some Desirable Changes in Criminal Jurisprudence

X. Absence of Substantial Improvement in Prison Conditions

IX. Capital Punishment 231

I. Historic Methods of Administering Capital Punishment

II. Capital Punishment in the Light of Scientific Criminology

X. Treatment Versus Punishment 265

I. The New Orientation

II. A Scientific Plan for the Repression of Crime

III. The Psychiatric Approach to the Treatment of Crime

IV. The Outlook

Index 285

THE STORY OF
PUNISHMENT

THE
STORY OF PUNISHMENT

CHAPTER I

Historic Methods of Ascertaining Guilt

I. Theories of Crime and Punishment as a Phase of Intellectual History

THE theories of crime, criminal responsibility and punishment which have held the field in various stages of human evolution have shown a close relation to the prevailing state of cultural development. The first theory which was advanced to explain criminal conduct was the theory of diabolical possession and instigation. This view flourished in primitive and oriental society. When metaphysics developed to the point where it became the dominant type of intellectual orientation and supplanted the theological interpretation of the universe among the Greeks, we find the rise of a new, but related, doctrine of the causation of crime. The individual was represented as a free moral agent who was at perfect liberty to choose between good and evil. One was held to be free to decide whether he would grant the victory to God or the devil; and the criminal had obviously decided in favor of Satan. The free moral agent theory, then, was only a further metaphysical elaboration of the primitive interpretation of diabolical possession.

With the rise of modern biology it was natural that the more advanced thinkers should give up these theological and metaphysical interpretations of the causation of criminal action and come to consider the physical causes of crime. This led the distinguished Italian physician and anthropologist, Cesare Lombroso (1836-1909), to work out a theory of

1

the criminal based entirely upon physical criteria. He held that the typical criminal was characterized by certain definite physical stigmata, such as, among many others, a low and slanting forehead, long ear lobes or none at all, a large jaw with no chin, heavy supra-orbital ridges, either excessive hairiness of the body or an abnormal absence of hair and extreme sensitivity or non-sensitivity to pain. He was brought to these conclusions by an observation of the large number of abnormal physical types in the Italian prisons of his day. He explained the presence of these traits among the criminals on the basis of biological reversion or "atavism." These somatological characteristics of the criminal, Lombroso held, were also the physical traits of primitive man, and he looked upon the criminal as a biological "throwback" to a primitive type.

Though some advanced thinkers of today, such as the late Thomas Mott Osborne, deny almost in toto the accuracy of Lombroso's theory, it would seem that his explanation of the criminal is not without significance. No one who has had any extensive contact with convicts can doubt the prevalence among them of these abnormal physical types which Lombroso so thoroughly described. The chief valid criticism of his theory is that it is not an adequate explanation of the entire criminal class. These physical stigmata which he alleged to be uniquely characteristic of the criminal are found with even greater frequency among the feeble-minded and other defectives than they are among convicted criminals. This means, in other words, that they are associated with degenerate human beings in general, and not with criminals alone. Moreover, Lombroso's theory does not account for the presence of a large number of relatively perfect physical specimens in our prison populations, or for the extensive manifestation of his classic stigmata among law-abiding citizens.

The inadequacy of Lombroso's doctrine led to the proposal of a large number of specific explanations of criminal conduct, chiefly psychological, as, for example, the pressure of physical want, the contagion of crime waves, the morbid suggestions of an unfortunate social environment, insanity and feeble-mindedness. It was obvious that all these interpretations possessed some value, but it was equally apparent that no single explanation was adequate, when taken by itself. We have many criminals who come from wealthy homes, others who commit crimes without any reference to a pattern or suggestion, and many who come from the best cultural groups in the community and who are neither feeble-minded nor insane.

What was needed was some mode of approach to the interpretation of the criminal which would combine in discriminating fashion all these various theories from Lombroso to the present. This was supplied by psychiatry or medical psychology. The advantage of the psychiatric approach is that it is possible for the psychiatrist to take into account all the possible influences operating upon the criminal, inasmuch as they all come to a focus in his mental activities. All good psychiatrists are adequately trained in biology, psychology and sociology, as well as in their own specialty, and are thus men uniquely fitted to investigate and evaluate the various influences which, in any particular case, impel an individual to execute an anti-social act.

The net result of the application of psychiatry to the problem of criminology has been the entire repudiation and elimination, once and for all, of the theological and metaphysical interpretations of criminal conduct and responsibility. It has been shown that a criminal act is absolutely determined for the individual on the basis of his biological heredity, his past and present experiences, or both. There is not the slightest modicum of freedom of choice allowed to either the criminal or the normal citizen in his daily conduct. Further, this modern scientific analysis of criminal conduct proves the absolute absurdity of the old notion that the degree of degradation of the criminal personality can, in any fundamental way, be measured by the nature of the crime.

Modern criminology has shown that the most hideous crimes may be committed by individuals of high intellect, with only slight mental disorders which are readily amenable to treatment, while many feeble-minded potential murderers may commit nothing more serious than petty larceny.

Again, psychiatry has tended to eliminate the element of mystery in regard to criminal activity. To the trained psychiatrist, as we have already intimated, the case of Leopold and Loeb would be as clear and simple to solve as it would have been for the skilful surgeon to diagnose a case of hernia or a facial cancer. A large amount of time was taken up in the courtroom by the circuitous and dilatory procedure required by our archaic criminal jurisprudence, in order that the psychiatrists might expound with formal legal correctness the simple fact that Leopold was suffering from a compulsion-neurosis on a homosexual basis which seemed headed toward a paranoid psychosis, while Loeb was in the initial stages of a dementia-praecox psychosis. Likewise, the famous Los Angeles "Bluebeard," who had murdered his nine wives, was suffering from a compulsion-neurosis created by overcompensation for an inferiority-complex generated by a slight physical defect.

The various doctrines which have prevailed with respect to the desirability and objectives of punishment have borne a very close and immediate relationship to the theories of crime and criminal responsibility. In primitive days, when the theory of diabolical possession dominated, the conventional notion of punishment was either to exorcise the devil or to exile or execute the criminal. In part, this doctrine was based upon the notion of protecting the community group against further outrages by the offending individual, but far more important was the notion of the necessity and the desirability of *placating the gods.*

The next stage in the evolution of the doctrine of punishment appeared when more stress was laid upon the element of *social revenge.* This attitude developed in conjunction with the notion of crime as the wilful act of a free moral agent. Society felt outraged at such an act of voluntary perversity and indignantly retaliated by a savage manifestation of group vengeance. Many forms of crime were identified with sin and were believed also to offer a challenge to God and orthodox religion. It scarcely needs to be pointed out that this theory of punishment is the one which still dominates contemporary criminal jurisprudence, however slightly it may be modified and mitigated by certain incidental innovations.

While revenge was the first important defense of punishment in the period of historical society, there soon developed an associated rationalization, namely, that of *deterrence*. The explanation arose that punishment was not really administered for the sake of social revenge. Rather, punishment had been established so that its infliction might be an impressive example which would deter potential wrong-doers from the commission of similar or worse crimes. Though social revenge is the real psychological basis of punishment today, the apologists for the punitive régime are likely to bring forward in their defense the more lovely and sophisticated argument that punishment deters from crime.

With the development of the biological theory of the criminal, as set forth by Lombroso and others, which was based upon the notion that the criminal represented a degenerate physical type incapable of reformation or notable improvement, the theory of the desirability of incarceration for long terms or for life developed wide popularity. It may be said, indeed, that this theory has been definitely accepted by the most advanced criminologists of today, in so far as it relates to the type of criminal that Lombroso had in mind. This solution was based upon the fundamental objective which dominates contemporary criminal science, namely, the *protection of society* from anti-social individuals.

The historian of crime and punishment must observe that social revenge is the only honest, straightforward and logical justification which can be brought forward in favor of punishing criminals. The claim for deterrence is belied both by history and by logic. History shows that severe punishments have never reduced criminality to any marked degree. For example, in England in 1830 very severe punishments were still administered for even petty crimes. Yet, with a population of some fifteen million, England had a criminal population of about fifty thousand distributed in prisons, prison hulks and penal colonies. In 1885, after the abolition of the brutal criminal code, though England's population had grown to about twenty-seven million, her criminal population numbered only nine thousand. The argument for deterrence cannot even be squared with the doctrine of the free moral agent, upon which the whole notion of punishment is based. If a man is not affected by his experiences it is obvious that he cannot be deterred from crime by the administration of punishment, however severe.

Punishment through imprisonment has never produced adequate social protection. With the exception of life prisoners the convicts are sooner or later returned to society to continue their depredations. Further, they are almost invariably made worse and more bitter criminals as result of their incarceration. Therefore, the net effect of imprisonment is to turn the criminals back upon society more competent and dangerous than they were at the time of their admission to the prison. Least of all can punishment be justified on the ground of its alleged reformative influences. Punishment, as thus far administered, whether by corporal punishment or imprisonment, has never been controlled and applied in such a fashion as to produce any real and widespread reformation on the part of convicts. It has almost invariably made the individual more of a personal and social wreck than before.

Therefore, only the motive of social revenge can be sincerely advanced in behalf of the existence and perpetuation of punishment. Those who retain this attitude towards the criminal are logically justified in arguing for the maintenance of punishment. Those who are unwilling to take such a stand must surrender their whole support of punishment and accept the alternative of scientific treatment of the criminal. Only scientifically conceived and rationally administered treatment can produce the desired results of deterrence, social protection and reformation.

Inasmuch as punishment for crime has inevitably and necessarily followed conviction of guilt, it is both logical and desirable to devote the majority of the first chapter of this work to a consideration of the historical methods of ascertaining guilt, from the primitive ordeal to our contemporary trial by jury.

II. METHODS OF ASCERTAINING GUILT IN EARLY SOCIETY

In the earliest stage of society there were no definite and well-established methods of formally ascertaining the guilt of a person who had committed a crime. It was necessary for him to have been detected in the overt act by the injured person or by a relative or clansman of the latter. Informal information sufficed to initiate proceedings against the accused. Such information would lead either to investigation and punishment of the guilty party by his own kinsmen or would launch a reprisal through blood-feud on the part of the clansmen of the injured. In due time, however, there developed the three classic methods of settling the matter of guilt or innocence in early society, namely, trial by battle, the ordeal, and compurgation.

By the method of settlement through the legal or judicial duel (trial by battle) the injured party or a near relative met the offender, and justice was satisfied by the outcome of the conflict. The gods were believed to give the victory to the innocent party. This was a considerable improvement on blood-feud, since it more strictly individualized the punishment and ended the former indeterminate strife. The duel, however, was by no means a satisfactory solution of the difficulties of blood-feud. If the offender was a great warrior he was likely to be victorious and not only escape unpunished but add to his crimes.

The ordeal thus was somewhat of an advance over the duel in such cases. The principle of the ordeal is based upon a semi-magical, semi-religious conception that the gods will aid the innocent. Therefore, by subjecting a man to torture or the performance of some difficult feat his success will manifest the interest of the gods in his case and their assumed declaration of his innocence. The details of the ordeal such as carrying a piece of hot iron, walking through fire, plunging one's arm in boiling water, running the gauntlet of a shower of spears, etc., are too well-known to call for any extended description. The gods manifested their will and knowledge through the results of the ordeal. If a man's hand healed rapidly after he had carried a hot stone or picked an object out of a pot of scalding water, he was adjudged innocent. If, however, his injured member did not make sufficient progress toward healing in the prescribed time, he was regarded as guilty and dealt with accordingly. As Hobhouse remarks, the theory was not entirely erroneous in either the duel or the ordeal, since one could fight or bear torture with better grace if innocent than if guilty.

The method of compurgation was also widely used and came closer to modern methods than any other. According to the accepted technique of compurgation, the accused person gathered together a group of reputable kinsmen or neighbors known as compurgators. These persons did not, as is so often assumed, swear that they believed the defendant innocent. The defendant swore that he was innocent and then the compurgators took an oath to the effect that they believed the accused was telling the truth in proclaiming his innocence. The number of compurgators was almost invariably twelve after this method came to be adopted by the Christians in the Middle Ages. The number twelve was insisted upon because of its remarkable religious significance in the Old and New Testaments.

Though it consisted in swearing as to the truth of the statement of the accused defendant, still compurgation differed widely from the modern evidence and oath. It was not so much a testimony as to fact as it was a matter of fulfilling the formal requirements of a specific number of compurgators and a certain method of rendering the oath. The clansmen of the parties were obliged to swear for their kinsman though they knew him to be guilty, and, as Hobhouse remarks, it was simply fighting for him with spiritual weapons rather than material. The decision was made according to the conclusiveness of the oaths. If no decision could be reached the ordeal or duel was resorted to or compensation was demanded.

With the appearance of the state and the increasing power of the central authorities we have the establishment of the court of law. It assumed the duty of ascertaining guilt and executing judgment. In the ascertainment of guilt the court retained the old supernatural ideas of the ordeal, duel and compurgation for a considerable time, but as the interest of the public in repressing crime grew stronger it was no longer content to use these methods of a bygone age. As a result, ordeals passed away, being condemned by the Lateran Council of 1215; the duel passed with the ordeal, being forbidden by St. Louis in France in 1260 while in England it might be avoided by appeal to the court. Compurgation became transformed into a testimony concerning the character of the offender. Finally, the old idea of vengeance divided into two parts: (1) criminal justice, which was dispensed by the judge according to the laws of the land and necessitated criminal punishment; and (2) civil cases which simply required restitution for material damages done to the injured party. Trial by jury gradually succeeded the earlier methods employed in the ascertainment of guilt. At this stage the distribution of justice had assumed in a crude manner the conceptions of the present age; and the execution of law had fully passed into the hands of the public authorities.

In the early period of the public control of crime the main zeal was unfortunately more keen for a repression of offences against the public order than for the exact dispensing of justice on fine points of equity. Hence is found the tendency to treat the accused as guilty and to give him grudgingly the partial means of proving his innocence as a privilege rather than as an inherent right. Torture was widely used on the continent of Europe in extorting confession and procuring evidence. Even where torture was not used it was customary to put the defendant at a disadvantage in calling witnesses and using counsel. While these formal inequalities were pretty generally removed in later times, the actual inequality still persists in the superior advantage of the wealthy in the matter of hiring counsel. As Hobhouse aptly remarks, the old trial by battle is still retained in the modern system of dispensing justice, the difference being that the fight is now by purse through the counsel and not by person as in earlier times.

III. Torture as a Method of Ascertaining Guilt

Torture is often regarded as a method of punishing the guilty. It is quite true that many forms of punishment which have been imposed upon those guilty of crime have been painful in the extreme and have literally been a case of torture to those upon whom the punishments were inflicted. In a technical and legal sense, however, torture has been applied, not for the purpose of punishing those already adjudged guilty, but as a device for extracting confessions of guilt or disclosing incriminating information relative to others. Hence, it is necessary to distinguish definitely between the application of torture to bring about confession and the application of cruel punishments after conviction. It was not, of course, unusual in periods like early modern times to employ methods of torture as a means of punishment after conviction, but we are here concerned with torture as a means of ascertaining guilt.

Torture has a long, terrible and bloody history, extending all the way from the savage devices of primitive man to the methods employed by our present-day police departments in applying the so-called "third degree." It is, however, to the credit of primitive man that the earliest forms of torture in no way approached those of historic society with respect to fiendishness of conception or ingenuity of execution. The savage was an amiable and unimaginative creature compared to the oriental potentates or early modern inquisitors. One could readily devote pages to the narration of the horrors of torture throughout historic society, but we shall content ourselves with a brief description of characteristic stages and methods of torture as applied in the criminal jurisprudence of the early modern period.

The period of active torture was usually preceded by imprisonment in a foul dungeon or a small cell. It was particularly common to incarcerate the individual in a cold, damp, vermin-infested dungeon or to put him in a cell so small that he could neither sit, stand nor recline with any comfort. He was ill-fed and was left in this uncomfortable and half-starved condition to contemplate the infinitely worse tortures which he was well aware remained in store for him. If it was winter time he was likely to be half frozen and in the summer he might be half suffocated.

In due time the accused person was brought into the torture room to face his accusers and those in charge of the application of torture. The general setting of the torture room was in keeping with the gruesome nature of the contemplated ceremonies. The officials were usually seated or standing about a long table covered with red cloth, and the room was frequently lighted with red fire. The first stage of torture was, then, primarily psychological and has sometimes been called the stage of *territion*. It was mental torture, produced by uncertainty of the nature of the impending torture, the terrifying nature of the torture chamber and the ominous conduct of the judges. A usual phase of the preliminary period of mental torture was to allow the prospective victim to view at length the various instruments of torture. Sometimes the victim was given a taste of the actual torture to come.

Next began the stages of actual physical torture. This was often initiated by tying the hands of the accused person behind his back and then drawing him up by a rope and pulley —the so-called "strappado." In being pulled up thus by his wrists his shoulders were wrenched from their sockets without leaving any outward mark.

The next stage of torture was most frequently devoted to the process known as stretching on a ladder. The accused person's hands were fastened to the top of the ladder and his feet tied to a pulley. He was then stretched until it was possible to see his visceral organs outlined against a light held behind his back. During this stretching process it was common to drop hot pitch or sulphur on the body of the person being stretched and to burn off the hair under his armpits.

The stretching or other preliminary processes were accompanied by much more painful applications. Thumb-screws were frequently employed. These were instruments whereby pieces of wood were closed down upon the thumb in such a fashion as to crush both the flesh and the bones of the thumb. The "Spanish boots" were a similar device, only that they were applied to the lower leg instead of the thumb. They enabled one to screw the pieces of wood down onto the shins in such a fashion as to crush the shin-bones. The pain was intensified by lining the inside of these pieces of wood with sharp iron spikes which penetrated the flesh before the wooden pieces began the crushing process. The accused was often stripped and drops of water allowed to fall steadily on his bare stomach or back. Again salt water was applied to the soles of the feet and goats allowed to lick them. These devices, while seemingly mild, produced great agony when prolonged. Another practice was that of putting heavy leather boots on the accused and then pouring hot water on the leather. This in due time led to the boiling and disintegration of the flesh of the foot and lower leg. Sometimes the legs were put in metal boots and molten lead poured in to consume flesh and bone.

Another popular form of torture in the fourth stage was what was known in German as the *Schnüre*. In this torture a rope was usually wound around the wrists of the accused and then drawn back and forth by the torturers with a sawing motion, thus cutting and rubbing away the flesh down to the bone. Another type of rope torture consisted in winding a rope about the arm so tightly that the flesh was pressed out between each coil of the rope. To increase the pain the torturer would then beat the arm with a cord or lash. Then the legs and feet were frequently bound tightly and securely together and wooden wedges driven between them with great force.

Common also was the combination of the water torture and strangulation. A piece of damp cloth would be placed upon the tongue and a stream of water allowed to trickle on it. In the process of breathing and swallowing the cloth would be drawn into the throat and produced partial strangulation. The cloth would then be pulled out and the act repeated. Upon being pulled out the cloth would frequently be found to be saturated with blood.

Another device was what was known in England as the "Scavenger's Daughter." In this form of torture—exactly the opposite to the rack in results—the knees were pulled up tightly against the chest and the feet against the hips. They were held in this position by iron bars, the tortured person being, as Wines remarks, "rolled up like a ball." This torture almost invariably forced the tortured person to bleed copiously from the nose and mouth and it very frequently crushed in the ribs and breast bone. Other types of torture resorted to in this fourth stage were such things as forcing on spiked collars, tearing out strips of flesh with pincers, poking the victims with white-hot irons, tearing out the tongue, gagging and choking, which at times tore open the mouth or broke the jaw-bones, and the most cruel and brutal forms of flogging. Mild applications of the rack, with results falling short of death, were often used in this stage of torture. Common also was the so-called "squassation," where a man with weights tied to his feet was pulled high in the air and then allowed to fall suddenly, so as to tear his tendons and dislocate his joints. Another very painful torture of this grade was to bind the person in a chair with the end of his spine pressing full weight on a sharp piece of steel or a pointed diamond. Women as well as men were subjected to torture of this sort, and, in addition, had inflicted on them specially painful types of torture such as having their breasts cut off with appropriately constructed shears. During the second, third and fourth stages of torture the less intensive and active intervals might be utilized by such diversions as driving wooden pegs under the finger and toe nails of the victim.

If confession was not forced by some one of the first four stages of torture the officials proceeded to the fifth stage which often led to death during torture. The spiked barrel and the spiked cradle were frequently employed. In the spiked cradle the victim was rocked back and forth in a V-shaped receptacle from which sharp-pointed nails protruded and penetrated the body of the victim as he was rolled to and fro. The spiked barrel represented a similar type of torture and is self-explanatory. Spiked stools were also widely used.

Among the fatal forms of torture utilized in the fifth stage were the rack, the "iron maiden," breaking-on-the-wheel, sawing or hacking the victim to pieces, and the pressure torture known as *peine forte et dure*. When the rack was used the hands of the individual were fastened firmly and then both of his legs were pulled by a rope attached to a windlass. When applied with thoroughness in the fifth stage of torture it meant death, as the stretching process continued until the body gave way under the strain. The iron maiden was a hollow statue, either made of iron or wood braced with iron strips. Long spikes protruded from the inside, and when the accused person was placed inside the statue and the latter was closed in upon him the spikes entered his eyes and body, thus producing certain death. In the torture known as breaking-on-the-wheel the victim was stretched out on a heavy platform or wheel with four spokes in the form of a cross. The elbows and knees were fastened to projections on these spokes, and then the torturer was able to break each of the arms and legs in two places with a heavy iron bar. Then the victim's broken and bloody limbs were tied together over the center of his body and he was turned rapidly on this wheel until death intervened.

The accused were frequently literally sawed in pieces while alive. A common method was to hang a man up by his feet and then saw him in two pieces longitudinally. In the case of the employment of the *peine forte et dure* the victim was placed on a large flat stone or a firm wooden floor, and then weights were piled on his breast until he was either crushed to death or agreed to plead. This mode of torture was continued in England until the middle of the eighteenth century.

The full four or five stages of torture were, of course, rarely employed. The resistance of the person being tortured usually broke down before his torturers could get to the final stages. The forms of torture which meant death were usually applied as penalties rather than as a phase of forcing confession.

IV. THE THIRD DEGREE: THE PERSISTENCE OF TORTURE IN MODERN TIMES

The average citizen today has a vague impression that cruel and brutal methods of torture were employed in the far-off fifteenth century to extort confessions from those accused of crime. He rarely has the slightest suspicion, however, that these methods have tended to hang over into contemporary America with a change only in the technique and instruments utilized in administering torture. In the so-called "third degree," now in almost universal use by the police departments of our country, we have literally a persistence of torture as the first stage in the attempt to ascertain the guilt of those accused of crime. Some of the methods employed are quite as painful as those which were utilized in the medieval torture chamber. Further, it is not infrequent or uncommon for those subjected to the third degree to die in consequence of their brutal treatment. When death results from the third degree the police usually escape punishment by contending that the injuries which caused death were received prior to arrest or were the result of resisting arrest or of an accident after arrest. Unless the person injured by the third degree is a man of great influence he is likely to be unable to secure redress or to give adequate publicity to police brutality.

No other phase of our abominable contemporary criminal jurisprudence so completely and perfectly perpetuates and reflects medievalism as the practices associated with the third degree. We may illustrate the nature and prevalence of these barbarities by reference to specific cases and literature on the subject. In an article in the *Welfare Magazine* for April, 1926, Mr. Sherman W. Searle, Assistant Director of the Department of Public Welfare of the State of Illinois, thus comments upon the third degree and its use by the police of his state:

The so-called third degree methods of forcing confessions from those charged with having committed crimes, is a relic of the barbarous past. It is condemned by all civilized people. It has been frowned upon for the past two hundred and fifty years. It is only practiced by the police authorities in secret. Those who do practice it shield themselves from exposure through threats and hide behind the universal prejudice toward those who have been convicted of committing violations of the law. The word of one having been convicted is always doubly discounted. The universal reply to their statements is that they are only seeking to escape punishment. Nevertheless, there is abundant evidence to show that the third degree is being practiced by police authorities in the state of Illinois.

Only recently a young man in one of the institutions, in talking with an officer of that institution, stated that he had been charged with the commission of a certain crime for which two other young men are serving in another institution. He had never seen the ones who were convicted and only knew of it through publication in the newspapers. His statement to the officer could not affect him one way or another. It was made in a casual way.

The story he told, however, of eight days of continuous persecution and cruelty by the police, makes one's blood run cold. For eight nights the most excruciating torture was applied to him. He was rendered unconscious several times from the application of these methods, among which was the withholding of food. In this weakened condition he was taken from his cell in the dead of night for eight nights. In his case he had been "identified" by three witnesses as one of three who committed the crime. Neither one of the three was convicted, but two others paid the penalty. The tortures were administered in an inner room where the cries could not be heard. The "gold fish," iron rods, and fists were used. The gold fish consists of a piece of copper cable used in wiring telephone switchboards. This cable is drawn through a rubber hose. The iron rods are used to strike the victim on the shins, while with the gold fish they tap them on the head and the back of the neck for hours, usually with short intervals of rest during which time they are continually questioned.

Repeated stories of this kind have come to the officials of the Department of Public Welfare. They have come from various cities of the state. An exposure of these methods in the city of Springfield has recently filled the columns of the public press. The public is more or less appalled when presented with the facts. They had supposed that with the banishment of the rack, the thumb screws, and other inquisitional devices of the medieval period such methods were taboo. The use of the "third degree" is a confession of the lack of intelligence on the part of the police in the administration of the law. In England, for example, nothing of the sort is allowed, yet crime is reduced to the minimum.

In an article in the New York *Nation* for June 15, 1927, Mr. A. C. Sedgwick thus describes the typical procedure in the third degree:

The detectives must have a "clean" confession. They know the prisoners shot at them in the chase which followed the hold-up. They think the same men did the "jobs" which are still on their books as unsolved. They "have the goods on them," but the men refuse to talk. The detectives must make them talk—must "go to work on 'em" till they do.

One detective takes a piece of rubber hose, which is part of the equipment of the detective bureau and is favored for use because it leaves no marks. Another takes out his black-jack. Others grab anything—black-jacks, revolvers, night-sticks. "I seen you before," bawls a detective. "No sir," the prisoner answers. The detective strikes him. This is the signal. The "shellackin'" has started. Blow after blow from the rubber hose, black-jacks, and night-sticks. The prisoners fall to the floor. The blood pours from their faces. They spit and cough blood. The detectives, still in a white rage, look at them. The door opens. A young policeman in uniform pokes his head in. "You fellers is easy with 'em," he says. "Is that so?" roars a detective and kicks a prisoner in the face, pulls him to his feet, props him against the desk, then with the butt end of his revolver makes a gash in his head. The three prisoners go to the hospital.

If it were asked of any official source what happened to these men it would be said that they received their injuries resisting arrest, or perhaps that the "sidewalk come up and hit 'em." Policemen are supposed to use only that force which is necessary in the effecting of an arrest. But force, third-degree methods are necessary, the policeman believes, necessary to himself especially, for by beating a prisoner he is not only showing his authority but he has a chance to get from the prisoner confessions which may win him publicity and promotion. The third degree is known to all who have associated with policemen, but it is one of those things which is winked at and tolerated. Who can prove to a judge that a prisoner has fallen victim to violence in a police station when all the witnesses are policemen?

Another representative case of the third degree was that of a Chinaman, Ziang Sun Wan, who was suspected of murder and was subjected to third-degree methods in the city of Washington. The facts are presented in a Supreme Court decision written by Justice Brandeis and published in large part in the *New Republic* for November 12, 1924. Though ill, Wan was subjected to an inquisition for some twelve days before a confession, later repudiated, was extorted from him. We quote some of the more relevant sections from Justice Brandeis' summary of the facts:

Wan was held in the hotel room without formal arrest, incommunicado. But he was not left alone. Every moment of the day, and of the night, at least one member of the police force was on guard inside his room. Three ordinary policemen were assigned to this duty. Each served eight hours; the shifts beginning at midnight, at eight in the morning, and at four in the afternoon. Morning, afternoon and evening (and at least on one occasion after midnight) the prisoner was visited by the superintendent of police and one or more of the detectives. The sole purpose of these visits was to interrogate him. Regardless of Wan's wishes and protest, his condition of health or the hour, they engaged him in conversation. He was subjected to persistent, lengthy and repeated cross-examination. Sometimes it was subtle, sometimes severe. Always the examination was conducted with a view to entrapping Wan into a confession of his own guilt and of that of his brother. Whenever these visitors entered the room, the guard was stationed outside the closed door.

On the eighth day, the accusatory questioning took a more excruciating form. A detective was in attendance throughout the day. In the evening, Wan was taken from Hotel Dewey to the Mission. There, continuously for ten hours, this sick man was led from floor to floor minutely to examine and re-examine the scene of the triple murder and every object connected with it, to give explanations, and to answer questions. The places where the dead men were discovered; the revolver with which presumably the murder was committed, the blood stains and the finger prints thereon; the bullet holes in the walls; the discharged cartridges found upon the floor; the clothes of the murdered men; the blood stains on the floor and the stairs; a bloody handkerchief; the coat and pillow which had been found covering the dead men's faces; photographs, taken by the police, of the men as they lay dead; the doors

and windows through which the murderer might have entered or made his escape; photostat copies of writings, by
means of which it was sought to prove that Wan was impli-
cated in a forgery incident to the murder; all these were shown
him. Every supposed fact ascertained by the detectives in the
course of their investigation was related to him. Concerning
every object, every incident detailed, he was, in the presence
of a stenographer, plied with questions by the superintendent
of police and the detectives. By these he was engaged in argument; sometimes separately, sometimes in joint attack. The
process of interrogation became ever more insistent. It passed
at times from inquiry into command. From seven o'clock in
the evening until five o'clock in the morning the questioning
continued. Before it was concluded, Li, who was again in
attendance, had left the Mission about midnight, worn out
by the long hours. The superintendent of police had returned
to his home, apparently exhausted. One of the detectives had
fallen asleep. To Wan, not a moment of sleep was allowed.

On the ninth day, at twenty minutes past five in the morning, Wan was taken from the Mission to the station house
and placed formally under arrest. There, the interrogation
was promptly resumed. Again the detectives were in attendance, day and evening, plying their questions; pointing out
alleged contradictions; arguing with the prisoner; and urging
him to confess, lest his brother be deemed guilty of the crime.
Still the statements secured failed to satisfy the detectives'
craving for evidence. On the tenth day Wan was "bundled
up"; was again taken to the Mission; was again questioned
there for hours; and there "the whole thing was again talked
of and enacted." On the eleventh day, a formal interrogation
of Wan was conducted at the station house by the detectives
in the presence of a stenographer. On the twelfth day, the
verbatim typewritten report of the interrogation (which occupies twelve pages of the printed record) was read to Wan,
in his cell at the jail. There, he signed the report and initialled
each page. On the thirteenth day, for the first time, Wan was
visited by the chief medical officer of the jail, in the performance of his duties.

The New York *World* of November 18, 1929, thus describes the administration of the third degree to Mrs. Parks
in Camden, New Jersey:

In order to force from Gladys May Parks a confession that she murdered the two Rogers children the criminal authorities in Camden have employed "third-degree" methods. Day after day, for long hours at a stretch, without sleep, without rest, she was questioned in the hope that she would break down. After previous failures, the detectives at last kept her on the rack for over twenty-five hours without intermission. Through it all the woman stuck to her first story that the two children came to their death by accident and that she had concealed their bodies. Although she was in a state of physical collapse, the police could get nothing further from her in support of their belief that she was guilty of murder.

We like to think that in this age we have discarded the mediæval mode of getting evidence by torture. We profess to look with horror on the use of physical violence for the purpose of compelling a prisoner to admit the commission of a crime. But how different in fact are these practices of the officers of the law in New Jersey from the use of torture in bygone ages? Only in a measure do the methods vary: the end is the same—by downright cruelty and mental pain to wring from the lips of a prisoner the final testimony that shall prove guilt beyond possibility of denial.

It is in the name of the law, presumably, and in furtherance of the administration of justice, that the District Attorney and detectives of Camden have conducted their preliminary examination of the Parks woman by hateful methods. Ordinarily where the police use the "third degree" they take pains to keep it quiet. In New Jersey the authorities, perhaps because there was little in the circumstances of the case to arouse sympathy for the defendant, have disregarded public opinion. It is time they were brought to a sharp halt. It is time they were taught that they cannot with impunity abuse their powers even against the most helpless of those who fall into their hands, and that they cannot use the law to cover up their own offenses against law and justice.

In the case of John Campanella, an Italian at East St. Louis in 1922, death resulted from the third degree. After he had died from the results of the beating administered during the third degree, the police officials who had conducted the torture hung up Campanella's body by the neck, so as to make those who found him believe that he had committed suicide. When

the coroner examined the body he found no evidence of strangulation. The police escaped with dismissal from their posts.
It is not generally known that in the Franks murder case,
before the arrest of Leopold and Loeb, two teachers in the
Lincoln School in Chicago were subjected to an unmerciful
beating with a rubber hose in order to extort a confession of
murder. These men were unable to secure any redress or damages from the city authorities. Mr. Villard thus describes the
confessions of the Chief of Police in Seattle in 1926 relative
to the use of the third degree:*

One of the devices he used was an electrically-wired carpet
covering the entire floor of the cell. When the current is turned
on, he said, "sparks fly and the prisoner leaps, screaming in
agony, into the air . . . It is not fatal, its effects are not
lasting, and *it leaves no marks.*" A method "highly recommended by the police of other cities" he described as follows:
"The prisoner is given a heavy iron ball and told to place
it in a slot in the end of his cell. This slot, they show him, is
opened by a trigger from which depends a length of stout
cord. The prisoner is then bound and thrown on the floor in
such a manner that his head is under the slot. One of his legs
then is lifted at right angles to his body and the release cord
is tied to his foot. So long as he can keep the leg upright he is
in no danger. While he is kept in this position, the prisoner is
questioned, the police commenting at intervals on the agony
he must be suffering in trying to hold the aching leg upright.
Prisoners sometimes become unconscious through fear and
pain. The 'catch' of the plan is that, while he is being bound,
a detective has removed the iron ball and has put in its place
a rubber ball!"

One of the most ingenious devices yet discovered among
the instruments employed to inflict the third degree was the
electric chair used by the Sheriff of Helena, Arkansas. It is
described in the following news report in the New York
Times of November 23, 1929:

Helena, Ark., Nov. 22 (A.P.).—A makeshift electric
chair, said to have been in use in the Sheriff's office here for

---

*O. G. Villard, in *Harper's Magazine*, October, 1927, pp. 611-12.

several years, today was ordered destroyed by Circuit Judge W. D. Davenport as a result of testimony of a negro that it was used to force from him a "confession" that he killed his 6-year-old stepson.

The negro was convicted and sentenced to life imprisonment.

The chair was brought into the court room by order of Judge Davenport during the trial of the negro, James McAllister, 21.

Sheriff J. C. Barlow testified that the chair, inherited with the office from a long line of former county Sheriffs, had been rebuilt and used three times by him to obtain statements from prisoners.

Judge Davenport described its use as "uncivilized" and added that "if these people are going to be mobbed before coming up here, there is no use of having a court."

The young negro squirmed in the witness chair as he described the alleged torture to which he was subjected in the "electric chair." He said he confessed to choking the boy, Joe Willie Hopkins, to death so the officers would turn off the current when the pain became unbearable. He then signed the confession, he said, "so they wouldn't put me in the chair again."

McAllister's attorney said the testimony concerning the chair would be used in an appeal to the Supreme Court.

The fear of third degree methods actually incites to suicide and crime. One of the most notorious examples of suicide was the case of Andrea Salsedo. Salsedo was a friend of Sacco and Vanzetti, and it was their knowledge of his death under torture which led them to attempt to dispose of radical literature in their possession, during which effort they were arrested on a charge of murder. Salsedo had been subjected to prolonged physical and mental torture by the Department of Justice until he became insane and leaped from the fourteenth story of the Park Row building in New York City. In the case of the young negro, Luther Boddy, who killed two policemen when they attempted to arrest him in New York City in 1922, it was proved that he committed this double murder in order to escape the horrors of a repetition of the third degree to which he had been earlier subjected.

Police officials frequently argue in support of the application of the third degree that it is absolutely essential in order to ascertain guilt. The untenable nature of this contention is well revealed by the procedure in England. Here the application of the third degree is explicitly forbidden and rigidly excluded. Yet, no one would think of contending that English authorities have proved less capable than the American police in detecting criminals and convicting them of their guilt. In no other civilized country is the third degree torture permitted as in the United States.

An even more fundamental refutation of this police contention is to be found in the fact that ascertainment of guilt is no part whatever of the police function. It is the province of the police solely and exclusively to apprehend those suspected of crime. Once they have done this, their part in criminal procedure ceases, except insofar as they may offer testimony at the trial relative to the reasons for which they made the arrest. In the United States, where the police are notoriously deficient in performing their legitimate functions of apprehension and arrest, they are particularly to be condemned for intruding into the second stage of criminal procedure, namely the ascertainment of guilt.

The police commissioner of one of our largest American cities freely admitted to a delegation of lawyers recently that his police force employed the third degree with great frequency; indeed, with almost complete uniformity on those with a previous criminal record. His argument was that the courts had broken down and convictions could not be secured. Hence, the only way he could keep crime in the city under control was to let criminals understand that if they were arrested they would be "beaten-up" severely. There is little doubt of the truth of the commissioner's charges against the courts in this metropolitan center, but this is no justification for the third degree. It is a situation which calls for a drive for judicial reform and the purification of the courts.

The commissioner could vindicate himself by showing a high ratio of arrests to crimes committed.

V. TRIAL BY JURY

We have not space here for a thorough review of the history of the jury, such as might be founded upon the illuminating researches of Brunner, Pollock, Maitland, Thayer and Haskins, but we may point out briefly the salient facts in the matter. In the first place, more than ninety-nine per cent of human history passed without any such institution as the jury having a place in criminal procedure. It had, indeed, a very recent origin. Even the highly developed Roman jurisprudence knew it not. Its beginnings in late medieval times in western Europe were due as much to accident as to design. During the greater part of the Middle Ages the ordeal, trial by battle and compurgation were the most widely used devices for ascertaining the guilt of the accused. But early in the period the political, rather than the juristic, conditions of the times were evolving machinery which, though far removed in its origin from court procedure, was destined ultimately to beget the modern jury.

Its remote origins are to be found in the nature of the *fiscus,* which was related to the royal revenue jurisdiction in imperial Rome. This power was carried over by the Franks, to whom the royal lands were known as fiscal lands. Among the more important administrative functions of the Frankish Empire was the inquiry into royal rights, and particularly into disputes over royal lands. In order to establish his rights the King would frequently direct an *inquisitio,* or inquiry into the actual state of affairs. The matter was usually settled after conversations and adjustments between the royal representatives and private citizens. In due time the *inquisitio* was extended still further. The King's representatives would summon a group of leading citizens and extract from them an opinion or statement as to the taxable wealth of their community, the state of the public order, and the prevalence of offenses against the King and his laws. This group of citizens or neighbors was known as a *jurata* and its report to the King or his representatives was called a *veredictum*. Here we have in embryo both the terminology and the procedure of the modern jury.

This first stage of its development, as primarily an administrative rather than a juristic instrument, was most perfectly realized by the Normans, who took the practice to England in 1066. There the royal inquisition soon came to be known as an assize. Exactly a century after the landing of William the Conqueror, namely, at the famous Assize of Clarendon in 1166, the grand jury took definite form. A varying number of country gentlemen and burghers were summoned before the royal representatives and compelled to tell whether they knew of anyone accused of crime in the neighborhood. At least twelve of those summoned had to agree as to the accuracy of the report in order to secure royal action. That so large a number was summoned was due to the fact that in the case of powerful violators of the King's peace a single individual feared to make accusation. This jury of accusation, which appeared shortly after the middle of the twelfth century, was, of course, the grand jury rather than the trial or petit jury of today. Those accused of crime by it were at first commonly subjected to the ordeal or duel in order to ascertain their guilt, though as early as 1166, in certain civil cases, Henry II is said to have allowed the accused to decline trial by battle and resort to a crude form of jury trial. The development of the trial jury, as we know it, however, was delayed for half a century or more.

The thing which did more than anything else to establish jury trial was Innocent III's condemnation of the ordeal in 1215. This strong pronouncement of the Church against the prevalent method of ascertaining guilt led to the gradual substitution of the jury trial, which had made its appearance in England by the close of the first quarter of the thirteenth century. At first, it was rather common for the grand jury to act also as a trial jury, but in due time the two bodies came to be definitely separated in composition and function. For a century or so a person who preferred to do so might decline a jury trial and resort to trial by battle or accept torture. The incentive in these cases was the fact that conviction by a jury led to the seizure of the property of the accused and the possible destitution of his relatives. Trial by battle was gradually outlawed, but torture remained legal in many countries to the close of the eighteenth century.

In the early juries there had been no definite uniformity as to numbers, with the exception that usually twelve of those chosen were compelled to agree before a decision could be made, but in the course of time the English jury came to consist definitely of twelve "good men and true." The choice of the number twelve unquestionably was based upon Scriptural precedent. The primordial jury was in this sense clearly related to the earlier device of compurgation, by which, in the absence of direct evidence, twelve friends of the accused could swear to their belief in the veracity of the defendant when he was protesting his innocence. The Holy Spirit was assumed to hover in close proximity to the compurgators, and when the jury developed it was believed that it watched with equal solicitude over the decisions of jurymen. The Holy Ghost was supposed to be particularly favorable to the number of twelve because of the fact that there had been twelve tribes of Israel and Twelve Apostles. It is probably only an accident that the sacred Hebrew number seven was not chosen instead of twelve. A definite deterrent advantage might certainly have arisen had the choice fallen on the number thirteen! The following quotation from *Duncomb's Trials* (1665) gives a good idea of the mystical and theological attitude towards the number twelve as applied to the jury system:

As to the sanctity and foreordained character of the number twelve, and first as to their (the jury's) number twelve; and this number is no less esteemed by our law than by Holy Writ. If the Twelve Apostles on their twelve thrones must try us in our eternal state, good reason hath the law to appoint the number twelve to try our temporal. The tribes of Israel were twelve; the Patriarchs were twelve, and Solomon's officers were twelve (I Kings 4:7). Therefore, not only matters of fact were tried by twelve, but in ancient times twelve judges were to try matters in law. In the Exchequer Chambers there were twelve counsellors of state for matters of state and he that appealed to the law must have eleven others with him who believe he says true and the law is so precise in their number of twelve that if the trial be by more or less than twelve it is a mistrial.

At the outset the trial jury performed the functions of the present jury plus that of the witnesses. The jurymen were usually men who had knowledge of the facts in question and they based their verdict in large part upon their own information or judgment. By the opening of the fifteenth century in England, however, the jury was gradually transformed into a body which founded its decisions mainly upon evidence supplied by witnesses. For a considerable period the only witnesses summoned were those for the prosecution, and the defendant was at a distinct disadvantage. Gradually, however, he was given the right, under progressively lessened handicaps, to call upon witnesses to testify in his behalf. Along with this went the development of rules of evidence, of the right to challenge jurymen, and of improved methods of impanelling the jury. The rules of evidence and the court-room procedure which prevail today are a curious mosaic, embodying elements which originated as early as the fourteenth century, in juxtaposition to such highly novel devices as the summoning of trained psychiatrists to aid judges and juries in their decisions. The modern rules of evidence and procedure, in other words, present a recapitulation of the entire history of trial by jury.

It should be quite evident from even this brief and casual sketch that the jury is far from the divinely created and sanctioned bulwark of human liberty which right-thinking men now suppose it to be. It took its origin in a non-juridical field and was clumsily adapted to its present purpose simply because nothing better was at hand. Far from being a rampart of human freedom or safeguard of democracy, it was in its origins one of the most potent and highly prized instruments of royal absolutism and monarchial oppression. Compared to other institutions of the time, trial by jury probably made a fairly respectable showing in the sixteenth century, when there were relatively few highly trained lawyers, and the men summoned for jury service represented the intelligent and cultured middle and upper classes. But the progress of medical knowledge, sociology, jurisprudence, and democracy since that time has made it as preposterous and out of date as the sun dial of James I or the coach of Charles II. Moreover, the average jury is today chosen from altogether less intelligent groups than those which furnished jurymen in the sixteenth century.

The complete futility and inadequacy of the trial by jury can best be indicated by a brief analysis of the actual procedure from the impanelling of the jury to the rendering of the verdict. The selection of the panel is determined by lot, the names of a definite number of citizens being drawn at random from a collection of slips or cards bearing the names of all the qualified citizens of the country. At best, any such panel can only at rare intervals include a better than average group of citizens. It cannot be limited to those possessing unusual intelligence or special knowledge of criminal matters. In the usual case, the panel is made up of a typical collection of farmers, shoemakers, barbers, plumbers, clerks, drummers, hodcarriers, and day laborers, with a few professional or business men sprinkled among them. In many cases, of course, the theory of a choice by lot has become a legal fiction, and accommodating commissioners of juries are willing, for a reasonable consideration, to draw the names of the men desired by district attorneys or lawyers for the defense. Such selected panels are by no means rare, and when one of them supplies a jury the outcome of the trial is assured before a single witness has been summoned. Even when a panel is honestly selected it fulfils exactly the democratic doctrine that special training is in no way essential to competence in the handling of public affairs. It is drawn from precisely the classes from which a mob might be raised by the Ku Klux Klan.

The courtroom presents a situation where those in charge of the practical procedure are not primarily concerned with the facts in the case, something which could not possibly exist where scientific procedure was really desired. The average district-attorney is usually interested in convicting the accused, whether innocent or guilty, in order to advance his political prospects or to promote his rise in the legal or judicial profession. The counsel for the defense is desirous of securing the discharge of his client, whether innocent or guilty, for the purpose of increasing his reputation as a successful criminal lawyer or justifying his charging an inordinate fee. Neither side, then, is really interested in the facts. Moreover, the court procedure is one which would make it relatively difficult to get at the facts even if the lawyers involved were enthusiastic about obtaining them. Imagine such a situation as the basis for attacking any problem in natural or social science!

The method of actually selecting the jury is one which makes it very hard indeed to provide a group of twelve men who are even up to the average in honesty and ability. We have a process of counter-selection in the procedure of excusing and challenging jurors, whereby there normally remain for service on the jury only the more illiterate, unintelligent or dishonest representatives of a relatively low stratum of human society. One of the most interesting cases of an attempt to select jurors favorable to a particular side in a case came out in connection with a recent murder trial in Massachusetts, *Commonwealth* vs. *Cero*. It was proved that before the trial the district attorney's office had drawn up a questionnaire which was put by police officers to all members of the panel of jurymen from whom the twelve good men and true were ultimately to be selected. The results of this questionnaire were in the hands of the district attorney before the trial. The questionnaire follows:

Date........

Name in full........
Residence........
Age........
Style of living........
Business........
Property-owner........
Married or single........
Living with wife........
Character and associates........
Habits........
Is he a man addicted to drinking?........
Does he lead a fast life?........
Politics........
Is he a college graduate?........
Lodge affiliations........
Affiliations with politicians........
Affiliations with law and lawyers........
Ever served on a jury?........
Is he related to any employee in City, County or State?.....
Was he ever in the employ of the city of Boston?........
Has he a criminal record?........
Is he related to any former Boston police officer who abandoned his duty on or about September 9, 1919 [the famous Boston Police Strike], or was discharged from the Department for causes arising out of that situation?........
General Remarks........
Investigating Officer........

Perhaps the most astonishing thing about the whole matter is to be found in the fact that this procedure of the district attorney was approved by the Supreme Judicial Court of Massachusetts when the case was argued on appeal.

All of our present psychological knowledge overwhelmingly demonstrates the futility and unscientific nature of the whole court procedure connected with the jury trial. In the first place, after a few hours or days of excitement or bewilderment in their novel situation, the jury lapses into a state of coma, indifference, or day-dreaming, which makes it impossible for them to follow the evidence presented in any intelli-

gent or consistent fashion. There has, perhaps, been no better
brief description of the jury and its attitudes than the following characterization by T. S. Matthews of the first jury
chosen to try the Gastonia strikers in the fall of 1929:*

As for the jury—this pitiful residue of many panels, this
result of nine days' weeding among good men and true to find
twelve citizens with no opinions—this jury is not prepossess-
ing in appearance. It is considered in some circles that the jury
is "pro-labor"—perhaps because one of them is an ex-member
of a union. The faces they show to the court, however, are the
blank, shy faces of private men in a public place. They squirm
uneasily on their seats through the long hot hours of testimony, and rise with alacrity when the Judge calls a recess.
They look by turns bewildered, bored, interested and sleepy.
In short, a jury.

Further, psychological studies of testimony have proved
most convincingly that even the most highly-trained witnesses, operating under the most advantageous conditions, can
rarely testify with accuracy or uniformity in regard to any act
which they have observed. Still further, even if witnesses possessed an adequate knowledge of the facts involved and were
desirous of telling these facts to the jury in a straightforward
and honest fashion, the present rules governing testimony and
evidence in the courtroom would make it practically impossible for them to achieve this end. The district attorney and
the counsel for the defense, instead of welcoming all possible
facts which might be introduced as bearing upon the case, are
usually determined to prevent the introduction of testimony
damaging to their side of the case, or, if the introduction of
such testimony cannot be prevented, are on the alert to divert
the attention of the jury from this evidence by all sorts of
rhetorical tricks and emotional appeals.

Therefore, the outcome of courtroom procedure before the
jury is essentially this: a body of individuals of average or
less than average ability who could not tell the truth if they

---

*New Republic, September 18, 1929.

wanted to, who usually have little of the truth to tell, who are not allowed to tell even all of that, and who are frequently instructed to fabricate voluminously and unblushingly, present this largely worthless, wholly worthless, or worse than worthless information to twelve men who are for the most part unconscious of what is being divulged to them, and would be incapable of an intelligent assimilation and interpretation of such information if they actually heard it.

The jury then proceeds to arrive at its verdict after consultation and conference in the secrecy of the jury room. Having followed little of the testimony in an intelligent fashion, and being further quite incapable of making up their minds upon the basis of a rational and competent analysis of concrete facts, the whole matter of the determination upon a verdict is largely the product of the instructions of the judge, of chance or of the personality types on the jury. An extremely impressive personality who by accident gets on the jury may bring about a decision entirely contrary to the evidence, while an unusually stupid, stubborn or corrupt moron may prevent agreement, in spite of overwhelmingly convincing evidence.

Further, one must remember that the jury trial is perverted not only by the inexperience and ignorance of the jurymen but also by the arrogance, bias and prejudice of the judge. Many of the most seasoned criminal lawyers have informed the writer that juries are frequently more influenced by the opinions, decisions, comments and summations of the judge than they are by the evidence. Many a lawyer, full of contempt and indignation in regard to the conduct of the trial judge, finds it necessary to suppress his feelings as he knows that he will be creating for himself an almost insuperable handicap if he arouses the antipathy of the judge and brings about the probability of adverse rulings throughout the case. The conduct of Judge Webster Thayer in the case of Sacco and Vanzetti, now happily accessible for all time to the candid scrutiny of students of legal history and criminal procedure, furnishes an admirable example of the degree to which a case can be influenced by the prejudices and irresponsibility of the trial judge. In an interesting article in the *American Mercury* for April, 1929, entitled "Trial by Jury or by Judge," Mr. Sterling E. Edmunds deals in illuminating fashion with the vast influence exerted by judges over the decisions arrived at by jurors and the ultimate outcome of the case on trial.

If, by chance, an intelligent verdict has been agreed upon, there is a reasonable probability that it may be set aside on the basis of the most absurd legal technicalities which have no bearing whatever upon the fact of the guilt or innocence of the accused. Mr. Mark O. Prentiss has gathered an interesting list of cases set aside on the basis of legal technicalities, from which we have selected the following representative illustrations:*

A defendant was convicted under an indictment charging the theft of $100, "lawful money." The conviction was set aside because the indictment did not say "lawful money of the United States." The court gave as the reason for granting the defendant a new trial that the victim might have been carrying around Mexican money. . . .

In Georgia a defendant was convicted under an indictment which charged that he stole a hog that had a slit out of its right ear and a clip out of the left. The appellate court granted the defendant a new trial because, while it was proved that the defendant stole the hog, the evidence disclosed that it was a hog with a slit out of its left ear and a clip out of its right ear. . . .

In another case a defendant was convicted of stealing a pair of boots. The judgment of the trial court was set aside by the higher court, because it appeared that while the defendant had stolen two boots, he had stolen two rights. . . .

In another case involving some offense along a public road the conviction was set aside because, while the proof showed that the road had been used for thirty years as a public road, it did not show that the road had ever been formally dedicated to the public. . . .

In another Alabama case a defendant was charged in the

Current History, October, 1925.

indictment with stealing a cow. The evidence proved him guilty of stealing a bull. In either event the defendant was guilty of grand larceny. The higher court, however, set aside the judgment of conviction.

Therefore, we may probably safely conclude that the modern jury trial offers no greater proof of certainty and accuracy of justice than the ancient ordeal or trial by battle.

Those who may agree with the writer as to the weaknesses and absurdities of contemporary criminal jurisprudence may well ask what can be suggested as a substitute. It is easy enough to outline the essentials of a scientific system for the apprehension and conviction of the criminal, but it is a far more difficult matter to secure the adoption of any such scheme. We should, in the first place, take the police system entirely out of politics and make it a highly trained technical profession similar, if not superior, to the present Canadian Mounted Police. Chief August Vollmer, Arthur Woods and others have indicated the requirements of any such adequate system of trained professional police. There should also be great improvement in the public detective service, which would put at the disposal of police and detectives all the technical devices which could possibly be employed by the criminal classes. In this manner we could make the apprehension of the criminal relatively speedy and certain. It is recognized by all criminologists worthy of the name, and fully proved by the example of England, that certainty of apprehension is far more of a deterrent than hypothetical severity of punishment. In the next place, the police should be encouraged to concentrate upon prevention of, and apprehension for, the commission of really serious crimes.

Instead of the present unintelligent lay jury we should have a permanent paid body of experts whose sole business it would be to deal with accused criminals by investigating the matter of their guilt or innocence and discovering the nature and causation of their criminal personality. Such a body of paid experts, made up of highly trained detectives, physicians, psychiatrists, sociologists and criminologists, would actually be interested in getting at the facts and would provide a procedure whereby the relevant facts could be obtained and scrutinized in a direct, speedy and intelligent fashion. Before such a body the rhetorical subterfuges, evasions, and bulldozing of the contemporary courtroom would be as ineffective as they would be unlikely.

Further, such a group of experts would not only be intimately interested in the matter of the guilt of the accused; they would be equally, if not more, interested in his personality. Even if the evidence pointed to the innocence of the accused, he would be held if it could be proved that he was suffering from some mental or physical disorder or defect certain to make him a potential menace to society. There would be no attempt to *punish* the individual for the particular crime committed; rather an effort would be made so to treat or segregate the accused as to make him no longer a menace or danger to society. These experts would be interested very literally and very directly in social protection and not in using the corpses of possibly innocent men as the stepping-stones to governorships, or in exploiting the discharge of dangerous crooks and criminals in the interest of enhancing their own legal prestige and private fortunes.

Perhaps a word should be said about the development of technical scientific aids in crime detection. Here we have scientific devices like the so-called "lie-detector" which registers changes in heart-beat, blood-pressure, reaction-time and the like. It is supposed to reveal attempts at lying on the part of the most hard-boiled and skillful evader. Blood analysis and the employment of various chemicals in identification tests have come into wide use. Doubtless we shall witness an ever greater effort to put refined scientific methods at the service of criminology. Yet there will be need for care and discrimination. Some of these devices can be administered in ways perilously near to the third degree. Indeed, one judge ordered the abandonment of the lie-detector as a third-degree instrument. In other cases we shall need to discriminate sharply between *bona fide* scientific agencies and the pretense of cranks and fakirs.

SELECTED REFERENCES

Bernaldo De Quirós, Constancio. *Modern Theories of Criminality.* Boston, 1911.

Borchard, Edwin M. *Convicting the Innocent.* New Haven, 1932.

Callender, Clarence N. *American Courts.* New York, 1927.

Carlin, Jerome E. *Lawyers' Ethics.* New York, 1966.

Davis, William S. *Life on a Medieval Barony.* New York, 1923.

Encyclopaedia Britannica, 11th ed., s.v. "Torture."

Frank, Jerome. *Courts on Trial.* Princeton, 1949.

Glueck, Sheldon S. *Crime and Justice.* Boston, 1936.

Glueck, Sheldon S. *Mental Disorder and the Criminal Law.* Boston, 1925.

Healy, William. *The Individual Delinquent.* 1915; Reprinted Montclair, N. J., 1969.

Hoag, Ernest B., and Williams, Edward Huntington. *Crime, Abnormal Minds and the Law.* Indianapolis, 1923.

Hopkins, Ernest J. *Our Lawless Police.* New York, 1931.

Jackson, Percival E. *Look at the Law.* New York, 1940.

Kalven, Harry, Jr., and Zeisel, Hans. *The American Jury.* Boston, 1966.

Lea, Henry C. *Superstition and Force.* Philadelphia, 1892.

Michael, Jerome, and Adler, Mortimer J. *Crime, Law and the Social Sciences.* 1933; Reprinted Montclair, N. J., 1971.

Moley, Raymond. *Our Criminal Courts.* New York, 1930.

Smith, Eugene. *Criminal Law in the United States.* 1910; Reprinted Montclair, N. J., 1972.

Smith, M. Hamblin. *The Psychology of the Criminal.* London, 1922.

Smith, Reginald Heber. *Justice and the Poor.* 1919; Reprinted Montclair, N. J., 1972.

Stalmaster, Irvin. *What Price Jury Trials?* Boston, 1931.

Stone, Irving. *Clarence Darrow for the Defense.* Garden City, N. Y., 1941.

Taft, Henry W. *Witnesses in Court.* New York, 1934.

Thayer, James B. *The Development of Trial by Jury.* Cambridge, Mass., 1896.

Waite, John B. *Criminal Law in Action.* New York, 1934.

CHAPTER II

Crime and Punishment in Early Society

I. LAW, CUSTOM AND RELIGION IN PRIMITIVE SOCIETY

THERE is no more interesting chapter in the history of human institutions than the account of the various types of conduct which society has regarded as a wrong, social or private, and of the means which it has adopted to repress these breaches of the peace. In this chapter the attempt will be made to trace the leading stages in this evolution of jurisprudence and criminal methods during primitive and early historic society. In primitive society there is no written law. This has led some of the earlier students and observers of savage races to declare them essentially lawless and possessed of no efficient means of social control. To show that this is an entirely erroneous opinion is not a difficult task. While primitive society has no written code, it has a method of enforcing sanctioned modes of conduct which is probably more powerful and vigilant than any written code which man has ever devised. This practically omnipotent force is custom.

Of the psychological origin of custom in suggestion, imitation and repetition, growing out of man's earliest struggles with his environment, nothing need be said here. It is sufficient to note that every recorded human society has possessed a fairly well-defined set of customary rules of conduct which are observed and enforced with a truly religious vigor. The actual significance of this tyrannical rule of custom in primitive society cannot be understood unless one puts himself temporarily in the position of the savage. The latter is constantly in fear of the ravages of the unknown, and nothing stands between him and these powers of darkness except the well-beaten path of custom. To deviate from this in the least is to be precipitated into the abyss of unforeseen and hideous disasters. To use the phrase of Professor Marett, primitive man's "custom is his luck." Not only does this transgression of the customary code expose the offending individual to untold woes, but it also renders his whole social group liable to the vengeance of the gods, for in early days responsibility is collective from the standpoint of both the natural and supernatural world. In primitive society a crime and a sin are practically identical. Hence, to supplement the individual fear of violating the prescribed modes of conduct on account of the dangers from unseen powers, there is the certain knowledge on the part of the offender that his group will summarily avenge themselves upon him for rendering it open to destruction from the intervention of both human and spiritual forces. As Marett says, the most generally accepted way of wiping out a crime and sin in primitive society is "to wipe out the sinner." Dr. Oppenheimer has well summarized the mystical and religious background of primitive punishments:

> Primitive punishment is inflicted either to remove the stain of impurity from society or to prevent a supernatural being from taking revenge on the tribe. Its object is in either case expiation—expiation, however, not for its own sake but expiation with a utilitarian background.

In view of the foregoing it is readily apparent that for anthropological and historical purposes the definition of law might well read that "law is any social rule to the infringement of which punishment is by usage attached." This conception of law will cover not only the codified law of the present but the customary law of the past. From this standpoint, then, there can be no question that there is law of the most effective kind in primitive society. Law seldom attracts attention, however, save when violated, and it is rarely in evidence in primitive society, since for obvious reasons few dream of violating the prescribed usages of the group. It must be admitted that, from the standpoint of his own code of conduct, the savage is far more law-abiding than the modern man, who fears only secular human authorities in the violation of the law.

II. CRIME IN EARLY SOCIETY

Recognizing, then, that we must seek the sources of primitive law in the customary usages of the group or "folkways" and not in a written code, attention may now be turned to the ways in which primitive society regards and represses the violations of its public and private tranquillity.

In present-day society there is found a two-fold division of the infractions of law: (1) the criminal cases calling for social action in apprehension and punishment, and (2) the civil cases (torts) which are a private matter and, while using much the same judicial channels and organs, are regarded as demanding only a restitution for damages done. The former class of cases are looked upon as threatening the stability of the whole social order and, hence, are of sufficient importance to demand the attention of the social group as manifested through its appropriate organs of control. The latter are considered as matters of equity which may be settled by private arrangement though the public organs of the law be summoned to aid in the process.

In primitive society a somewhat analogous condition was to be found. There were here also two classes of crimes, public and private: those which threaten the whole social group and those which are simply wrongs to private individuals. The whole social group would aid in the repression of the former cases, while the adjudication of the latter was left to the injured parties and their clansmen or kinsmen. While the theory involved is essentially identical, there is a vast difference between the nature of the crimes which are included under the categories of public and private in the conception of primitive and modern society. Those of the former type will first be analyzed.

In the light of the fact that the most serious disasters to society are thought in primitive times to come from the intervention of supernatural agencies in the affairs of men, it is perfectly natural for early man to regard as the most heinous crimes those which violate the customary rules for placating these supernatural powers and, hence, expose the whole group to the perils of their relentless wrath. Of this class of offences by far the most important was the violation of some fundamental taboo which furnished the basis for the common code of conduct.

While these taboos were many in early civilizations, the one which was most respected, since it furnished the basis for the whole system of relationships in tribal society, was the taboo against endogamy or incest. Therefore, its violation was most severely punished. The other major public crime of early days was witchcraft or sorcery. This consisted in using magical powers to bring disaster upon the group and to secure individual revenge or advancement. It was nothing else than betraying the group to the mercy of the evil spirits. Naturally, the presence of such a person as a sorcerer in the group was a source of ever-present danger and due cause for a panic in the social body. In addition to these two most important public crimes, there were several others which were usually deemed of sufficient importance to attract group attention. One of these was treason, namely, betraying the group into the hands of another or revealing the most precious possession of primitive peoples, to wit, their initiation secrets. Another was cowardice, or the failure to defend the group against its enemies. Cowardice, however, was by no means considered to be as serious a crime as treason. A third was sacrilege. Of less importance than treason, cowardice and sacrilege were a number of miscellaneous crimes, most of them sexual. The most common of the non-sexual crimes in this category were poisoning and the breaking of the rules concerning hunting-grounds.

To turn next to those crimes which are considered a matter for private revenge on the part of the individual or his clansmen, there were in early days four or five which would never be overlooked by the injured or his relatives: murder, adultery, theft, slander and assault. There is little which needs to be discussed in regard to certain of these crimes since their nature is essentially the same now as then. The crimes of adultery and slander, however, deserve special mention. In regard to adultery, the punishment of the male offender was usually a matter for clan decision. The punishment of the woman, at least after the development of patronymic tribal society, was, however, largely a domestic case handed over to the husband. Adultery in primitive and early historic society was considered a serious crime because of the necessity of leaving legitimate offspring to carry out sacrificial rites. Slander, while still punishable, is now a minor crime. In primitive times, however, owing to the greater mystical and material value of a good name (a savage's name being considered as much a part of his material property as his spear or arrows), slander was a serious wrong and among many early peoples a frequent cause of blood-feud.

In addition to these two main types of crimes in primitive society there was a third class which comprised a few crimes which were not subject to the punishment of the entire tribal group or of the clan or local group. These were largely offences within the family and, in most cases, had no specific punishment allotted.

III. PUNISHMENT OF CRIME IN PRIMITIVE SOCIETY

In treating this subject, as well as in differentiating among the crimes of primitive society, there are many complications which arise. This is due to the fact that the various classes of crimes call forth a different manner of punishment and also to the fact that the manner of punishing all crimes varies in the different eras of primitive society. Certain broad principles and stages, however, are easy to distinguish.

First, to consider the punishment of the public offences, we find that, since most of them imply the previous passage from the horde stage of society into tribal society, we may leave the former stage out of consideration. The punishment of the breaking of taboos, particularly that against endogamy, and of witchcraft, was, as might be expected, carried out with great severity. The whole group (tribe or village), including all the neighboring clans or the whole village, turned out to eliminate the criminal with the greatest expedition. The offender might be hacked to pieces in the frenzy which overcomes the mob or otherwise brutally but surely exterminated. He might even be eaten. One can well compare the panic which seizes the primitive group at the commission of such a crime to that which seizes the individual, particularly a child, when attacked or frightened in the dark. The commission of such a crime renders the group liable to the depredations of the offended spirits whom they cannot see but whose existence and power are real enough from the primitive man's point of view. The wife and children of the witch or sorcerer were also killed and his house burned. All taint was thus removed.

When the nature of the offence is looked at from their standpoint, the fury of the primitive mob is easily explainable. Probably the fierceness of the punishment was not so much the result of a desire to inflict pain upon the offender as it was to get rid of him and hence remove the source of their danger from the powers of darkness.

Treason was also summarily dealt with and the traitor was consigned to the regions beyond in no uncertain manner. In this case the element of public vengeance was probably more evident than in the former cases. With the coward the punishment was usually a matter of gross humiliation or corporal punishment rather than death. He might be deprived of his weapons, made to eat with dogs, or to run a gauntlet of a shower of spears or clubs. The other public crimes mentioned above were punished in various ways by different people. Exile was very frequently ordered. Thus did society in the earlier days purge herself of those who threatened the security of the group.

To punish or repress crimes of a private nature the earliest society had no developed organs; so it was left to be settled by private means. In the earliest or horde stage of primitive social organization the settlement of private wrongs was a purely personal matter. In the case of murder the offender might escape unscathed unless some of the immediate relatives of the deceased took up the cause of the latter. In practically all other cases the aggrieved party settled with the offender directly and the adjustment might issue simply in a greater grievance. While this conception of crime and this method of punishment were probably rather general among all peoples when they were in this period of their historic evolution, there are only a relatively few savages who remain today in the horde stage of social organization. Among these are the Veddahs of Ceylon, the Mincopis of the Andaman Islands, the Bushmen of central Australia and southern Africa, the Yahgans of Terra del Fuego, the Innuit of the Arctic regions, and certain very backward Indian tribes of western United States and Brazil.

In developed tribal society, however, we have a much more compact social organization and hence a much better system of adjusting the wrongs done to any member of the social body. In general, we have two types of developed tribal society based upon different methods of tracing relationship: the *matronymic*, where relationship was traced through mothers, and the *patronymic*, where relationship was traced through fathers. In both, however, the unitary group was normally the clan, be it maternal, as in the former case, or paternal, as in the latter. While varying somewhat in detail, the method of punishment in these two types of primitive society was essentially the same in principle and may be treated as a whole except where the differences were considerable. It is necessary to bear in mind, of course, that in many areas primitive man never developed the clan organization, but lived in the local group-village type of society. The theories of crime did not differ markedly here from those which prevailed in kinship society, but the clan basis of the recognition and repression of crime did not exist.

In most tribal society the unitary group was not the family, as now understood, but the clan which was composed of all who claimed common descent from some ancestor whether this be traced through mother or father. In primitive society the clan both supervised the administration of many types of private vengeance and took charge of the retaliation against another clan for any damage done to clan number one or any assaults upon any of its members. The control of private revenge, then, was divided in primitive society between the clan and the family group.

It was a religious duty of each clan to avenge summarily any wrong to its members. In summing up the general principles of clan punishment or blood-feud, as it is commonly called, the following fundamental ideas should be mentioned: First, the word "retaliation" was more applicable to the conditions in the system of blood-feud than punishment or repression. Second, the injury ceased entirely to be a private matter between the individuals concerned and became collective. An injury to any member of a clan was an injury to the whole clan. Third, the method of retaliation came to be collective, all members of a clan being compelled by the rule of custom to avenge the wrong done to any clansman. Fourth, the responsibility was also collective; if the offender could not be found then the revenge might be wreaked upon his clan. Of course, this latter principle rendered it obligatory on the clan of the offender to defend him since it meant also a defence of themselves. Fifth, the intention of the offender was entirely ignored, it making no difference whether the crime was premeditated or accidental. Sixth, owing to clan exclusiveness, no clan was concerned with the wrongs to a member of another, nor was a man usually considered a criminal in the light of his clan for injury done by him outside of his own clan. Such were the fundamental principles of blood-feud varying, of course, in detail among different peoples.

Next, what were the details which were observed in the actual carrying out of the principles of clan retaliation? Blood-feud was usually regulated by customary rules of procedure in retaliation. The basis of this procedure was the well-known *lex talionis,* the "eye for an eye and tooth for a tooth" principle. The exact literalness of this method of retaliation, in which the punishment was made exactly to fit the crime, is most astonishing. Several interesting examples may be cited. Hobhouse quotes one illustration from the *Leges Henerici;* "a man who has killed another by falling on him from out of a tree is himself put to death in exactly the same method—a relation of the deceased solemnly mounting the tree and, much one would say at his own risk, descending upon the offender." A murderer was usually executed by one of the clansmen of the deceased by the use of the same method as had been used in committing the murder. This exactness of retaliation was even carried to animals and inanimate objects, as for instance the killing of the ox who had gored a man or burying or breaking the weapon which had been used in murder.

Finally, there remains to be reviewed briefly the punishment of the third class of crimes mentioned above, namely those which took place within the family. Probably the most effective method of punishing this class of offences was outlawry or exile from the gods of the family. This was a very serious punishment for primitive man, as it removed him from all succor or protection, either from the powers of this world or those of the world of spirits, and made him the prey of anyone without involving responsibility for his injury.

In primitive society the punishment inflicted was either ceremonial or corporal, though they might be combined. The most frequent type of religious or ceremonial punishment was exile or banishment from the group and from the protection of the group gods. In early historic society this became transmuted into outlawry. In early stages of primitive society corporal punishment seems to have taken the form of any type of summary physical vengeance. Later it was developed with some ceremonial exactness into the famous *lex talionis,* according to which the physical revenge duplicated with exactness the damage originally done to the injured party. Flogging and mutilation were also utilized by primitive man, often with a ceremonial coloring. Professor Robert H. Lowie points out that the Uganda tribes in Africa make use of the confinement in the stocks as a method of punishment. The early equivalent of fines appear, as we shall see, in the practice of composition and the exaction of *Wergeld.* There is, however, little trace of imprisonment in primitive society, except in connection with cannibalism or in detention preceding the determination of guilt and punishment. By and large, the most usual types of public punishment in primitive society were death, exile and compensation. The flogging, clubbing, mutilation and the like, of which we hear so much, were chiefly examples of mob law or of private vengeance.

The attempt to repress crime through the infliction of various types of corporal punishment continued from primitive society to the close of the eighteenth century of the Christian Era. In the next chapter we shall describe briefly the various methods of applying corporal punishment. There were no remarkable phases of progress in the application of corporal punishment from the early historic period to the opening of the nineteenth century. Therefore, any attempt to trace the history of corporal punishment, epoch by epoch or state by state, from the ancient Orient, through Greek and Roman history and the Middle Ages, would involve needless and monotonous repetition. It is far better to adopt the topical treatment and to describe in some detail the leading forms of corporal punishment as they have been employed in historic times. We shall deal with this matter in the following chapter. Those who desire to examine in detail the nature of the punishments inflicted in early oriental and classical society will find an excellent summary in H. Oppenheimer's *The Ra-*

tionale of Punishment, Book II, Chapter iii ("Ancient Punishments").

IV. The Mitigation of the Principle of Blood-Feud

The system of unrestricted blood-feud was attended with many difficulties and limitations, and changes were gradually introduced to make up for the more obvious defects. The most serious of the many shortcomings of the system of clan retaliation was that it provided no satisfactory method of bringing a quarrel to an end. If a man from clan A injured a man from clan B, the matter was not settled by the revenge which was visited by clan B upon the man from clan A or upon the entire clan, but simply gave clan A a reason in turn to revenge itself upon clan B. This was due to the fact that no clan recognized a wrong against another clan or the right of another clan to avenge an injury upon one of its members. Therefore, an injury once perpetrated started a perpetual *vendetta* which was likely to render life extremely precarious to members of both clans.

A very widely practiced and successful principle of mitigation was that of compensation or composition, namely, restitution for injury through fines or money payments. This principle, of course, could not be applied to public crimes but only to the individual wrongs. Along with the principle of compensation came many other interesting reforms. Among the most important of these were distinctions in the degree of responsibility. The more remote relatives were eliminated from responsibility, and responsibility tended, in general, to be individualized. Distinction between accident and intent in the commission of crime came more and more to be recognized. In addition to the changes which might be called positive reforms there were other interesting ideas and practices which appeared with compensation. The amount of compensation varied according to the nature of the crime, the age, rank, sex or influence of the injured party. Moreover, a crime which might be settled by compensation, if committed against an average man, might call for blood revenge if committed against a nobleman. "A free born man is worth more than a slave; a grown-up more than a child, a man more than a woman, and a person of rank more than a freeman," were the usual principles governing compensation. From these differences in the amount of damages according to crime, age, sex, rank, degree of relationship, etc., there grew up such a complicated system of regulations that the earliest codified law of many peoples, particularly of the Anglo Saxon race, is in considerable part devoted to this subject of blood-fines or *Wergeld*.

In his *Introduction to the Middle Ages* Professor Ephraim Emerton presents us with an admirable account of the development of the practice of composition among the early Germanic peoples. He makes plain the nature of the process and points out the refinements which it ultimately took on:*

The same process of transition from a notion of law which made it right for every man to revenge his own wrongs by taking a life for a life, an eye for an eye, and a tooth for a tooth, to the more civilized notion of paying a well-defined penalty for such an offence, is seen in the whole matter of crimes among the Germans. Through all the folk-laws there appears one curious fundamental idea, that a man's life has a given worth in money. No doubt this was a pretty late stage in the legal growth of these people; it could hardly have been true until the idea of the common use of money as a measure of values had made its way among them. The value of a man was called his "Wergeld" (man-money), and varied considerably among the different tribes. It rested perhaps originally upon the amount of land owned by the given man, but that had been forgotten, and it depended upon the rank of man in society. The Wergeld, like all other values, was reckoned in shillings (solidi), an amount which we cannot estimate with any great certainty; but we may form some idea of how much a man was worth from the fact that in the law of the Alemanni a first-rate cow was worth one solidus and two-thirds, while the Wergeld of a freeman was two hundred solidi. According to the Salic law the ordinary Frankish freeman was

*Emerton, *op. cit.*, 87-90.

worth two hundred and the ordinary Roman landholder one hundred; but if these were in the special service of the king *(trustis)* their Wergeld was tripled. The Frisian noble was worth eighty shillings; the freeman, fifty-three shillings and one penny; and the serf *(litus)*, twenty-seven less one penny.

Lesser offences were formerly, no doubt, settled on the eye-for-an-eye principle; but in process of time a given value had come to be fixed upon each offence, and the effort of the law was to induce men to make use of these fines instead of claiming the ancient right of retaliation. The most singular nicety in this regard is seen in the Frisian law, one of those in which the original German character had been most carefully preserved.

Long experience in deciding actual cases had probably taught the judges about how much the criminal would be willing to pay rather than resort to arms, and when the law came to be written down, these figures were given to serve as the rule of the future. Thus, in the Frisian law, if a man's nose were cut off, he received twenty shillings; if it were only pierced through, fifteen. An eyebrow was worth two shillings; a canine tooth, three; a molar, four. A hand cost almost as much as the full Wergeld; a thumb, thirteen and a third shillings; the forefinger, seven; the middle finger, six and two-thirds; the ring finger, eight; the little finger, six. If several wounds were made with one blow, they were measured, and the longest one was paid for according to its length, but just how much we are not told. Evidently this latter provision was not definite enough to suit the needs of justice, for in the later "additions of the wise men" we find that in this case of several wounds made by one blow, the wounded man must first swear that such was the case, and then each wound was to be paid for as follows: if it was as long as the first joint of the forefinger, one shilling; if as long as the first two joints, two shillings; if as long as the first two and half of the third, three shillings; and if the full length of the forefinger, four shillings. Then another shilling was added for the length of the space between the forefinger and the thumb; another, for the lower thumb-joint, making six; but if the wound was as long as the whole span, from the tip of the forefinger to the tip of the thumb, the price jumped suddenly to twenty-four shillings; and if it was longer only by the difference between this span and that of the thumb and the middle finger, the price rose to thirty-six. Evidently the good men who made these changes, lived at a time when strong efforts were being made to tame these wild men of the northern marshes, by making the punishment for wrong more severe than it had been.

It is, perhaps, worth pointing out that in this respect our barbarian ancestors were wiser and more just than we are today. They adopted thoroughly the theory of restitution to the injured, whereas we have abandoned this practice, to the detriment of all concerned. Even where fines are imposed the state retains the proceeds.

V. The Growth of Public Control of the Adjustment of Private Wrongs

With the growth of the various agencies for mitigating the principle of blood-feud there was appearing the basic modern principle of the public control of private wrongs. The beginnings of the court, or that impartial third party which was lacking in primitive days, appear in the elders or council of the tribe or clan, to whom appeal might be taken, though neither party was at first obliged to abide by its decision. The court in this early appearance had peace-making rather than effective judicial functions. What was needed to give it the necessary powers was the backing of a dominant public authority which would enable the court to enforce its decrees in a fearless manner.

This need was realized with the establishment of the kingship and the firm though tyrannical central authority which went with it. The kingship, like all human institutions, grew slowly, but when it had thoroughly established itself as a strong central authority a great change came over the conception of the nature of crime and, consequently, over the method of treating it. Even the crimes formerly settled by blood-feud were no longer a private matter to be handled largely by private means. They became an offence against the king's peace, an insult to his formal vanity, and a breach of the public tranquillity which was a matter for the public authorities to settle.

With the growth of this conception of crime as an offence against the public welfare, as exemplified in the majesty of the king, there was a corresponding decline in the principle of compensation, which ultimately became obsolete. Of course, revenge did not immediately disappear, and it is found lingering on, subject to certain restrictions. For instance, it might be taken at the moment of the commission of the crime, or with the consent of the court, or in cases of the murder of a close relative or violation of marriage laws. In due time it practically disappeared though vestiges still remain in the so-called "unwritten law."

In the early days of vigorous public control of crime great rigor was practiced in the treatment of those convicted of crime. Crime now being regarded as a revolt against public authority, it was viewed as a challenge to civil and ecclesiastical power and an affront to the king's station. Hence, it was crushed out with tremendous severity. This abnormal severity in punishment is probably to be explained for two main reasons. First, order is always hard to maintain in the early days of royal power, owing to the influence of powerful families and the use of wealth. Therefore, great severity was thought desirable whenever the king had an opportunity to show his authority. Second, in the first enthusiasm of its use of its new instrument—public punishment for crime—society was supremely confident in the efficacy of the deterrent principle supposed to be found in severe punishment and was determined to use this agency to the extreme if necessary. Mr. Ives thus describes the gradual substitution of public justice under the growing royal rule for the earlier system of compensation:*

About the tenth century, after the ending of the Danish troubles, and in the eleventh under the Norman rule, the king was strong enough to extend his power and protection. In the

*G. Ives, *A History of Penal Methods*, pp. 9-10.

twelfth the old system of *bōt* and *wer,* designed to compensate
the injured and keep the peace among the fierce and warlike
race of freemen, began to give place to one under which the
king exacted punishment and tribute, which he administered
and collected through itinerant judges, sheriffs, and other
officers.

The heavy fines imposed on places and people became an
important source of revenue to the crown and to the barons
and the lords of manors when they held rights of private
jurisdiction (Sake and Soke, Courts Leet, etc.), which were
frequently delegated.

The State was growing strong enough to take vengeance;
the common man was no longer feared as had been the well-
armed Saxon citizen of old, and to the "common" criminal
was extended the ruthless severity once reserved for the slaves.
Then likewise Glanville and the lawyers, under the influence
of Rome and Constantinople, drew a sharp and arbitrary distinction between the criminal and the civil pleas, and the idea
of compensation began to wane before the revenge instinct
now backed by power. If there was money obtainable, the
king's judges would seize it; the idea of damage done to the
individual was merged and lost in the greater trespass alleged
to have been committed by the offender against the peace,
against the code and king.

VI. Summary

Briefly to review the main stages in the early history of
criminal jurisprudence, one may point out the following steps
in the process. In the first place, the few crimes which were
considered a danger to the public and, hence, punished by the
whole local group, were those which exposed the group to
outside dangers from spiritual or human enemies, particularly
the former. The crimes against persons were not punished by
the tribe, but rather by the kinship group of primitive times
—the clan—under the well-known principle of blood-feud,
or by the family. Under the unrestrained action of this principle, responsibility and retaliation for crimes were collective
on both sides and the intention of the offender was entirely
ignored. Worse than all else, the revenge failed to put an end

to the affair and furnished the means of keeping up a perpetual feud between clans.

Owing to the disadvantages of the principle of blood-feud, agencies for mitigating and reforming it arose in the duel and compensation or composition. Growing up out of and along with these new principles came the impartial third party which is now considered the essential element in adjudication, namely, the court. This at first had merely peace-making rather than judicial functions, but with the rising power of the central authority the powers and functions of the court expanded and the principle of blood-feud and its ameliorating agencies correspondingly declined. Responsibility then became individualized and intent was considered. As the power of the king and the central authorities grew, nearly all violations of the legal code were looked upon as public matters and were handled accordingly by the public organs. But the old principle of vengeance was retained, being transformed from private into public revenge. To it was added the element of deterrence, and there ensued a period of great severity in the determination of guilt and the punishment of the guilty. In due time, however, increasing enlightenment disclosed the fallacy in this theory. Some of the barbarities have been gradually removed. The old idea of vengeance and the later one of deterrence were giving way to those of social protection and reformation.

SELECTED REFERENCES

Andrews. William L. *Bygone Punishments.* 2d ed. 1931: Reprinted Montclair, N. J., 1972.

Du Cane, Edmund F. *The Punishment and Prevention of Crime.* London, 1885.

Earle, Alice Morse. *Curious Punishments of Bygone Days.* 1896: Reprinted Montclair, N. J., 1969.

Ewing, Alfred C. *The Morality of Punishment.* 1929: Reprinted Montclair, N. J., 1970.

Hentig, Hans Von. *Punishment, Its Origin, Purpose and Psychology.* 1937; Reprinted Montclair, N. J., 1972.

Hobhouse, Leonard T. *Morals in Evolution.* 7th ed. London, 1951.

Hoebel, Edward A. *The Law of Primitive Man.* Cambridge, Mass., 1954.

Ives, George. *A History of Penal Methods.* 1914; Reprinted Montclair, N. J., 1970.

Letourneau, Charles J. M. *L'évolution juridique dans les diverses races humaines.* Paris, 1891.

Lowie, Robert H. *Primitive Society.* Rev. ed. New York, 1947.

Marett, Robert R. *Anthropology.* New York, 1912.

Murdock, George. *Our Primitive Contemporaries.* New York, 1934.

Oppenheimer, Heinrich. *The Rationale of Punishment.* 1913; Reprinted Montclair, N. J., 1972.

—Pike, Luke Owen. *A History of Crime in England.* 2 vols. 1873-76; Reprinted Montclair, N. J., 1968.

Steinmetz, Sebald R. *Ethnologische Studien zur ersten Entwicklung der Strafe.* 2 vols. Leiden, 1928.

Sumner, William G. *Folkways.* Boston, 1911.

Tozzer, Alfred M. *Social Origins and Social Continuities.* New York, 1925.

Westermarck, Edward. *The Origin and Development of the Moral Ideas.* 2 vols. New York, 1906-1908.

Wines, Frederick H. *Punishment and Reformation.* Rev. ed. New York, 1919.

CHAPTER III

Methods of Inflicting Corporal Punishment

I. Flogging

IN the preceding chapter we have outlined the chief aspects of the process of dealing with anti-social action in primitive society. From the earliest days to the close of the eighteenth century the almost universal method of punishing crime was the application of some type of corporal punishment. Not until the time of the American Revolution did western civilization begin seriously to consider the substitution of imprisonment for corporal punishment. In this chapter we shall deal with the most common kinds of corporal punishment which have been employed during the course of human history. We shall limit ourselves chiefly to forms of corporal punishment which fell short of producing death by intent. The description of the historic methods of inflicting the death penalty will be reserved for a later chapter.

As the most widely employed form of corporal punishment flogging has enjoyed a long history from primitive times to our own day. Flogging has not only been one of the most popular methods of punishing public crimes; it has also been almost universally utilized as a method of preserving family, domestic, military and academic discipline. In the Mosaic code flogging was prescribed as a method of punishment for crime: "The judge shall cause him to lie down and be beaten before his face, according to his fault, by a certain number. Forty stripes he may give him, and not exceed; lest if he should exceed, and beat him above these with many stripes, then thy brother should seem vile unto thee." Parental flogging is commended in Proverbs: "He that spareth his rod hateth his son, but he that loveth him chasteneth him betimes."

For all of the above purposes flogging has continued down to the twentieth century. As a method of punishing criminals it has been one of the most frequently utilized of all types of corporal punishment, which have included, along with flogging, branding, mutilation, ducking, the stocks and pillory, as well as varied and ingenious methods of inflicting the death penalty. About 1800 imprisonment was gradually substituted for corporal punishment and flogging fell into relative disuse. It is still frequently employed, however, being legal in Delaware, Canada, Great Britain and some Continental and Asiatic lands as a punishment for certain crimes, chiefly assault, robbery and rape. As late as 1920 the British Parliament legalized the use of the "cat-o'-nine tails" in flogging those convicted of robbery. Where flogging was forbidden as a method of punishing criminals its use was often continued within the prisons as a favorite method of enforcing penal discipline. Throughout the nineteenth century, prison investigations revealed the scandalous prevalence of flogging as a method of disciplining convicts. It has by no means disappeared as yet from our prison system. Exponents of severity in dealing with convicts are still found warmly urging the revival of flogging in the United States.*

The flogging of slaves, children, pupils in schools, soldiers and sailors has been universal through the ages, though the severity differed widely in relation to the age and status of the person flogged. Slaves were frequently flogged to death when they were sufficiently numerous so that they had little pecuniary value. The amount of flogging of negro slaves in the southern United States prior to the Civil War was exaggerated in Abolitionist literature, inasmuch as the negro slaves were too valuable to reduce their efficiency by oversevere punishment. In Jewish and Christian civilization, prior to the rise of modern genetic, dynamic and educational psy-

---

*E.g. M. Kavanagh, *The Criminal and His Allies*, Chap. XXIII.

chology, scriptural precepts and natural inclination made it appear that proper discipline was lacking in the home and school unless children were frequently and instructively flogged. In preserving discipline in the army and navy flogging was relied upon and practiced with great brutality.

The instruments and methods of flogging have varied greatly. In maintaining discipline in the home, sticks, rods, straps, whips and other handy objects have been drafted into service. Rods, straps and whips with a single lash have dominated in the schools, though more recently short pieces of rubber-hose have been found highly effective and physically but slightly injurious in pedagogical service. In punishing criminals and maintaining discipline in army and naval circles the lash, with a variety of diabolically ingenious elaborations, has dominated. One of the most popular refinements of brutality with the lash has been the so-called "cat-o'-nine-tails." This gained the name because this flogging device was constructed of nine knotted cords or thongs of rawhide attached to a handle.

Even more effective in producing pain and ultimately death was the Russian *knut*. This was an instrument constructed of a number of dried and hardened thongs of rawhide interwoven with wire, the wires often being hooked and sharpened on the end so that they would tear the flesh when the blow was delivered. Severe punishment with the *knut* almost invariably meant death. A particularly painful, though not so deadly, type of flogging was the peculiarly oriental device known as the "bastinado," or blows delivered upon the soles of the feet with a light rod or a knotted cord or lash.

In the period before the reaction set in against corporal punishment flogging was executed with great brutality. The backs of the condemned were frequently cut in strips and blood gushed from their wounds. Not infrequently salt was thrown upon the bleeding backs to increase the pain. When the *knut* was used, pieces of flesh were literally torn from the back as the hooked points were jerked loose. The following quotation from Charles White's *Convict Life* presents a good picture of the incredible brutality associated with the practice of flogging criminals as late as the first half of the nineteenth century:*

At a convict station of the interior a witness on his way to the Court had to pass the triangles which had been in use that day. "I saw," he observes, "a man walk across the yard with the blood that had run from his lacerated flesh squashing out of his shoes at every step he took. A dog was licking the blood off the triangles, and the ants were carrying away great pieces of human flesh that the lash had scattered about the ground. . . . The scourger's feet had worn a deep hole in the ground by the violence with which he whirled himself round on it so as to strike the quivering and wealed back, out of which stuck the sinews, white, ragged and swollen. The infliction was one hundred lashes at about half-minute time, so as to extend the punishment through nearly an hour. They had a pair of scourgers who gave each other spell and spell about, and they were bespattered with blood like a couple of butchers."

Not only in the Old World, but also in the New, was flogging employed with the most fiendish cruelty. The following description reveals the brutality of M. Duroux, who was in charge of a French colony on Ship Island in the Gulf of Mexico off the mouth of the Mississippi River. One of Duroux's victims thus describes the experience of himself and his brother:†

Because I was unable to do the work assigned to me, I was brought to him (Duroux) for an explanation. I swore to him that I had done my best, but that my strength was insufficient for the labor imposed upon me. He set four men upon me. They threw me to the ground, stripped me naked. Duroux himself applied the whip. He struck me again and again until I lost consciousness. One eye was put out by a blow from the butt of the whip.
He ordered the four men to take me far enough from his dwelling so that my cries would not disturb his rest at night.

---

*Cited in Ives, *op. cit.*, p. 152.
†Lyle Saxon, *Fabulous New Orleans*, p. 131.

There I was bound to a tree. In my nakedness I was a prey to the mosquitoes which settled upon me in swarms. I remained there for two days and two nights without food or water.

My brother, who had made some attempt to soften his heart, was tied naked to a tree nearby. In this position, standing with his back to the tree, and with his body exposed to the sun, he presented a pitiful sight. His body was covered with blood and was black with flies and mosquitoes. He was released at the end of thirty-six hours, but died the following day.

At times there have been as many as fourteen men, naked and tied to stakes in the sun on the beach. Duroux walked up and down before them, prodding them in the softer parts of their bodies with his sword, enough to draw blood.

Convict whippings in some southern states today thoroughly match the brutality of this case.

II. MUTILATION

Another type of corporal punishment which was widely used down to the time of imprisonment was mutilation. This was early employed in connection with the *lex talionis*. As we have already seen, this procedure directed that punishment be inflicted by a method which exactly duplicated the injury originally inflicted. If a person cut off the hand of another, he lost his own hand, etc. As mayhem, or various forms of mutilation, was a common crime in primitive and early historic society, the infliction of mutilation according to the principle of the *lex talionis* had a wide application.

Another justification of mutilation as a punishment appears to have been based upon the desire to prevent the repetition of a particular crime. Thus thieves and counterfeiters had their hands cut off, liars and perjurors their tongues torn out, spies their eyes gouged out, those guilty of rape, castrated, and women guilty of adultery had their noses cut off or were otherwise disfigured in such a manner as to make further sexual intercourse with them unattractive or difficult. The preventive *motif* in regard to mutilation appears very early. The Egyptians punished rape by castration and other forms of sexual mutilation. The Assyrians punished the male adulterer with castration and, under certain conditions, disfigured his female partner. A woman who aided an adulterous rendezvous lost her ears if detected.

Even more horrible was the inflection of extensive mutilation for the purpose of creating a deterrent example and producing a gruesome object lesson to discourage other potential criminals. King Canute, of England, who developed for himself an unusual reputation for probity and justice, nevertheless gave out the following legislation prescribing mutilation as a common method of corporal punishment:

Let the offender's hands be cut off, or his feet, or both, according as the deed may be. And if he have wrought yet greater wrong, then let his eyes be put out and his nose and his ears and his upper lip be cut off, or let him be scalped, whichever of these shall counsel those whose duty it is to counsel thereupon, so that punishment may be inflicted and also the soul preserved.

The theory of mutilation as a deterrent example was also well stated in a decree of William the Conqueror:

We decree that no one shall be killed or hung for any misdeeds, but rather that his eyes be plucked out and his feet, hands and testicles cut off, so that whatever part of his body remains will be a living sign to all of his crime and iniquity.

The pain involved in these mutilations, inflicted as they were without any anæsthetic, may well be imagined. Further, loss of blood and infection were likely to produce death in the case of major mutilations. Indeed, in a medieval English law it is stated that if a man survived three days unaided after the amputation of his legs, he might be nursed back to health and freedom if the bishop of the diocese consented. Mutilation continued even in England until after the beginning of the sixteenth century. The cutting off of the ears and hands persisted until the eighteenth century.

III. BRANDING

Branding has been very generally used as a method of corporal punishment. The branding of prisoners of war, slaves and criminals, was common in late oriental and in classical societies. The Romans tended to brand criminals with some appropriate mark upon the forehead. In late medieval France the criminal was branded with the royal emblem, the *fleur-de-lis* on the shoulder. Later this was changed to the initial letter of the particular crime committed. The English made wide use of branding, as late as 1699 it being ordered that criminals should be branded upon the face. The letters used in branding bore at least a rough general resemblance to the nature of the crime committed. Murderers were branded with an "M"; thieves with a "T"; vagrants with a "V"; idlers with an "S" (meaning slave); and fighters and brawlers with an "F." Most widely used was the letter "M" meaning malefactor. Branding was also common in American colonial jurisprudence and criminal procedure. In the laws of colonial New Jersey it was stipulated, for example, that for burglary the first offense was to be punished by branding with a T on his hand, while the second offense was to be punished by branding an R on his forehead. Not until the last half of the eighteenth century was branding abolished in England, then the most enlightened European state.

Closely associated with branding was the piercing of the tongue with a hot iron. This punishment was particularly popular for lying, perjury and blasphemy.

IV. STOCKS AND PILLORY

The stocks and pillory were used as a method of corporal punishment, particularly in early modern times. The pillory was not abolished in England until 1837. When the pillory was employed in a simple fashion and not accompanied by any other mode of punishment, its operation was chiefly psychological, and it was designed to bring about the feeling of humiliation naturally attendant upon the infliction of public disgrace. Unfortunately, the stocks and pillory were very rarely utilized merely as a method of confining a person in public and exposing him to the contempt of his fellow citizens. This confinement was very frequently supplemented by making the person thus detained a legitimate target for decayed vegetables, rotten eggs and even stones. Occasionally persons in the stocks and pillory were pelted to death while thus confined. The victim might also be whipped or branded while in the stocks or pillory. It was a very common custom to nail the ears of the person confined to the beams of the pillory. When they were released they would be compelled either to tear their ears loose from the nails or have them cut away carelessly by the officer in charge. Mr. Ives thus describes the operation of the pillory in early modern England:*

This well-known instrument was made of all shapes and sizes, and varied from a forked post or a slit pillar to what must have looked like a penal dovecote made to hold several prisoners. The convicted were sometimes drawn thither on hurdles, and might be accompanied by minstrels on the way. The hair of the head and beard were shaved off, and sometimes the victims were secured by being nailed through the ears to the framework, and might also be branded. With faces protruding through the strong beams, and with hands through two holes, secured and helpless, they were made to stand defenceless before the crowd as targets for any missiles that might be thrown. To those who were hated this was a serious ordeal, for they would be so pelted and knocked about by the mob as to be badly wounded, if not actually done to death. On one occasion two informers were killed in the pillory for getting certain lads hanged for the sake of the reward. At length those who had stood their time were released, and those who had had their ears nailed would be cut free, and then they might slink away from the scene of shame, or be carried back to prison to endure additional punishment.

Somewhat similar to the stocks and pillory as a method of

*Ives, *History of Penal Methods*, p. 55.

producing humiliation was the employment of devices known
as the "Spanish Mantle." This was a barrel with a hole for
the head and arms. The prisoner was compelled to wear this
while being marched through the street subject to the derision
of onlookers. Another device similar to the Spanish Mantle
was an iron frame fastened about the body. Iron masks and
cage-like helmets were also put on criminals to produce shame
and humiliation. They were usually of a special and ingenious
design, so as to indicate the particular form of crime which
was being thus punished. Prisoners were frequently confined
in "jougs" or iron collars attached to a wall or post.

V.   Other Sundry Punishments

Confinement in irons was a common and brutal form of
punishment. A prisoner might be confined in his cell, both
hands and feet being fastened by heavy chains to the sides,
ceiling or floor of the cell. It was not uncommon for prisoners
to be chained in a reclining position upon angular bars of
iron and left in such a position for days or weeks at a time.
As late as 1830 an investigating committee in the state of
New Jersey discovered that convicts were being strapped on
their backs to a plank and left there in some cases as long as
twenty days at a time. As we shall point out in a subsequent
chapter, chain gangs are still common in the southern portion of the United States. Mr. Ives thus portrays the manner
in which men in irons were compelled to labor in the Australian chain gangs in the middle of the last century:*

But the most grievous part of the chain-gang punishment
consisted of the fetters which the men wore. The chains
weighed from six to seven and sometimes nine pounds. They
were riveted on by blacksmiths, and were examined every
morning and evening lest they should be tampered with.

In these they lived throughout the length of their sentences,
which might be six months, twelve months, two years, in
the ironed gangs. In chains they laboured like beasts of burden through the Australian heat, sometimes with legs chafed

*Ives, op. cit., pp. 157-58.

and galled by the iron clasp; and fastened they lay at night, though it might be with torn backs and much-smarting tendons after having had fifty lashes at the hands of the scourger, or twice that number if returned after flight. Even upon removal to the hospital, although the parti-coloured clothing was given up, the chains were kept on by official orders; and convicts were often interred in them.

The ducking-stool was a well-known expedient employed as a form of corporal punishment for lesser crimes. It was particularly applied to village scolds and gossips. As its name implies, this was a device in which one was strapped to a chair fastened to a long lever. The culprit thus adjusted was submerged in the water at the pleasure of the operator who manipulated the affair from the bank of the stream or pond. Crowds would usually gather to jeer at the culprit, thus increasing the psychological aspects of the punishment.

We have now briefly reviewed the method of applying some of the more common forms of corporal punishment other than those which obviously and directly involved the infliction of the death penalty. We shall postpone the discussion of the divers methods of imposing the death penalty until we take up the subject of capital punishment in a special chapter. Suffice it to say that the various methods of producing death which have been employed in regard to criminals have frequently been much more terrible and painful than any of the milder forms of corporal punishment which we have described in the preceding pages. The only extenuating feature of the fatal forms of capital punishment is to be discerned in the fact that the suffering did not usually last as long as in the case of severe mutilations and the like.

When one considers the methods of torture which we have already described, the modes of inflicting corporal punishment, and the varieties of the death penalty, we may well be both amused and astonished that anyone should object to the doctrine of evolution on the ground that it holds that man is an animal and directly related to other types of simian life. It would seem more logical and appropriate that the objection should come from our simian relatives who might present legitimate reasons for disliking to be associated with a cousin capable of the fiendish and deliberate cruelties which we have all too briefly catalogued above. Certainly no other branch of the simian world can be legitimately accused of anything of the sort. It is to be doubted, indeed, whether any other member of the animal kingdom has ever given evidence of such cruelty and brutality as has *homo sapiens* in dealing with the criminal group. If certain Catholic opponents of evolution like Mr. McCann and Father O'Toole are repelled by the notion of our physical descent from the simians, how much more humiliated should they feel at the thought of spiritual descent from the medieval and early modern inquisitors.

The Quakers, or members of the Society of Friends, appear to have been the only considerable religious group in Europe in early modern times who discerned any discrepancy between the religion of love and the infliction of brutal corporal punishments upon their fellow men or fellow Christians. They were greatly repelled by the disgraceful cruelties and protested vigorously against them. Unfortunately, they were greatly outnumbered in Europe and could do little beyond raising their voices against the usual barbarities of the age. In America, however, they controlled for a time the destinies of two English colonies. Here they introduced for the first time a criminal code which dispensed with corporal punishment, except in the case of murder. To the Quakers, then, we owe the first successful and significant protest against the savagery of corporal punishment. The great mass of Christians not only failed to demand reforms, but were themselves in the vanguard of those who wallowed in the blood of their co-religionists. In a later chapter we shall trace the effects of the Quaker protest in the gradual rise of imprisonment.

SELECTED REFERENCES

Andrews, William L. *Bygone Punishments.* 2d ed. 1931; Reprinted Montclair, N. J., 1972.

Caldwell, Robert G. *Red Hannah, Delaware's Whipping Post.* Philadelphia, 1947.

Clarke, Marcus. *For the Term of His Natural Life.* London, 1885.

Davis, William S. *Life on a Medieval Barony.* New York, 1923.

Du Cane, Edmund F. *The Punishment and Prevention of Crime.* London, 1885.

Duff, Charles. *A Handbook on Hanging.* London, 1928.

Earle, Alice Morse. *Curious Punishments of Bygone Days.* 1896; Reprinted Montclair, N. J., 1969.

Falk, Herbert A. *Corporal Punishment.* New York, 1941.

Ives, George. *A History of Penal Methods.* 1914; Reprinted Montclair. N. J., 1970.

Lea, Henry C. *Superstition and Force.* Philadelphia, 1892.

Maine, Henry S. *Ancient Law.* New York, 1931.

Napier, C. J. *Remarks on Military Law and the Punishment of Flogging.* London, 1837.

Pike, Luke Owen. *A History of Crime in England.* 2 vols. 1873-76; Reprinted Montclair, N. J., 1968.

Pollock, Frederick, and Maitland. F. W. *The History of English Law before the Time of Edward I.* 2d ed. 2 vols. London, 1898.

Salt, Henry S. *The Flogging Craze.* 1916; Reprinted Montclair, N. J., 1972.

Stephen, J. F. *History of the Criminal Law in England.* 3 vols. New York, 1883.

Thompson, J. J. "Early Corporal Punishments." *Illinois Law Quarterly,* December 1923.

White, Charles. *Convict Life.* Bathurst, Australia, 1889.

White, Walter F. *Rope and Faggot: A Biography of Judge Lynch.* New York, 1929.

Wilson, Margaret. *The Crime of Punishment.* New York, 1931.

Wines, Frederick H. *Punishment and Reformation.* Rev. ed. New York, 1919.

Wood, Arthur E., and Waite, John B. *Crime and Its Treatment.* New York, 1941.

CHAPTER IV

Transportation as a Method of Punishment

I. The British Experience With Transportation

THE sending of a criminal into exile was a common form of punishment in primitive society, but this practice carried with it certain religious and ritualistic accompaniments not found in the modern historic employment of transportation. The primitive device of exile developed in historic times into the practice of outlawry, in which the earlier religious element in exile had been largely supplanted by the political motive present in outlawry. In oriental and classical times, criminals were frequently sent away as slaves to work on galleys, in mines and the like. The experience of Great Britain with the transportation of criminals in the period following 1600 was far more the product of new historic situations and problems than a direct development from the earlier practices of exile and outlawry.

The development of the transportation of criminals in England in early modern times was the outgrowth of two different factors. During the Middle Ages and down to the time of Elizabeth many criminals sentenced to death and many captured outlaws had been sent to sea as galley-slaves. By the close of the sixteenth century the galley ceased to be an effective warship and was replaced by vessels which relied entirely upon sailing power. This meant that the day of galley-slaves was over forever. It also meant, of course, that a substitute must be found for the galleys as a place of destination for the prisoners who had heretofore been consigned to the sea. At this very time there was a marked increase of crime in England, due to the confusion and misery which accompanied the transition from medieval to modern times. These conditions are well known to all social historians of England and received their classic description in the opening pages of Sir Thomas More's *Utopia*.

This disappearance of the galley and the increase in the number of criminals brought up a very real problem as to their disposition. Even the barbarous authorities of those days could not bring themselves to the thoroughgoing application of the death penalty which was prescribed for the great majority of crimes at the period. Therefore they turned to the possibility offered by the newly founded colonies and decided to ship convicts overseas as a means of ridding England of this undesirable type of citizen. Indeed, the first legislation ordering deportation came before England had established any permanent colonies in America. It is apparent that at the outset the movement for deportation was motivated more by the desire to rid England of the criminals than to provide the colonies with man-power. The first law authorizing deportation was passed in 1597 and read as follows:*

If any of the said Rogues shall appear to be dangerous . . . or otherwyse be such as will not be reformed, That in every such case it shall & may be Lawfull to commit that rogue to the Howse of Correccion or otherwyse to the Gaole . . . there to remain untill the next Quarter Sessions . . . & then such of the Rogues so committed as . . . shalbe thought fitt not to be delivered, shall . . . be banyshed out of this Realme and all the domynions thereof . . . and shall be conveied unto such partes beyond the seas as shalbe at any tyme hereafter for that purpose assigned by the Privie Counsell. . . . And if any such Rogue so banyshed as aforesaid shall returne agayne into any part of the Realme . . . without lawfull Lycence or Warrant so to do, that in every such case the offence shalbe Fellony and the Party offending therein Suffer Death as in case of Felony.

This right of deportation was still further elaborated by an order of the Privy Council in 1617:†

*Ives, *op. cit.*, p. 107.
†J. E. Gillespie, "The Transportation of English Convicts After 1783," in *Journal of Criminal Law and Criminology*, November, 1922.

Whereas it hath pleased his Majestie out of his singular Clemencie and mercy to take into his princely consideration the wretched estate of divers of his Subjects who by the Lawes of the Realme are adjudged to dye for sondry offences though heynous in themselves, yet not of the highest nature, soe as his Majestie both out of his gracious Clemencye, as also for diverse weighty Considerations Could wishe they might be rather Corrected than destroyed, and that in theire punishmentes some of them might live, and yealde a profitable Service to the Common wealth in partes abroad, where it shall bee founde fitt to employ them, for which purpose his Majestie having directed his Commission under the greate Seale of England, to vs and the rest of his privy Counsell, gyving full power warrant and Authoritye to vs or and Sixe or more of vs whereof the Lord Chancellor or Lord Keeper of the Greate Seale, to be two, to Reprieve and stay from execution suche persons as now stand Convicted of any Robbery or felony (Willfull murther, Rape, witchcraft or Burglary onely excepted) who for strength of bodye or other abilityes shall be thought fitt to be imployed in forreine discoveryes or other Services beyond the seas. . .

The final legislation legalizing transportation was embodied in the Act of 1717 which ran as follows:*

That the present laws are not effectual to deter from crime; that many offenders to whom the royal mercy hath been extended upon condition of transporting themselves to the West Indies, have often neglected to perform the said condition, but returned to their former wickedness, and been at last for new crimes brought to a shameful ignominious death. And whereas, in many of His Majesty's colonies and plantations in America, there is great want of servants, etc., be it enacted . . . that any person convicted of any offence for which he is liable to be whipt or burnt on the hand, or shall have been ordered to any workhouse . . . may be sent to some of His Majesty's colonies and plantations in America. And the court before whom he is convicted shall have power to convey, transport, or make over such offenders to any such person as shall contract for the performance of such transportation, and to his assigns, for such term of years as the Act empowers, and they shall have property and interest in the service of such

*E. F. Du Cane, *The Punishment and Prevention of Crime*, pp. 113-14.

person for such term of years. Offenders returning before expiration of term to be liable to death. The king may pardon an offender sentenced to such transportation, the offender paying his owner. Contractors to give security for performance of contract, and to obtain certificate from the governor of the colony of having fulfilled it.

By 1775 England was sending about two thousand convicts annually to the English colonies in America, mostly in the form of indentured servants. There is no way of determining exactly how many criminals Great Britain exported to America during the colonial period, but the more conservative estimates put the number between fifty thousand and one hundred thousand. Their condition upon arrival in America varied greatly. If they fell into the hands of a kind master who was living in a prosperous area, their lot might be relatively fortunate and happy. If they were unlucky enough to be owned temporarily by a brutal master who was himself suffering hardships, their condition might be terrible indeed. The following estimate by Mr. Ives in his *History of Penal Methods* appears to the writer to be a fair and just one:*

What then had been the actual condition of those transported to the American and island plantations? The colonial evidence is extremely various: many, if not most, convicts desired and urgently petitioned to be sent out; yet others dreaded it more than death. Although the pioneers underwent very great hardships, yet the conditions of those who came afterwards were largely determined by their personal qualities and equally by those of the masters they served under.

Often the food was meagre and the life rough and hard, and these conditions pressed with fatal severity upon those who were in any way degenerate and sickly, and numbers were. We can still read the piteous lamentations of one Richard Frethome. He wrote that since he landed he had eaten nothing but pease and cobboly, "and had to work both early and late for a mess of water gruel and a mouthful of bread and beef; a mouthful of bread for a penny loaf cannot serve four men." He had nothing at all, not a shirt to his back but two rags, nor no clothes but one poor suit, nor but one pair

*Op. cit., pp. 120-23.

of shoes, but one pair of stockings, but one cap, but two bands. "Oh that you did but see my daily and hourly sighs and groans, tears and thumps that I afford mine own breast, and rue and curse the hour of my birth with holy Job. I had thought no head had been able to hold so much water as hath and doth daly flow from my eyes." The poor creature died but a few months afterwards.

Besides the inevitable hardships of their situation, the indentured servants had frequently to endure their masters' violence. In Virginia their lives are said to have been protected only in theory, and of Barbadoes in the early period a witness exclaims, "Truly I have seen such cruelty there done to servants as I did not think one Christian could have done to another." The most common punishment was, of course, flogging; servants were generally flogged where freemen were fined; and in Virginia, ten to thirty lashes were the usual number inflicted, but the actual severity would depend on the overseers and the instruments they employed.

In 1705 a law made it necessary to get a Justice-of-the-Peace order to be allowed to flog a Christian white servant naked; under a penalty of 40s. The servants would frequently run away from bad masters, and became liable to severe penalties if recaptured; to whipping, branding, and to having their serving time extended by from one to seven years; and they might have to labour in chains. Yet from the natural facilities of the country they escaped in great numbers, and some of them fled to the woods and mountains and stayed there, and so went out of civilisation for good and all.

But were they not better off than those in prison or penal servitude? As a class, they were beyond measure happier than the inmates of any walled-in penal institutions. In the early days the struggle was mainly with nature, for food and shelter, when master and slaves contended together in common cause. In later times the serfs' position grew worse in some ways from their association with the downtrodden negro slaves; on the other hand, they gained advantages from some later laws. Except in those cases where they served under the worst masters, their position had many aspects that were human and even hopeful for their future in the colonies. An old writer on the state of Virginia has remarked about the convicts that "Their being sent thither to work as Slaves for Punishment is but a mere notion, for few of them ever lived so well and so easily before, especially if they were good for anything." "These are to serve seven and sometimes fourteen years and they, and servants by indenture, have an allowance of corn and cloathes when they are out of their time."

As soon as they (the convicts) were landed in America, says another author, they were no longer convicts but servants by indenture or custom of the country, and at the end of their term of bondage it was the custom to give them the plant to start with, including raiment, tools, and implements, and also three barrels of corn. Sometimes a grant of fifty acres was added; and in any case land was obtainable easily. In the year 1690 Governor Howard directed that every servant should receive a patent of fifty acres in fee on attaining his freedom. So that a man or woman had a real chance to retrieve past faults or misfortunes and was not merely cast forth to attempt the (almost) impossible. And in consequence many did well, and out of the fifty thousand or more who had been sentenced to transportation some rose to attain high honour and position.

The American Revolution and the separation of the thirteen British colonies from Great Britain in 1776 put an end to transportation of convicts to America. The large supply of available convicts in England was, however, in no wise diminished by the Revolution in America. Therefore, the British had to consider what was to be done with them. Many were placed upon old boats, the notorious prison hulks, which will be described fully in a later chapter. This did not provide adequate relief, however, and it was decided to send the convicts to other parts of the British Empire. A few were sent to Africa, but they perished quickly when exposed to the tropical climate and the diseases of that area. Hence, on January 23, 1787, it was decided to deport convicts to the newly discovered areas in Australasia. This meant a considerable change in the earlier practice of transportation. The transformation has been well described by Professor James E. Gillespie in the following paragraph:*

Thus was inaugurated, in a somewhat hasty manner, a system totally different from any hitherto tried. Previously

*Gillespie, loc. cit., p. 361.

convicts had been sent to serve as bond servants to colonial planters. Masters of merchant vessels had assumed the responsibility for the transport and disposal of the convicts as bond servants to the planters in a colony where such servants formed the unimportant minority of the whole colonial population. Under the system used in Australia, the majority of the colonists were to be convicts, and they were directly controlled by the government which founded the colony for their disposal.

The first expedition was made up of about seven hundred and fifty convicts, on board six transports and accompanied by two war vessels and three provision ships. It left England on May 13, 1787, and arrived off what is now the city of Sydney in 1788 after an eight months' trip. Upon landing a rude prison was erected under military guard and supervision and the prisoners were put at work in the effort to conquer the virgin territory of Australia. The original penal colony was threatened with famine, but in the middle of the year 1790 relief arrived from Great Britain.

The transportation conditions at the outset were terrible beyond description. Instead of sending the convicts under governmental supervision and at government expense, contractors were engaged at so much per head to transport the convicts to Australia. Professor Gillespie thus describes the situation:*

Hired transports were employed to convey the convicts from England to New South Wales. Contractors received between £20 and £30 per head. The more convicts carried the greater the profit would be, thus as many were usually crammed on board as the ships would hold. As a result of such a state of confinement the most loathsome disease was common and the death rate was extremely high. Out of 502 who were placed on the "Neptune" in 1790 for conveyance to Australia, 158, and in 1799, 95 out of the 300 on board the "Hillsborough" died on the voyage. Those who did arrive were so near dead that they could not stand, and it was necessary to sling them like goods and hoist them out of the ships,

*Gillespie, p. 362.

and when first landed they died at the rate of ten or twelve a day. The government attempted in 1802 to correct these evils by sending convicts twice a year in ships specially fitted out for the purpose, and placed under the direction of a transport board and commanded by naval officers. Although the transports continued to be crowded, health conditions apparently were greatly improved as it was reported in 1819 by Sir T. B. Martin, the head of the transport board, that within the past three years only 53 out of 6,409, or at the rate of 1 in 112, had died. Out of the 10 transports which had recently sailed only one or two had died.

Dr. Vanderkemp, a Moravian missionary, has left his impressions of the voyage on the convict ship "Hillsborough" in 1799:*

About 240 of these miserable creatures were chained in pairs, hand to hand or leg to leg, with no light but what came in at the hatchways. At first the darkness of the place, the rattling of the chains, and the dreadful imprecations of the prisoners, suggested ideas of the most horrid nature, and combined to form a lively picture of the infernal regions. Besides, in a short time a putrid fever broke out among the convicts, and carried off 34 before the ship reached the Cape, and the ship became loathsome beyond description.

The condition of convicts upon arrival in Australia is well indicated in the following passage from Mr. Ives' *History of Penal Methods*:†

When the "Neptune," "Scarborough," and "Surprise" entered Sydney Harbour, the Chaplain, Mr. Johnson, climbed on board the last-named. "Went down amongst the convicts," he writes, "where I beheld a sight truly shocking to the feelings of humanity—a great number of them lying, some half, and others entirely naked, without either bed or bedding, unable to turn or help themselves. Spoke to them as I passed along, but the smell was so offensive that I could scarcely bear it. I then went on board the 'Scarborough,' and proposed to go down amongst them, but was dissuaded from it by the Captain. The 'Neptune' was still more wretched and intolerable, and therefore I never attempted it." The con-

---

*Cited by Du Cane, *op. cit.*, p. 126.
†*Op. cit.*, pp. 132-33.

victs sometimes concealed the fact of a death amongst them, in order to devour the dead man's rations, and then each hidden carcass added its quota to the pestilential atmosphere.

"Some of these unhappy people died after the ships came into the harbour before they could be taken on shore . . . The landing was truly affecting and shocking; great numbers were not able to walk, nor move hand or foot; such were slung over the ship's side in the same manner as they would sling a cask, a box, or anything of that nature. Before their being brought up to the open air some fainted, some died upon deck, and others in the boat before they could reach the shore. When they came on shore many were not able to walk, to stand, or to stir themselves in the least, hence, some were led by others. Some creeped upon their hands and knees." . . . The existing sick at Port Jackson had been under fifty; the new comers swelled the list up to close on five hundred.

The best authorities estimate that about one hundred and thirty-five thousand convicts in all were sent to Australasia between 1787 and 1857 when the practice was virtually abandoned. The convicts were distributed about in various parts of Australasia. They were located not only in Australia but also in Tasmania and on Norfolk Island, the latter of which was some one thousand miles east of Australia in the lonely Pacific. The Norfolk Island colony is particularly important because it was here, in 1840, that Captain Alexander Maconochie introduced his scheme of commutation for good behavior which was later adopted in the famous Irish prison system developed in the middle of the last century by Walter Crofton. The Irish prison system was the most important foreign stimulus to the group of reformers who established the Elmira Reformatory in the United States about 1875. It should not, of course, be supposed for a minute that Maconochie's enlightenment was at all characteristic of the treatment of criminals in the Australasian penal colonies. It was but a momentary flash in an unbroken night of dismal and unrelieved savagery. It received no support in Australasia, and became of historical significance only because it attracted Walter Crofton and other reformers at home.

The conditions among the convicts in Australia were deplorable in the extreme—indeed almost incredible. In America the deported convicts had been handed over to responsible masters who possessed a real reason for desiring to keep them alive and decently healthy. The official and military government of the Australian convicts removed this motive for the preservation of the life and health of the convict population. The chain gangs, the flogging and other brutalities almost defy description. Further, the moral conditions among the convicts were indescribable. Particularly notorious was the development of the prevalence of homosexuality, owing to the few women among the convicts. We have already quoted above descriptions of life in the chain gangs and of the terrible Australian whipping posts. The Parliamentary Committee of 1838 thus compared the transportation of convicts to America and to Australasia:*

The offenders who were transported in the past century to America were sent to communities, the bulk of whose population were men of thrift and probity; the children of improvidence were dropped in by driblets among the mass of a population already formed, and were absorbed and assimilated as they were dropped in.

In New South Wales, on the contrary, the community was composed of the very dregs of society—of men proved by experience to be unfit to be at large in any society, and who were sent from the British gaols, and turned loose to mix with one another in the desert, together with a few taskmasters who were to set them to work in the open wilderness, and with the military who were to keep them from revolt.

The consequences of this strange assemblage were vice, immorality, frightful disease, hunger, dreadful mortality among the settlers. The convicts were decimated by pestilence on the voyage, and again decimated by famine on their arrival; and the most hideous cruelty was practised towards the unfortunate natives.

*Cited in Du Cane, *op. cit.*, pp. 123-24.

One of the most comprehensive and graphic descriptions of life in the Australian penal colonies is contained in the following paragraphs of Mr. Ives' classic work:*

It would be hard to conceive a worse place than Port Macquarie, or a more dismal convict settlement than Port Arthur; men dragged out their days in chains and gloom, and often died and were put away underground in fetters unfreed; things can't be much worse than that. But Norfolk Island was the worst place of all in several ways. The sentences were generally longest; a number were there for life (especially in the latter days), and the colonially-convicted were frequently sent out to the settlements "for the remainder of their sentence" of transportation, which might easily involve them in a life doom (or sometimes for a comparatively short term, for much the same sort of crime). The sentences, too, were often increased in the penal settlements at Norfolk Island; many of the prisoners never returned till the place broke up (most of them were taken away in the year 1855), and one writer states that two-thirds of them perished there.

Moreover, at Norfolk Island especially, but not exclusively under Price, they employed gags, bridles or head-stalls, and a veritable engine of torture known as the Stretcher, which has been described as an iron frame some six feet by three, not unlike a bedstead, the sides being kept in position by round iron bars twelve inches apart. Upon this frame the victim was fastened, the head extending over the edge and without support. One man is said to have been placed upon the instrument in a dark cell and left in this fashion for the space of twelve hours; he was found to be dead when ultimately they came to him.

Another medieval method was to suspend chained prisoners by one hand; and one of the most dreaded penalties sometimes resorted to was to sentence a man to work—often with unhealed wounds from quite recent flogging—in the Cayenne pepper mill, the fine stinging dust from which was especially maddening.

But the hellish conditions prevailing in all those inhuman prisons for colonial penal servitude can best be conceived from sidelights thrown upon them by the behaviour of the wretched prisoners.

---

*Ives, op. cit., pp. 167-70.

As we shall find them doing at English convict prisons many years afterwards, the prisoners would injure and mutilate themselves—as for instance by putting lime in their eyes —to get in the hospital. I will reproduce an official description of all they had upon Norfolk Island for the care of two thousand men. "The hospital," observes Mr. Stewart, "is a low building containing three wards, two of them accommodating five beds each, the other ten. The mode of ventilation is objectionable, as a thorough draught cannot be avoided; the wards are exceedingly hot in summer and cold and damp in winter. They open upon a narrow verandah into an enclosed yard about 80 feet by 20; this is the only place in which the patients can take exercise. . . . The smell is always offensive in consequence of the want of a proper sewer, but during the hot season the stench is excessive. Twenty beds, and a detached cold convalescent ward are the extent of hospital accommodation."

Likewise, at each and all of the penal settlements, the prisoners committed desperate assaults, often upon each other by pre-arrangement, "from absolute weariness of their lives," in order to get away from those dreadful places, if only as witnesses, or even as persons accused of murder. At Macquarie Harbour, on one occasion, three prisoners tossed: one was to be slain, another was to strike the fatal blow, the third was to be the witness of the planned deed; so they would get a respite —a grim "holiday." At Port Arthur one man murdered his own particular friend and companion, that both might get free from it.

The same hideous tragedies took place also at Norfolk Island; crimes were committed to obtain the journey to Sydney, even if it were to be upon a capital charge. There, too, the "parts" to be taken were often decided by lot, and they always tried to furnish the greatest possible number of witnesses. The appearance of these has been described by Sir Roger Therry, who at that time was attorney-general. They had been two or three years upon Norfolk Island, and "Their sunken, glazed eyes, deadly pale faces, hollow fleshless cheeks, and once manly limbs shrivelled and withered up as if by premature old age, created a thrill of horror amongst the bystanders. They were all under thirty-five years of age." The authorities met this terrible state of things in a manner typical of nineteenth-century prison boards. In 1834 the New South Wales Governor was empowered to convene a Criminal Court upon Norfolk Island, to be composed of a barrister and five officers. Henceforth these desired journeys to the trials at Sydney would be denied; the abuses they let alone, and the outrages might continue, but all was to be settled out at the prison; and the gallows would swing men there.

Nevertheless, striking and accurate as Mr. Ives' paragraphs may be, they can give one no real notion of the actual horrors of Australasian convict life in the first half of the nineteenth century. To get any adequate impression of the real state of affairs one must read widely in the clinical literature. Important here are such books as Charles White's *Convict Life,* a careful historical summary; Marcus Clarke's famous novel, *For the Term of His Natural Life,* based on a faithful study of the records; *Adventures of an Outlaw: the Memoirs of Ralph Rashleigh,* a recently recovered and published diary of a convict in Australia from 1825 to 1854; Rolf Boldrewood's *Robbery Under Arms,* a description of bushranging; and Henry Kingsley's *Geoffry Hamlin,* which portrays early Australian life, particularly as affected by convict labor and the fear of bushrangers.

There was little or nothing to mitigate the sufferings of the convicts. They came to Australasia, starved, diseased, and weakened from the effects of the long sea voyage passed under the worst conceivable conditions. They were at once put to work at the hardest kinds of tasks in clearing and breaking land, mining, burning lime and the like. Their inexperience added to the severity of the conditions. They were controlled and supervised by brutal and sadistic overseers, whose chief pleasure seemed to consist in finding excuses for cruel and repeated floggings. When they were not employed by the government at the above occupations the convicts were let out to farmers. But the latter were almost invariably ex-convicts who had won their freedom. They tended to take out on their convict helpers the venom they had accumulated when being inhumanly treated as convicts themselves. The abusiveness of the farmers frequently equalled that of the government overseers. While the convicts were assigned to the hardest type of labor for long hours, their food was very inadequate and their clothing scanty. There was great suffering from cold in winter, and convicts were often compelled to work with bare feet where tough shoes would have been quickly scuffed to pieces. The horrible life which they lived was a natural incentive to attempt escape. Many who succeeded in breaking away became bushrangers. Securing arms, they scoured the countryside committing murder, robbery and arson, not failing in the process to even up old scores with brutal former overseers and employers. Revenge of this sort, while often carried out with revolting cruelty, is almost the only chapter in the history of Australasian penal administration which one can read with any real satisfaction.

As an indication of the depths to which the human animal can descend when entrusted with power over his fellowmen, we may quote the following passages from the description of Ralph Rashleigh's experiences in the camp of convict lime-burners in Australia:*

The lime-burners' camp consisted of two lines of hovels, enclosed by a tall palisade made of strips of the outer coat of the cabbage palm. The convicts here were the exiles and outcasts of the criminals from whose ranks they derived, only the weak, the vicious and the untameable being sent here from the horrors of Newcastle. As Rashleigh arrived they were busily employed loading boats with marine shells, which were burned, but not slaked, for making lime. This loading was done by means of baskets which were filled and carried through the surf on the convicts' backs to the boats, into which the shells were tipped.

Rashleigh was at once given a basket and ordered to join the rest. He appealed to the overseer to be allowed to do some other kind of work, urging the soreness of his back, raw from a hundred lashes yesterday, as an excuse for his request. The overseer affected sympathy and asked to be shown the sore place, and when Rashleigh gingerly peeled off the piece of rough rag which he had secured as a dressing, the brute in

*The Adventures of an Outlaw: The Memoirs of Ralph Rashleigh, pp. 247-53.

charge flung into the sore a handful of quicklime, and cut him sharply across the spot with his stick.

"Get to your work, you blasted, crawling caterpillar," he shouted, "or I'll soon serve you ten times worse than that!"

Rashleigh took up his basket and waded out into the salt water, which set the lime sizzling in his festering wound, while the brine seemed to eat into the raw cuts left by the lash. Almost mad with the pain, he was nevertheless kept steadily on the run until about ten o'clock at night, when the last of the boats were loaded, and the worn-out, hungry wretches, who had been in and out of the water at this work for sixteen hours, were at last allowed to go to their comfortless hovels and rest. One or two of the hundred and fifty men had some-how managed to make themselves bedding of dried seaweed, but the vast majority slept on hard wooden slabs which were the substitute for beds.

The living conditions of the emaciated wretches who were condemned to work at the lime-burners' camp were incredibly severe at this time. The only clothing which was permitted did not vary in the heat of summer or the bitterness of winter, and consisted of the rag apron worn for the sake of decency. Every man wore not less than two sets of leg-irons—many had four and six as punishment for excessive delinquencies— and at all hours, governed only by the state of the tides, they were compelled to work breast-high in the sea in order to un-load their baskets in the boats which drew about three to four feet of water. In the summer their bodies were peeled of skin, and in the winter they were frozen and frost-bitten; huddling together at night on the floor of their sleeping-hovels in order to generate some warmth. Their weekly allowance of food was three and a half pounds of maize in cob, and an equal weight of ill-cured salt beef, and even this was reduced by the commissariat overseers, who stole freely from the common stock. The convicts were powerless to complain of these pec-ulations by their immediate superiors, who held the power to punish them with lawless fury. There were no stated hours for labour, it being a compulsion on the overseers to work the men as long as they could be made to stand, and it was usual for the convicts to be driven for fifteen hours a day.

The crown of the lime-burners' misery, however, was the treatment meted out to them on the periodical visits of the commandant of the district during his tours of the out-stations. Rashleigh had learnt at Newcastle the almost insane devotion of this despot to the infliction of pain upon the wretches under him, and he guessed that the severity of punishment would increase on this side of the river, inhabited as it undoubtedly was by the most incorrigible ruffians in the ranks of the convicts. The commandant always came with two scourgers, each of whom carried three or four "cat-o'-nine-tails," and his method on arrival was to go from one working party to another, pick out any poor exhausted devil who was working less industriously than his mates, tie him to the nearest fence and have him lashed with never less than fifty strokes. Their backs running with blood his victims were at once ordered to resume their work.

To Rashleigh it seemed that this man's temper was completely perverted. Scenes and sounds which aroused pity and loathing in any ordinary man were a source of fiendish delight to him, and it was a habit of his suddenly to spring at the scourger and belabour him with his riding-whip in order to make him flog the tied convict with harder blows. His especial pleasure was to select men from the boat-loaders' gangs, and have them flogged until their backs were raw, so that he could enjoy the sight of the writhings and the sound of the shrieks as he compelled them to place their baskets of lime on their bleeding backs and wade out into the stinging salt water. His eyes would dilate with satisfaction at the pain caused by the lime slaking in the blood of the wounds. Several times during his stay there, Rashleigh saw men drown themselves before the eyes of their torturer, whose comment was always to the effect that it would save the Government rope and the hangman a job. . . .

There was danger for any man who was fortunate enough to receive a soft bone with his meat allowance. The greedy envious eyes of his companions would watch him as he voraciously ground it in his teeth and when, his jaws wearied, he flung down a portion of the bone, there would be a wild scramble for it. On the second day of his internment Rashleigh learnt how terrible a thing hunger could be.

He had flung down a bone, and in the scuffle that ensued for its possession two men grabbed different ends of the bone, and as neither would admit that the other had priority of claim, Rashleigh was asked to decide who should have it. He suggested dividing it, but the famished wretches would not agree, and at last he decided in favour of one of them. The man who had lost the bone, looking murder at Rashleigh and the man with the prize, fell away from the group, while the possessor partly crushed the bone between two stones, and sat down with his back to a shed and began to gnaw it.

Rashleigh stared at the man in pity, wondering how long it would be before he were reduced to a similar state of bestial acquisitiveness, when he saw the second man standing over the eater with a great iron shell-rake raised ready to strike. Rashleigh shouted a warning and sprang forward to prevent the blow, but was too late. As he sprang the rake crashed onto the head of the unsuspecting man with a force which crushed his skull and spattered the brains around.

"Ha, ha, I've got it now!" cried the murderer, snatching up the half-gnawed bone, covered with the blood and brains of his victim, cramming it into his mouth and holding out his hands to the overseer who came running up to handcuff him. His hunger was appeased for the moment: what did punishment and hanging matter!

Rashleigh was appalled to learn, on questioning his mates about this episode, that such atrocities were by no means rare; and one of the men—who had come over with him on the ship from England—warned him never to save any portion of his food for another meal, as there were many among the older, brutalized convicts who would not hesitate to kill him for a handful of maize or a bit of rotten meat.

In spite of the above, and many similar occurrences narrated in the work, Lord Birkenhead could write in a Foreword to Rashleigh's memoirs as follows:

There is no just cause to feel shame that such experiences as are here recorded could befall Britishers. One may, perhaps, regard the disappearance of the transportation system, and all that it connoted of human suffering, with relief and satisfaction; but in an historical sense it can be said that the wisdom and justification of that system lay in the incontrovertible fact that it worked well.

Such a statement might be permissible in an ardent Irish nationalist, who might well find nothing too bad to "befall a Britisher," but it is a strange utterance to proceed from a distinguished English jurist. Rather, we should say that the experiences recorded in the authoritative books on Australasian

convict life should bring shame to the human race as a whole.
They are a standing blot on the character and behavior of the
species. The worst charges which the most soured and con-
firmed misanthrope could bring against the human animal
would be supported by ample clinical evidence in the record of
penal servitude in Australasia less than a century ago.

The following account presents an excellent illustration of
the horrible revenge which bushrangers frequently took on
brutal former overseers. In the description which we shall cite,
McCoy, Foxley and Smith were bushrangers, and Huggins
was an overseer who had earlier inflicted severe punishment
on McCoy:*

Huggins seemed to shrink with fear before the concentrated
venom of the man, and in his rabid terror began again to pour
out supplications for mercy.

"Shut up, you worm!" cried McCoy. "Take a look at me.
Don't you know me?"

Huggins looked, but failed to recognize the man.

"Aye, but you do know me," continued McCoy; "you
know Sandy McCoy. It's not twelve months since I was under you, in your bloody gang. One day when I wanted to see
the doctor you put me in the lock-up for six-and-thirty hours
handcuffed to a beam over my head, so that all my weight
was on my wrists and my toes just touching ground. Christ!
If you forget, I remember. Now it's our turn, and you may as
well say your prayers, for you're standing on your grave."

"He did that trick on you, did he, McCoy?" said Foxley;
and listening to his story, Rashleigh could understand the
hard ruthlessness of the bushrangers. "That's a common
hobby of his and his kidney. Not a month since, one of his
deputy-overseers was tried for killing a poor devil who was
sick, like you, and wanted to go to hospital. But Mr. Huggins ordered him to be triced up, and his deputy did as he was
told, and left him there two days and two nights. The first
night the deputy was told the man was dying, but he answered, "Let him die, and be damned too!" So the next night,
when the doctor came at last to see him, the poor devil was
dead—stiff as a rod. That crawler, though he was committed,
managed to get clear. But I'll take damned good care you

*The Adventures of an Outlaw, pp. 188-91.

don't escape from justice, you murdering swine, for I'm judge and jury in this here court, and I never acquitted a tyrant in my life."

Huggins now threw himself on the ground in an agony of despair and terror, beating his head on the rock. Then he knelt to Foxley, alternating supplications with imprecations, until at length the leader of the gang broke out:

"Blast the crying beggar! He'll make us all deaf. Gag him."

As he spoke Foxley suddenly leapt up and began to act like one demented. Swearing and roaring, he jumped about, rolled on the ground, and finally began to tear off his clothes until he stood stark naked: whereupon he recommenced his wild dancing antics, whistling, shouting, singing, halloing and swearing all in a breath. It was some minutes before Smith, McCoy and Rashleigh understood the cause of this quaint exhibition. The more to enjoy his triumph over Huggins, Foxley had sat down incautiously near a huge nest of ants, of a species vulgarly known in the colony as light-horsemen. They are phenomenal pests upward of an inch and a half long, blue and green in colour, and are the fiercest and most virulent biters among all bush insects. While Foxley had sat still they had not molested him, but when he had moved, they had stung him by scores, and now his body was smothered with swellings the size of hazel nuts. His companions judged how intense the pain must have been from the fact that he, who was then grimacing and yelling with pain, had been seen to endure the most severe floggings without so much as wincing.

Foxley at last gathered up his clothes and shook them free from the ants, cursing the now prostrate Huggins as the cause of it all.

"Blast you!" he roared, with demoniac ferocity. "You can lie there; but I'll waken you with a vengeance before I'm done. Make me some ropes," he ordered the others with a snarl. He himself joined them in the task of improvising ropes out of rolled bark lining, and when the cords were made, set about cutting and trimming a number of stakes, which he sharpened at the end. He then made Smith and McCoy gather all the logs and short timber lengths that they could find, while Rashleigh looked on wondering what new diabolism was in preparation.

The three bushrangers approached Huggins and stripped him of every stitch of clothing, and dragged him—despite all his violent resistance—over to the ant-bed. Then Rashleigh understood. They were going to tie the man down and leave him to one of the most dreadful deaths ever conceived by the debased imagination of man. He began to beg Foxley to desist, using every argument that his frenzied mind could lay hold of, finally reminding the outlaw that sooner or later his turn to suffer for the crimes he committed must come. . . .

"Hi! you," yelled Foxley to Rashleigh, "come and help get this dog tied up."

He had no alternative but to obey, except the death to which they had condemned Huggins, and so Rashleigh was obliged to carry the practically senseless man back to the ant-heap. The ants were angered and scared by the second thud of his body, and in a few moments had completely covered him. The bushrangers began coolly to tie the wretched man down with cords fastened to the stakes which Foxley had prepared, securing him as firmly as the Lilliputians did Gulliver. The agony which he was suffering from the myriad bites of the swarming ants set him struggling like a madman, but the only effects of his efforts were that he still more infuriated the ants, and tightened the bonds against which he struggled. Rashleigh was dizzy with sickness and fell to the ground in a faint, striking his head upon a sharp stone. Almost instantly he recovered consciousness, and was allowed to go, under the guidance of McCoy, in search of water. After a prolonged search they found enough for their immediate purposes, and he prepared a meal of what remained of their provisions. Presently Foxley and Smith came up, and the leader, noticing how scanty was the fare, swore that had he known how depleted was the larder, he would have cut a steak off Huggins's body before giving it as a meal to the ants. Rashleigh could not suppress an expression of mingled incredulity and disgust at the loathsome suggestion.

"Aye, softy," said the brutal Foxley, "I tell you there isn't a tastier morsel in this world than the heart of a tyrant."

For a bitter instant Rashleigh was tempted to retort that Foxley should himself make the most toothsome meal that ever could be cooked, but checked himself in time.

After supper the party lay down to rest, and started out again at an early hour in the morning towards the Western Road, whence they had come after meeting the luckless Huggins. They passed the spot where he had been tied to the ant-heap, and Rashleigh was swept with nausea again to see that nothing but the untouched head and the clean, stripped bones remained of the thick-set overseer. To this kind of end did the criminal penal code lead; for, undoubtedly, he reflected, the man would never have been killed but for the fact that he had been so brutal in his punishment of McCoy, and Foxley himself had suffered at the hands of other overseers before making his escape.

A number of influences combined to bring about the abandonment of the practice of sending British convicts to Australasia. The discovery of gold in the middle of the nineteenth century brought in a large group of non-convict inhabitants. Further immigration was stimulated by the discovery of the possibilities of sheep raising and wheat cultivation in Australia. The non-convict population resented the sending of more convicts and petitioned the home government to abandon the practice. The humanitarians in England were shocked by the conditions which were shown to exist in the Australian penal colonies. Finally, the imitation of the American prison system led to the building of elaborate prisons in England to receive the British convict population on home ground. Therefore, a strong agitation against transportation began in the '40's and the whole enterprise was practically abandoned in the '50's. It was entirely suppressed in 1870, and there thus disappeared one of the most gruesome episodes in the history of organized and systematic human cruelty.

II. OTHER EXPERIMENTS WITH TRANSPORTATION

France essayed to imitate the British scheme of transportation in 1791 when it ordered life transportation of all convicts convicted of a felony a second time. It was planned to use the island of Madagascar as a penal colony. The destruction of the French navy prevented the execution of this enterprise, but in 1851 the proposal of transportation was revived. French Guiana was selected as the location of this French penal colony and full legislative sanction was provided by an act of May, 1854. In 1863 New Caledonia, an island in the southern Pacific some seven hundred miles east of Australia,

was chosen as the second French penal colony. French Guiana
and Devil's Island off the coast, together with New Caledonia,
remain to the present day the two penal settlements maintained by France. They are still in active and extensive use.
There is no doubt whatever that the most incredible and indefensible brutalities to be found today in the treatment of
criminals by a civilized nation exist in these two French penal
colonies. The noted traveler, Mr. Harry A. Franck, writing in
the New York *World* in 1926, commented in the following
fashion on his observation in the main prison located in Cayenne, the capital of French Guiana:

I have never been able to understand why the French, with
so many admirable qualities, can be so brutal to helpless beings under them as they are to the exiled convicts. To be sure
they are "tough guys." I doubt if our own prisons could produce as vicious, as heartless a set of murderers and cutthroats
as the criminal element of Paris. . . .
The guardians of the prisoners in French Guiana apparently consider it a punishment themselves to be sent there and
are inclined to take it out on the convicts. The principal
seemed bent on impressing upon me his efficiency as a warden
by showing how brutal he could be to the wretches under
him. One living skeleton shaking with fever lay on his plank
covered with a dirty strip of cloth. "Where did he get that?"
shrieked my guide to the trembling trusty in charge of the
room. It was an old flour sack, replied the trembling trusty;
the invalid had complained of cold.
"Let him shiver," shouted the principal. "This is no rich
man's hospital. Give it to the guard outside before I send you
out with a shovel again." Another sick man failed to rise to
his feet and take off his hat as we passed until the warden
bawled at him that such an act of "insubordination" merited
the dungeon.
The atmosphere of the whole place was that of a den of
vicious animals, between whom and their keepers there was
not the suggestion of a bond of human sympathy.
Not all those sentenced to Cayenne are professional criminals from the underworld. One sewer digger working barefoot
under the deadly sun was pointed out to me as once a noted
Paris lawyer. The high official, who stole several millions of

public funds when the churches of France were declared state property, brought up in Cayenne.

Sometimes it is a political prisoner who is no criminal at all from our point of view, but merely the victim of his rival politicians. But high or low, they are all thrown together, and a few months, or at most years, of hard labor under an equatorial sun with scanty food and hopeless surroundings, gives them all, the Parisian Apache or the high official gone wrong, the same gaunt, yellow, whipped-dog appearance.

I asked the warden whether he noticed any great difference between men of education and comfortable circumstances who came to him and the vicious scum of France that undoubtedly makes up the majority of the unwilling guests of the colony. His reply was illuminating, symbolical of France's great American prison. "Bah!" he cried, "Give us a month and you cannot tell one from the other."

The condition and treatment of the convicts in the French penal colony in French Guiana and the adjacent islands has been made the subject of a recent powerful and illuminating book by Blair Niles, entitled *Condemned to Devil's Island*. The work is a first-hand study not only of Devil's Island itself but of the whole French penal colony. Presented in somewhat dramatic fashion as the interpretation of the mental reactions of condemned prisoners, it is one of the two or three most forceful books ever contributed to the exposure of the perennial cruelty associated with prison methods. As a revelation of the conduct in French penal colonies it occupies a place comparable to that of Marcus Clarke's famous novel of Australian prison life, entitled *For the Term of His Natural Life*. The horrors of life in this French penal colony can only be appreciated by one who takes the pains to consult Mrs. Niles' moving work. Suffice it to say that, except for the floggings, nothing which we know of Australia a century ago surpasses for fiendish and studied cruelty the human hell which exists in French Guiana. The book created something of an international sensation and led to at least certain gestures of reform on the part of the French government. Indeed, it was recently reported in the press that the French government was contemplating the abandonment of the transportation of convicts to French Guiana and Devil's Island.

The other country to experiment extensively with transportation was Russia,* which established penal colonies in Siberia, on the islands off the coast in the Pacific and in Turkestan. As might be expected of a state much more barbarous and backward in its policies and administration than either France or England, the conditions of the Russian prisoners in the Siberian prison camps defy verbal description. It was the same old story of vermin-infested prisons, chain gangs and brutal floggings. Nowhere else in modern times, among supposedly civilized nations, have the convicts been treated with more indefensible and uniform barbarism than they were in the old Siberian penal settlements. The classic description of life in the Siberian prison camps is contained in Feodor Dostoyevsky's famous work, *The House of the Dead*, based upon the four years' experience of the author as an inmate of one of the Siberian penal colonies.

In the early days of the Bolshevik Revolution in Russia there was a notable relaxation in the brutal treatment of criminals, and more stress was laid upon rehabilitation. For some time this was widely praised by open-minded observers of Communist Russia. But exile to Siberia was continued on a considerable scale, especially for those anti-Bolsheviks who were not killed off during the Revolution. When Stalin came into power, a harsh totalitarian system was introduced, the number of political prisoners was greatly increased, and those not executed were sent off to Siberian labor camps where their treatment was fully as brutal as that of those exiled under the Tsars. A million or more of the prosperous peasants or *kulaks* were killed off and those that survived suffered, in Siberia, what was often worse than death.

Transportation, then, which, in its rudimentary form of exile and outlawry, was one of the earliest recorded forms of

---

*Italy maintains penal colonies in northern Africa and on Mediterranean islands, in which the customary brutalities are practised. See F. Nitti, *Escape.*

punishment, still remains actively with us as one of the vestiges of barbarism in a supposedly civilized era. The annals of the practice are among the darkest stains in the history of a subject which is as a whole perhaps the most repulsive phase of human history.

SELECTED REFERENCES

Ballagh, James Curtis. *White Servitude in the Colony of Virginia.* Baltimore, 1895.

Barry, John Vincent. *Alexander Maconochie of Norfolk Island.* New York, 1958.

Belbenoit, René. *Dry Guillotine.* New York, 1938.

Boxall, George E. *A History of Australian Bushranging.* 4th ed. London, 1916.

Browne, Thomas Alexander [Rolf Boldrewood, pseud.] *Robbery Under Arms.* New York, 1954.

Cash, Martin. *The Adventures of Martin Cash . . . in Tasmania . . . in the Year 1843.* Hobart, Australia, 1870.

Clarke, Marcus. *For the Term of His Natural Life.* London, 1885.

Dostoyevsky, Feodor. *The House of the Dead.* New York, 1915.

Gibb, Eric. *Thrilling Incidents of the Convict System in Austral-Asia.* London, 1895.

Gillespie, J. E. "The Transportation of English Convicts after 1783." *The Journal of Criminal Law and Criminology,* November 1922.

Griffiths, Arthur. *Memorials of Millbank.* London, 1875.

Hunter, John. *Historical Journal.* London, 1793.

Kennan, George. *Siberia and the Exile System.* 2 vols. New York, 1891.

Kingsley, Henry. *Recollections of Geoffrey Hamlin.* New York, 1894.

Krarup-Nielson, Aage. *Hell Beyond the Seas.* New York, 1936.

Lang, John D. *Transportation and Colonisation.* London, 1837.

Lipper, Elinor. *Eleven Years in Soviet Prison Camps.* Chicago, 1951.

Niles, Blair. *Condemned to Devil's Island.* New York, 1928.

Nordhoff, Charles, and Hall, James N. *Botany Bay.* Boston, 1941.

O'Brien, Eris M. *The Foundation of Australia, 1786-1800. A Study in English Criminal Practice and Penal Colonisation in the Eighteenth Century.* London, 1937.

Rashleigh, Ralph [pseud.]. *The Adventures of an Outlaw: Memoirs of R. Rashleigh, a Penal Exile in Australia, 1825-1844.* New York, 1929.

Smith, Abbott E. *Colonists in Bondage.* Chapel Hill, N. C., 1947.

Solzhenitsyn, Alexander. *One Day in the Life of Ivan Denisovich.* New York, 1963.

Tench, Watkin. *A Complete Account of the Settlement at Port Jackson in New South Wales.* London, 1793.

Ullathorne, William B. *Autobiography.* 2 vols. London, 1891-92.

White, Charles. *Convict Life.* Bathurst, Australia, 1889.

CHAPTER V

The Reform of the Criminal Law
(1750–1850)

I. THE INTELLECTUAL BACKGROUND OF THE
REFORM MOVEMENT

O NE of the most striking phases of cultural progress
from 1500 to 1800 was the remarkable development
of natural science from the age of Copernicus to the
days of Newton and Lavoisier. This put at man's disposal a
vast amount of new knowledge concerning the nature of the
physical universe, the processes of physical nature, the structure, growth and decay of organic substances, the processes
involved in the physical life of man, and the relationship
between man and other members of the animal kingdom. It
also tended to emphasize the character and productivity of the
new scientific or inductive method of searching for truth, as
opposed to the older deductive religious and metaphysical
techniques.

At first, this scientific mode of approach was confined to
the physical and biological sciences, but its development and
success there made it inevitable that it would ultimately
come to be applied to man and his social relationships as
well. By undermining those views of man which had rested
upon the religious outlook, it also helped to make it seem
more worth while to study man simply as a human being
in a secular setting. The discoveries overseas served to help
along this scientific movement by stimulating the spirit of
curiosity and by bringing in a large amount of highly varied
information about the physical universe as observed from
new angles. This embodied the flora and fauna of the world,

new rocks and chemicals, geographic conditions, and, above all, the customs of man in all parts of the planet and in all stages of cultural evolution.

The implications of the new natural science and the overseas discoveries for philosophy and social science were exploited chiefly by the British Deists and Rationalists and by their followers on the Continent, who are usually known as the French *Philosophes*. These writers, among whom were Lord Herbert of Cherbury, Alexander Pope, the third Earl of Shaftesbury, John Locke, David Hume, Thomas Chubb, Henry St. John Bolingbroke, Conyers Middleton and Tom Paine, attacked the savagery in orthodox Christianity, argued for a more urbane and genteel attitude toward God, contended that religion should appeal to man's reason, questioned miracles, and, in particular, supported toleration and freethinking. Alexander Pope and others attacked the conventional Christian tendency to degrade man as man and to regard man in his secular sense as a vile entity unworthy of interest or study. The Deists as a group upheld man as the supreme achievement of God's creative ingenuity to date and contended that to depreciate man was an indirect insult to God.

By thus rehabilitating man in his mundane setting, as he had not been since Greek days, the Deists and *Philosophes* made possible the rise of the social sciences which are devoted to a study of the nature of man and of his social relationships. Hitherto, theology had been regarded as the "queen of the sciences," because it was man's soul which was important and theology was the technique for exploring and saving the soul. With the growth of interest in man as man there inevitably came a great increase in the desire to improve social conditions by eliminating abuses and oppression and thus increasing human happiness. In other words, secularism immediately suggested reforms in institutions, something in which a logical orthodox Christian could scarcely find any absorbing interest. A Christian was chiefly concerned with salvation. In any event, he expected secular civilization and material things to pass away fairly soon. This interest in reform was best expressed by Helvetius, Condorcet and Bentham. The whole rationalistic philosophy in all of its aspects was best summarized in the various writings of Tom Paine, not an original author but an organizer and expositor of a high order and a noble crusader for truth and justice.

While this rationalistic movement began in England, it soon gained headway on the Continent. Voltaire visited England in his earlier years and became the greatest of all exponents of the philosophy of freedom and enlightenment because of his versatility, his courage and zeal, and his international reputation. Diderot and the Encyclopedists first systematized, classified and rendered available to the reading public the essentials of the new learning and the new rationalistic philosophy. The Abbé de St. Pierre, Helvetius and others were among the leaders of those who aroused an interest in social reform and called for the reconstruction of social ideals and practices.

II. BECCARIA AND HIS WORK

While Montesquieu, particularly in his *Persian Letters,* attacked the abuses in the existing criminal law, and while Voltaire took an active part in the campaign for the reform of criminal law and criminal procedure, neither the British nor the French Rationalists produced the most effective work in the field of the reform of criminal jurisprudence. This honor was reserved for an Italian admirer of the British and French Rationalists, Cesare Bonesana, Marchese di Beccaria (1738-1794). There was little about Beccaria's personality or life to merit special mention. He was born of a noble family and lived in easy circumstances throughout his life. He was a man of thoughtful, retiring disposition, somewhat timid and lethargic. His early life was spent primarily in leisure and literary pursuits. From 1768 to 1770 he was a professor of political economy (the second to hold such a title in Italy) in the Palatine School in Milan. The remainder of his life was divided between retirement and occasional service as a magistrate and a member of commissions. While he wrote on economics, æsthetics and criminal law, his literary product of greatest historic moment was his famous *Trattato dei delitti e delle pene* (Essay on Crimes and Punishments), published in July, 1764.

The framework of Beccaria's thought was provided by his intensive cultivation of the French and English Rationalists of this period. He freely confessed his indebtedness to them. He was familiar with writings of the whole group, but a few in particular seem to have had a special influence upon his thinking and aspirations. Montesquieu's *Persian Letters* stimulated him to take cognizance of the stupidities and the oppressive nature of many European institutions at that time, and especially to note the barbarities in the system of criminal procedure. The same writer's *Spirit of Laws* impressed upon him the fact of the relativity of the excellence of laws, depending largely upon their adaptability to the people and the times. From Hume and Helvetius he derived much of his humanitarianism, his hedonism and his utilitarian view of ethics. The Encyclopedists supplied a broad comprehension of eighteenth century learning and enlightenment. Voltaire, as well as Montesquieu, drew his attention to the notorious abuses and cruelties in the body of criminal law and in the methods of treating criminals which prevailed at the time. Finally, his intimate friend, Alessandro Verri, was a prison official in Milan. Beccaria frequently visited the institution, and the revolting scenes which he invariably beheld during these visits furnished the clinical information and the moral stimulus to the execution of the literary work which had more practical effect than any other treatise ever written in the long campaign against barbarism in criminal law and procedure.

Beccaria was in no sense a professional lawyer, jurist or technical student of criminology. Therefore, he was equally free from the paralyzing weight of tradition and convention and the limited perspective of professional activity. He wrote as an intelligent outsider, who handled the problem completely divorced from tradition but filled with the humanitarianism, enlightenment and courage of contemporary Rationalism. The play of such a mind upon his chosen subject was bound to work a revolution. It was an almost perfect example of common sense applied to law. His classic work was composed between March, 1763, and January, 1764, and was published in July of that year. It was written at the insistence of, and in collaboration with, his friend Pietro Verri, the brother of Alessandro. Pietro was a man of marked literary ability. He actually wrote parts of the *Dei delitti* and carefully revised the whole work.

In order to appreciate the timeliness and novelty of the book it is necessary to recall the situation at the time, characterized as it was by secret accusations, almost complete absence of provision for the defense of the accused, extensive use of the most savage types of torture, an incredibly large number of capital crimes, and barbarous lesser punishments, such as whipping, branding and mutilation. Space does not permit a careful analysis of his famous *Essay,* but we may summarize concisely the essentials of the system which he recommended:

(1) The basis of all social action must be the utilitarian conception of the greatest happiness for the greatest number. (2) Crime must be considered as an injury to society, and the only rational measure of crime is the extent of this injury. (3) Prevention of crime is more important than punishment for crimes; indeed, punishment is justifiable only on the supposition that it helps to prevent criminal conduct. In preventing crime it is necessary to improve and publish the laws, so that the nation may know what they are and be brought to support them, to reward virtue, and to improve education both as to legislation and life. (4) In criminal procedure secret accusations and torture should be abolished;

there should be speedy trials; the accused should be treated humanely prior to trial and must have every right and facility to bring forward evidence in his behalf; and turning state's evidence should be done away with, as it amounts to no more than a "national authorization of treachery." (5) The purpose of punishment is to deter persons from the commission of crime and not to provide social revenge. Not severity, but certainty and expedition in punishment best secure this result of deterrence. Punishment must be sure and swift and penalties determined strictly in accordance with the social damage wrought by the crime. Crimes against property should be punished solely by fines, or by imprisonment when the person is unable to pay the fine. Banishment is an excellent punishment for crimes against the state. There should be no capital punishment. Capital punishment does not eliminate crime. Life imprisonment is a better deterrent. Capital punishment is irreparable and hence makes no provision for possible mistakes and the necessity of later rectification. (6) Imprisonment should be more widely employed, but its mode of application should be greatly improved through providing better physical quarters and by separating and classifying the prisoners as to age, sex and degree of criminality.

Beccaria's conclusions state his viewpoint with clarity and conciseness: "In order that every punishment may not be an act of violence committed by one man or by many against a single individual, it ought to be above all things public, speedy, necessary, the least possible in the given circumstances, proportioned to its crime, dictated by the laws." Excepting only the modern psychiatric analysis of the criminal, with its substitution of the conception of treatment instead of punishment, one may safely say that Beccaria's little treatise envisaged the major criminological advances during the next century and a half.

Beccaria's brochure had an enormous influence upon his contemporaries and successors, only the outstanding phases of which can be mentioned here. The French Rationalists, especially Voltaire, welcomed it with great enthusiasm. Voltaire proclaimed that it would assure to its author immortality and would work a revolution in the moral world. Eminent writers on law and criminal reform, such as Sonnenfels in Austria, Filangieri and Renazzi in Italy, and Blackstone, Howard, Bentham and Romilly in England, were profoundly influenced by Beccaria's doctrines and freely acknowledged their indebtedness to him.

Much in the way of practical reform of criminal jurisprudence also grew out of his *Essay.* Among such evidences of progress, which were in greater or less degree influenced by Beccaria, may be mentioned the reforms in Austria under Maria Theresa and Joseph II, those carried out by Leopold of Tuscany, the criminal code of the French Revolution, the abolition of the barbarous criminal code of England, and the reform of the criminal law in the United States after 1776. Catherine the Great was much impressed by Beccaria's work and invited him to St. Petersburg to aid her in drawing up a new code of laws. He was obliged to decline on account of delicate health.

III. THE REFORM OF THE CRIMINAL LAW IN ENGLAND

We have just pointed out how Beccaria and other continental reformers had stimulated an interest in the reform of the criminal law throughout Europe. We may now survey briefly the nature and results of this movement for the reform of the criminal law in England in the century following the work of Beccaria.

The most important figure in arousing British interest in the atrocious treatment of criminals in the latter half of the eighteenth century was John Howard (1726-1791). Howard thus describes the origins of his interest in the reform of prisons and the criminal law:*

---

*Cited in E. C. Wines, *The State of Prisons and Child-Saving Institutions.*

The circumstance which excited me to activity in behalf of prisoners was the seeing some who by the verdict of juries were declared not guilty, some on whom the grand jury did not find such an appearance of guilt as subjected them to trial, and some whose prosecutors did not appear against them, after having been confined for months, dragged back to jail and locked up again till they should pay sundry fees to the jailer, the clerk of assize, etc. In order to redress this hardship, I applied to the justices of the county for a salary to the jailer in lieu of his fees. The bench were properly afflicted with the grievance, and willing to grant the relief desired, but they wanted a precedent for charging the county with the expense. I therefore rode into several counties in search of a precedent, but I soon learned that the same injustice was practised in them; and, looking into the prisons, I beheld scenes of calamity which I grew daily more and more anxious to alleviate. In order, therefore, to gain a more perfect knowledge of particulars and the extent of the evil by varied and accurate observation, I visited most of the county jails in England. Seeing in two or three of them some poor creatures whose aspect was peculiarly deplorable, and asking the cause of it, I was answered, "They were lately brought from the bridewells." This started a fresh subject of inquiry. I resolved to inspect the bridewells, and for that purpose I travelled again into the counties where I had been, and indeed into all the rest, examining bridewells and city and town jails. I beheld in many of them, as well as in the county jails, a complication of distresses; but my attention was principally fixed by the jail-fever and the smallpox, which I saw prevailing to the destruction of multitudes, not only of felons in their dungeons, but of debtors also.

While Howard devoted himself primarily to the investigation of prisons and to agitation for prison reform, the publicity which he gave to the treatment of criminals was one of the most powerful influences leading to the movement for the reform of the British criminal code.

Next to Howard the most influential person in England in arousing a sentiment for the reform of criminal law and prison conditions was the leader of the British utilitarians, Jeremy Bentham (1748-1832). Bentham's interest in the reform of the criminal law was a joint product of his humanitarianism and his desire to provide more scientific and modernized legislation. He wrote extensively on all aspects of criminal jurisprudence and prison administration, and many supposedly contemporary suggestions in these fields can be discovered in the voluminous writings of Bentham. He was the great intellectual ferment lying back of the reform of the criminal law as well as of many other types of social progress in England between 1775 and 1850. If his *felicific calculus* is no longer taken seriously as a key to human behavior, yet one can but admire his rationalistic courage and his comprehensive humanitarianism. He applied his *felicific calculus* to the theory of criminal law reform. He recommended that penalties be fixed which would impose an amount of pain just in excess of the pleasure which might be derived from the crime. This prospect of deriving more pain than pleasure from a crime would, Bentham believed, deter men from committing crimes. Bentham was, of course, sufficient of a student of social conditions to realize that crime could best be prevented by eliminating those general conditions which promote its development. Bentham's philosophy was digested, clarified and widely disseminated on the continent of Europe by Pierre Etienne Louis Dumont.

The four figures most intimately bound up with the practical movement for the reform of the brutal English criminal code, with its two hundred and twenty-two capital crimes, were Romilly, Mackintosh, Peel and Buxton. Sir Samuel Romilly (1757-1818), an able Whig lawyer, was the first great leader in the direct and persistent agitation for the reform of the English criminal code. He devoted his main efforts to this enterprise in the generation preceding his death in 1818. His reputation for reform in this field spread all over Europe. Though the inertia and conservatism of his country at the time made it impossible for him to achieve any sweeping results during his life, yet he launched the program of education and legislative agitation that was carried to success by his followers. Especially important was his notion that the improvement of living conditions—namely, preventive measures—would be far more effective in repressing crime than the most severe penalties. In other words, he took the enlightened view that prevention is more effective than punishment.

The two men who took up the mantle of Romilly were Sir James Mackintosh (1765-1832) and Sir Thomas Foxwell Buxton (1786-1845). Mackintosh was a distinguished Whig publicist, jurist and the predecessor of Macaulay as the historian of the English revolution of 1688. He bore the brunt of the fight against the barbarous British code after the death of Romilly. Sir Thomas Foxwell Buxton (1786-1845), married the sister of Elizabeth Fry, a well-known prison reformer of that age. Like Bentham he was interested in general humanitarianism, and the reform of the criminal law and prison conditions enlisted his interest and active support. The immediate legislative activities in behalf of the reform of the criminal code devolved primarily upon Sir Robert Peel (1788-1860). Due in large part to his efforts, the program of Romilly, Mackintosh and others was formulated, put into specific legislation and ultimately engineered through Parliament in piecemeal installments. Particularly famous was Peel's great speech of March 9, 1826, in support of legislation abolishing the barbarities in the existing British code.

As a result of the activity of the above persons and their supporters the British criminal code was completely transformed between 1820 and 1861. At the beginning of this period some two hundred and twenty-two offences were punishable by the death penalty. In 1820 the law was repealed which made it a capital offence to steal five shillings worth of goods from a shop. In 1822 the death penalty was removed on some hundred offences. In 1823 deportation was substituted for death in case of making false entries on a marriage license. In 1832 the death penalty was abolished for house-breaking, the stealing of horses and sheep and counterfeiting. In 1837 the death penalty was abolished on a number of other offences including smuggling and rioting. In 1861 the death penalty was finally removed on all offences except murder, treason and piracy.

The reform of the criminal law naturally led to a sweeping modification in the treatment of criminals. To be sure, the death penalty had not been carried out with any thoroughness, it being very usually commuted into confinement in the prison hulks or transportation to the American colonies and later to Australasia. While the practice of transportation to Australasia endured until past the middle of the nineteenth century, the reform of the British criminal code was accompanied by an ever greater interest in the use of imprisonment as a method of punishing crime. The British prisons at the middle of the nineteenth century were a product of both native ingenuity and the imitation of foreign innovations. Englishmen like Sir Thomas Beevor had established impressive local prisons in England and led to admiring comment on the part of his fellow countrymen.

Even more influential, however, was the example of the United States. The establishment of the Pennsylvania and Auburn systems of prison discipline in the first quarter of the nineteenth century attracted world-wide interest, and in 1832 Mr. William Crawford (1788-1847) was sent to America to investigate and report on these American prison systems. He was partial to the Pennsylvania or solitary system which, with modifications, was adopted by Great Britain. The melancholy results of this decision are well described by Mr. George Ives in his *History of Penal Methods* (pp. 182-200). We may now turn to the reform of the criminal code in the United States following the Revolutionary War, with special attention to the developments in Pennsylvania which was the center of reform from which the other states derived their incentive to progress.

IV. THE TRANSFORMATION OF THE CRIMINAL CODE
IN AMERICA (1776-1825)

There were two main causes for the reform of the barbarous provincial criminal code when Pennsylvania obtained
its independence. The first was the feeling that the code of
1718 was not a native colonial and national product, but
that it was the work of a foreign country, forced upon the
Province by taking advantage of its early religious scruples
and divisions. Especially was this view taken by the Quaker
element in Philadelphia and eastern Pennsylvania. Therefore,
it was natural that a reaction against the English criminal
jurisprudence should be one of the first manifestations of
national spirit after 1776. The second chief cause of reform
was the growth of enlightenment and criticism abroad. The
movement represented by Montesquieu, Voltaire, Diderot,
Beccaria, Paine, Bentham and others, which we have described above, had affected the leaders of colonial thought
in Pennsylvania to such an extent that reform would probably have been inevitable without the strong local impulses
which existed at home. This background of the reform of
criminal jurisprudence in Pennsylvania has been well summarized by one of the ablest contemporaries of, and participants in, the movement, William Bradford, Justice of the
Supreme Court of Pennsylvania, Attorney-General of the
United States and designer of the reformed Pennsylvania
penal codes of 1790 to 1794. Writing in 1793, he thus
explained the transformation of the criminal codes of Pennsylvania:*

We perceive, by this detail, that the severity of our criminal
law is an exotic plant, and not the native growth of Pennsylvania. It has been endured, but, I believe, has never been a
favorite. The religious opinions of many of our citizens were
in opposition to it: and, as soon as the principles of Beccaria
were desseminated, they found a soil that was prepared to
receive them. During our connection with Great Britain no

---

*H. E. Barnes, *Evolution of Penology in Pennsylvania*, pp. 105-6.

reform was attempted; but, as soon as we separated from her, the public sentiment disclosed itself and this benevolent undertaking was enjoined by the constitution. This was one of the first fruits of liberty and confirms the remark of Montesquieu, "That, as freedom advances, the severity of the penal law decreases."

It was natural that when the American reaction against English jurisprudence took place in Pennsylvania, it should take the form of a return to the doctrines and practices of Penn. The new state constitution of September 28, 1776, directed a speedy reform of the criminal code along the line of substituting imprisonment for the various types of corporal punishment. It was here directed that:

The penal laws as heretofore used, shall be reformed by the future legislature of the State, as soon as may be, and punishments made in some cases less sanguinary, and in general more proportionate to the crimes.

To deter more effectually from the commission of crimes, by continued visible punishment of long duration, and to make sanguinary punishments less necessary; houses ought to be provided for punishing by hard labor, those who shall be convicted of crimes not capital; wherein the criminals shall be employed for the benefit of the public, or for reparation of injuries done to private persons. And all persons at proper times shall be admitted to see the prisoners at their labor.

The absorption of attention and energy by the military struggle with England prevented any immediate reform of the criminal code, but on September 15, 1786, an act was passed which aimed to carry out the provisions of the constitution of 1776. The juristic conceptions of the framers of the act were expressed in the following paragraph:

Whereas, it is the wish of every good government to reclaim rather than to destroy, and it being apprehended that the cause of human corruptions proceed more from the impunity of crimes than from the moderation of punishments, and it having been found by experience that the punishments directed by the laws now in force, as well for capital as for other inferior offences do not answer the principal ends of society in inflicting them, to wit, to correct and reform the offenders, and to produce such strong impression on the minds of others as to deter them from committing the like offences, which it is conceived may be better effected by continued hard labor, publicly and disgracefully imposed on persons convicted of them, not only in the manner pointed out by the convention, but in streets of cities and towns, and upon the highways of the open country and other public works.

It was enacted, accordingly, that every person henceforth convicted of robbery, burglary, sodomy or buggery, instead of suffering the death penalty, should forfeit all property to the state and serve a sentence of not to exceed ten years at hard labor in the jail or house of correction in the county or city where the crime was committed. Horse stealing was penalized by full restoration to the owner, the forfeiture of an equal amount to the state and imprisonment at hard labor for a term not to exceed seven years. Simple larceny, over twenty shillings, was to be punished by full restitution, forfeiture of like amount to the state and imprisonment at hard labor for a term not to exceed three years. Petty larceny, under twenty shillings, was to receive a like punishment, except that the maximum term of imprisonment was limited to one year. It was further decreed that a mother could not be convicted of the murder of a bastard child unless it could be shown that the child was born alive. Finally, it was stipulated that any other crimes not capital, in the earlier code, but punishable by "burning in the hand, cutting off the ears, nailing the ear or ears to the pillory, placing in or upon the pillory, whipping or imprisonment for life," should thereafter be punished by imprisonment at hard labor for not more than two years. In this manner there disappeared from the statute books the most brutal and revolting phases of the criminal jurisprudence and procedure of the colonial period, although the death penalty was still retained for some ten crimes.

The important act of April 5, 1790, establishing the

Pennsylvania system of imprisonment in solitary confinement, while primarily a law concerned with penal administration, specified the penalties for crimes committed, but this part of the act simply repeated the terms of the law of September 15, 1786. The act of September 23, 1791, while chiefly devoted to the details of criminal procedure, made some advances with respect to ameliorating the severity of the criminal code. It repealed the death penalty for witchcraft, and ordered that there should be no more branding, whipping or imprisonment at hard labor imposed for adultery or fornication. These crimes were to be punished by a fine of not more than fifty pounds and imprisonment for three to twelve months.

The next great step in the progressive reform of the criminal code of Pennsylvania came in an act of April 22, 1794, but before analyzing the content of this act it will be useful and interesting to examine the chief doctrines of the able and influential pamphlet, published by William Bradford in 1793, on the desirability of reducing the number of capital crimes in Pennsylvania.* This work is most important in a number of ways. In the first place, it summarizes and indicates the sources of the doctrines of the jurist who drafted the revised penal code of Pennsylvania, as passed in installments by the legislature during the years 1786 to 1794. In the second place, it was very influential in bringing about the acceptance by the legislature of the law of 1794 reducing the list of capital crimes in Pennsylvania to that of murder in the first degree alone. Finally, as the product of the ablest legal mind in America at the time, it attracted wide attention at home and in Europe, and furnished the reformers with a valuable instrument for aiding in their assaults upon the old order in criminal jurisprudence.

Throughout the work, Mr. Bradford gave evidence of the fact that the works of Montesquieu, Beccaria and Blackstone

*W. Bradford, *An Enquiry How Far the Punishment of Death Is Necessary in Pennsylvania,* 1793.

were not only the chief source of his own conviction that the mitigation of the criminal laws was an indispensable and immediate necessity, but that he regarded them as the main inspiration which had produced the newer and more humane conceptions in criminal jurisprudence. At the outset Mr. Bradford laid down the dictum that the only object of punishment is the prevention of crime. The purpose of the death penalty, then must be solely to prevent the person executed from participating in another like crime and to deter others from committing crime through fear of death. If these ends can be accomplished by other modes of punishment, then the death penalty is unjustifiable. Mr. Bradford contended that solitary confinement at hard labor would accomplish all that had been claimed for the death penalty. He showed that history proves that mild penalties do not encourage the commission of crime nor severe penalties deter from criminal action. The example of Rome and England, he held, demonstrates this conclusively. Rome never imposed the death penalty except upon slaves, and yet it was much more orderly than England with its unprecedentedly long list of capital crimes. The experience of America had been similar to that of Rome and England.

Mr. Bradford then turned to a scientific examination of the effect of the ameliorating law of September 15, 1786, in Pennsylvania, upon the commission of those crimes which were removed from the list of capital offences. He concluded that, when all disturbing influences were eliminated, the results revealed the fact that the number of commissions of these crimes was less in the six years after 1786 than in the six years previous to that time. Mr. Bradford stated that he believed that society might safely dispense with the death penalty in the case of all crimes except premeditated murder and high treason. Finally, it might be that, sooner or later, the progress of intelligence would be sufficient, so that capital punishment could be wholly abolished. His conclusion is significant:

The conclusion to which we are led by this enquiry seems to be, that in all cases, except those of high treason and murder, the punishment of death may be safely abolished, and milder penalties advantageously introduced. Such a system of punishments, aided and enforced in the manner I have mentioned, will not only have an auspicious influence on the character, morals and happiness of the people, but may hasten the period, when, in the progress of civilization, the punishment of death shall cease to be necessary; and the legislature of Pennsylvania, putting the keystone to the arch, may triumph in the completion of their benevolent work.

Mr. Bradford had the satisfaction of seeing his theories enacted into law in the act of April 22, 1794, "for the better preventing of crimes, and for abolishing the punishment of death in certain cases." It was declared that,

It is the duty of every government to endeavor to reform, rather than to exterminate, offenders, and the punishment of death ought never to be inflicted where it is not absolutely necessary to the public safety.

Accordingly, it was enacted,

That no crime whatsoever, hereafter committed, except murder in the first degree, shall be punished with death in the State of Pennsylvania.

It was specified that murder in the first degree would be constituted by all premeditated murder and by all murder committed in attempting rape, arson, robbery or burglary. All other types of murder were to constitute murder in the second degree. The death penalty for murder in the first degree was to be inflicted "by hanging by the neck."

In addition to this remarkable reduction of capital crimes, the act provided reduced penalties for the crimes which were eliminated from the list of those punishable by death. The following were the penalties prescribed: *murder in the second degree*, imprisonment of from five to eighteen years; *manslaughter*, imprisonment for from two to ten years, with from six to fourteen years for a second offence; *murder or con-*

cealment of the death of a bastard child, imprisonment up to
five years or a fine at the discretion of the court; *high treason,*
imprisonment for from six to twelve years; *arson,* imprisonment from five to twelve years; *rape,* imprisonment for from
ten to twenty-one years; *malicious maiming,* imprisonment
for from two to ten years and a fine up to one thousand
dollars, three-fourths of which was to go to the party injured; *counterfeiting,* imprisonment from four to fifteen years
and a fine up to one thousand dollars. "Benefit of clergy" was
"forever abolished."

It was provided that if a person be convicted a second
time of a crime which was capital on September 15, 1786,
he should be confined for life in the solitary cells of the Walnut Street Jail, unless the inspectors saw fit to remove him
from these cells. The only exception to this rule was in case
the second offence was committed after escaping or being
pardoned; in such instances the penalty for a second commission of the crime was to be imprisonment for twenty-five
years. With some minor revisions, especially in the Act of
April 23, 1829, the law of 1794 remained the basis of the
criminal code of Pennsylvania until the systematic revision
of the code in 1860.

A slight increase in the severity of the penal code was produced by an act of April 4, 1807. The act of September 15,
1786, had decreed a punishment of not to exceed two years'
imprisonment for those crimes, not capital in 1786, but
which had been punished by the brutal forms of corporal
punishment and by imprisonment for life. This act of April
4, 1807, raised the maximum limit for these crimes to seven
years imprisonment, though it specified that this increase
should not apply to bigamy, accessory-after-the-fact in a
felony, or the reception of stolen goods. From this time until
the revision of April 23, 1829, there were no important
alterations in the criminal code of Pennsylvania.

We have devoted special attention to the reform of the
criminal law in the state of Pennsylvania because this was

the germinal center of progress in this field in the United States at the close of the eighteenth century. The innovations in Pennsylvania stimulated other states to follow her example, and within a half century following the Declaration of Independence all the American states had abolished the older and barbarous methods of corporal punishment and had substituted imprisonment therefor. In the next chapter we shall take up the subject of the rise of imprisonment as the normal and conventional method of punishing crime. We shall there indicate how the Pennsylvania system of prison discipline arose, how it stimulated the rise of the competing Auburn system, and how the struggle between these two systems colored the whole development of prison discipline during the first half of the nineteenth century.

SELECTED REFERENCES

Atkinson, Charles Milner. *Jeremy Bentham: Life and Work*. London, 1905.

Barnes, Harry Elmer. *A History of the Penal, Reformatory and Correctional Institutions of the State of New Jersey, Analytical and Documentary*. Trenton, 1918.

Cantù, Cesare. *Beccaria et le droit pénale*. Paris, 1885.

Dictionary of National Biography, s.v. "Romilly, Sir Samuel."

Halévy, Elie. *La formation du radicalisme philosophique*. Paris, 1904.

Hall, Arthur C. *Crime in Its Relation to Social Progress*. New York, 1902.

Ives, George. *A History of Penal Methods*. 1914; Reprinted Montclair, N. J., 1970.

Klein, Philip. *Prison Methods in New York State*. New York, 1920.

Landry, Eugenio. *Cesare Beccaria*. Milan, 1910.

Lewis, Orlando F. *The Development of American Prisons and Prison Customs, 1776-1845*. 1922; Reprinted Montclair, N. J., 1967.

McGiffert, Arthur C. *Protestant Thought before Kant*. New York, 1936.

Mackintosh, Robert James. *Memoirs of the Life of Sir James Mackintosh*. Boston, 1853.

Maestro, Marcello T. *Voltaire and Beccaria as Reformers of Criminal Law*. New York, 1942.

Masmonteil, Ernest. *La législation criminelle dans l'œuvre de Voltaire*. Paris, 1901.

Parmelee, Maurice. *The Principles of Anthropology and Sociology in Their Relation to Criminal Procedure*. New York, 1908.

Phillipson, Coleman. *Three Criminal Law Reformers:* Beccaria, Bentham, Romilly. 1923; Reprinted Montclair, N. J., 1970.

Ranston, M. *The Pioneers of the French Revolution*. Boston, 1926.

Riley, Isaac W. *From Myth to Reason*. New York, 1926.

Rusche, Georg, and Kirchheimer, Otto. *Punishment and Social Structure*. New York, 1939.

Stephen, J. F. *History of the Criminal Law in England*. 3 vols. New York, 1883.

Teeters, Negley K. *They Were in Prison*. Philadelphia, 1937.

Vaux, Roberts. *Notices of the Original and Successive Attempts to Improve the Discipline of the Prison at Philadelphia and to Reform the Criminal Code of Pennsylvania*. Philadelphia, 1826.

Wallas, Graham. *The Life of Francis Place*. New York, 1919.

Wilson, Roland K. *History of Modern English Law*. London, 1875.

Wines, Frederick H. *Punishment and Reformation*. Rev. ed. New York, 1919.

CHAPTER VI

Prisons: Their Rise and Development

I. The Late Origins of Penal Institutions.

THERE is an old and well-worn adage that "no prophet is without honor save in his own country," and it would seem fairly accurate to hold that the same sentiment may at times apply to prison systems and types of prison reform. While the writer was born within five miles of Auburn, New York, had passed by the Auburn prison hundreds of times, and had visited it in a score of instances, it was not until years afterward, as a result of a historical study of penology, that he received the slightest intimation that it had any historical significance other than that which might attach to any prison structure which could point to an existence of a century. Further, it may be doubted if there are a half-dozen citizens of the city of Auburn who realize that the somber gray stone walls, surmounted by the stolid figure of "Copper John," enclose a structure that, with one possible exception, is, historically considered, the most important penal institution in the Western Hemisphere, if not in the world—one which furnished the architectural and administrative pattern for an overwhelming majority of the prisons of the United States, and was visited and studied by the leading penologists and jurists of every important European country during the first half of the last century.

It will be the purpose of this chapter briefly to indicate the historical background and origins of the Pennsylvania and Auburn systems of prison administration and their influence upon contemporary penology. In view of the limited space at our disposal it has seemed best to omit most details of local antiquarian interest and thereby to make possible the treat-

113

ment of the much more vital general historical circumstances which combined to produce these important types of prison discipline.

The prison, viewed as an institution for detaining men against their will, originated in the most remote antiquity. It probably goes back as far as the time of the general practice of cannibalism, when future victims were held in stockade to be fattened. Throughout recorded history one frequently meets with reference to prisons used for the confinement of political and religious offenders. Yet the prison system of today, which is the agency through which imprisonment is made the mode of punishment for the majority of crimes, is an innovation of relatively recent origin. It is quite impossible to fix the exact date of the general beginning of imprisonment as a punishment for crime, and it may, indeed, be seriously doubted if any such date exists, except in a metaphysical sense. All that can be stated with accuracy is that at the beginning of the eighteenth century imprisonment was unusual, except as applied to political and religious offenders and debtors, while before the middle of the nineteenth century it was the conventional method of punishing crime in both Europe and America. The eighteenth century was the period of transition from corporal punishment to imprisonment, and, though the process of change was most rapid after 1775, there can be no doubt that the general movement was in progress during the entire period.

During the colonial period there were two institutions in existence, the combination of which later produced the modern prison. They were the jails, or prisons of the time, and the workhouses. The jails or prisons were chiefly used for the detention of those accused of crime pending their trial and for the confinement of debtors and religious and political offenders. They were rarely used for the incarceration of what were regarded as the criminal classes. At each session of the court there occurred what was called a "gaol delivery," when the jail was practically emptied of its inmates, to be filled again during the interval between the delivery and the next session of the court. Only political and religious offenders, debtors, and the few criminals who had received the rare penalty of imprisonment, remained in the jails or prisons longer than the period which elapsed between successive sessions of the courts. The workhouses, on the other hand, which began to appear about the middle of the sixteenth century, and reached their highest early development in Holland, were not for more than two centuries after their origin penal institutions in any strict sense of the word. They were utilized almost solely to repress vagrants and paupers and were not open for the reception of felons.

It was the great contribution of the West Jersey and Pennsylvania Quakers to the development of modern penology to have produced the two-fold achievement of substituting imprisonment for corporal punishment in the treatment of criminals and of combining the prison and the workhouse. In other words, they originated both the idea of imprisonment as the typical mode of punishing crime, and the doctrine that this imprisonment should not be in idleness but at hard labor. Of the priority of their accomplishment in this regard there can be no doubt. A century later they added the principle that imprisonment at hard labor should be in cellular separation, and thus created a modern prison system in its entirety.

II. The Convict Hulks

The earliest application of imprisonment as a widespread method of dealing with criminals was carried on not in prisons but in the prison hulks which Great Britain legalized following 1776. The placing of criminals on galleys had been a common practice in ancient times, and it was widely employed during the medieval period. The lot of these unhappy wretches was about as terrible as could be imagined. They were chained to their seats and compelled to work like animals upon the threat of the most severe flogging. Mr.

Ives has thus described the life of criminals condemned to the galleys in the Middle Ages and early modern times: *

What sort of life did they actually undergo? Doubtless it varied much under different overseers. We must imagine them chained to their crowded benches, often for six months at a time and perhaps for longer, or penned in prison-like barracks at the seaports. Their heads and their beards were shaved every month, and their garments ranged from non-existence in the African waters, to red caps, coats, shirts, and rough canvas breeches for those enslaved in colder, more decorous latitudes. The rowers were exposed to all weathers, and were fed on hard fare, and frequently much stinted in water-supply. Captives of all ranks were herded and chained together promiscuously, and doubtless grew to be as filthy and verminous as their shaven heads and paucity of clothing permitted them to become.

But the worst horrors of their position appeared in action, whenever their boat was either pursuing or being chased. We know how men will strain themselves in a contest, we know how a race-horse may be punished with whip and spurs. We can only imagine, and happily have not seen, how slaves could be urged by their overseers when they rowed for their rulers' lives. In the battle-race they were lashed by the overseers with whips, and indeed, by the fighting men generally, with rope-ends or anything that came handy. They were stimulated by sops of bread soaked in wine; in the frenzy of flight they were sometimes implored and entreated by those who might share their doom if the ship were taken; they were knocked about till covered with blood and wounds, and if, from any possible cause, one could work no further, all that was left of him would be thrown overboard. The galley in war-time was indeed a dreadful picture of pain and struggle; to be fastened there was a fate far worse than that endured in all the grime and dust of a steamship's stokehole. It was a phase of pitiable human agony which has gone to return no more.

When the galley was replaced by the ship which traveled entirely under sail power this form of savagery disappeared. The next form of confinement of convicts on shipboard was

*Ives, op. cit., pp. 104-5.

associated with the rise of the prison hulks. We pointed out in a previous chapter how the blocking of further transportation to the American colonies by the American Revolution made it necessary for Great Britain to seek other methods of disposing of her criminal population. A substitute for transportation to America was found in the utilization of the prison hulks and transportation to Australasia, the latter of which has already been described. The use of these prison hulks, which were usually broken-down war vessels, began in 1776 and lasted until the middle of the last century. A hulk was maintained at Gibraltar until 1875. While not as many convicts found their way into the hulks as were transported to Australasia, nevertheless these old vessels were very extensively used as a place for the confinement of convicts. As late as 1828 there were no less than four thousand convicts confined in the British prison hulks. The condition of convicts confined on these hulks was what one might logically expect from the penal methods of the age. The ships were unsanitary, ill-ventilated and full of vermin. Frequently a contagious disease would sweep through a ship carrying off the greater number of those confined therein. Brutal punishments, particularly severe floggings, were universally administered. There was little work except when a hulk might be tied up in a harbor and the more able-bodied prisoners employed on the docks or fortifications. The effect of this idleness was inevitably demoralizing. Even where disease and brutality were not rampant, moral degeneration inevitably followed in the train of the promiscuous association of prisoners of all ages and degrees of criminality. Mr. Ives thus sums up the conditions which were charactistic of life in the convict hulks: *

In 1776 the county authorities were told to prepare and enlarge the gaols to meet new conditions, an order to which they do not appear to have paid much attention. And as there was still not room enough within walls, new Acts

*Ives, op. cit., pp. 124-26.

were passed from the year 1776, authorising that prisoners, failing the possibility of their being transported, should be kept upon hulks. These, as their name implies, were old sailing-vessels, generally men-of-war, permanently made fast in rivers or harbours; within, they were as like the old-fashioned prisons as possible, being crowded, dirty and verminous, with the men and boys all in irons, often in double irons, for greater security.

Those who were able to do rough work were employed on shore on various dockyard tasks, such as digging and dredging, and worked the same number of hours as the free labourers. They were allowed some beer (without which nobody in those days was considered able to live!), generally small beer, a weakened variety, when they were set to do anything specially arduous, and when they got back to the ship at evening they appear to have had a good deal of freedom in spite of fetters and to have been allowed a little tobacco with which to console themselves. There prevailed, indeed, the usual stagnation of prison life, particularly for those who were unable to go outside with the land parties; bad language, some pilfering, and occasional violence, both by convicts and overseers.

The former were all liable to be flogged with a severe sort of cat, to the extent of two dozen lashes, but applications of the birch were common enough and were not considered worth noticing or recording. There were a great number of feeble degenerates placed on board, including some dazed and deadened by solitary confinement sent out from Millbank and other prisons; and there were a good many palpable lunatics on the ships as well, who were often troublesome and who were soundly flogged just like other captives; the authorities evinced neither surprise nor objection to the presence of mad people, only the very violent ones being sent to asylums, and the condition of these has been already described.

The prisoners of the hulks were, as usual, sadly neglected. Upon the hospital ship at Woolwich, for instance, neither towels nor even combs were provided, and most of the patients were infested with vermin. Whenever new cases had to be taken in, the previous occupants of the beds were turned into hammocks, and then the recent arrivals used the old sheets, which had not been changed, and some of the sick, especially if insane, lay in a horrible condition of filth and wretchedness. The senior medical officer of the hulks on the

Thames had a private practice to distract his attention, and the assistant surgeon was not a qualified man at all, but a medical student who was working for his degree. Among the criminals, lunatics, feeble-minded, and outcasts of all kinds who were cooped up for periods generally varying between one and seven years (the latter sentence was to be equivalent to fourteen years' transportation; all persons respited after sentence of death were to be specially dealt with by the Home Secretary) were young boys. An old table gives the number upon the hulks at that time, and we find the record of: one child of 2, two of 12, four boys of 14, four of 15, and altogether twenty persons less than 16 years old. About 1824 they appear to have placed the boys on a special ship, the hulk "Euryalus," and there the youngest "villain" was nine years old; some of the boys, the inspector reported, "are so young that they can hardly put on their clothes." Two-thirds of them are described as having been natural or neglected children. The Government had a place for at least a few of the Nation's babies, in convict prisons. For some thirty years after their inception the hulks received a large proportion of the condemned, and were used until 1858, or between eighty and ninety years.

The following extract from the Report of the Parliamentary Committee of 1832 emphasizes particularly the demoralizing influence of the promiscuity among the prisoners, entirely aside from the presence of brutality and disease:*

The great principles which your Committee have endeavored to establish are the necessity of a separation of criminals, and of a severity of punishment sufficient to make it an object of terror to the evil-doer. In both these respects the system of management in the hulks is not only necessarily deficient, it is actually opposed to them. All that has been stated of the miserable effects of the association of criminals in the prisons on shore, the profaneness, the vice, the demoralisation, that are its inevitable consequences, applies in its fullest extent in the case now under consideration. The convicts, after being shut up for the night, are allowed to have lights between decks in some ships as late as ten o'clock; that, although against the rules of the establishment, they are per-

*Cited by Du Cane, *op. cit.*, p. 120.

mitted the use of musical instruments; that flash songs, dancing, fighting, and gaming take place; that the old offenders are in the habit of robbing the newcomers; that newspapers and improper books are clandestinely introduced; that a communication is frequently kept up with their old associates on shore, and that occasionally spirits are introduced on board. It is true that the greater part of these practices is against the rules of the establishment, but their existence in defiance of these rules shows an inherent defect in the system. The convicts are also permitted to receive visits from their friends, and, during the time they remain, are excused from working, and it is stated that instances are frequent of their exemption from labour being extended to several days at the request of their friends. It is obvious that such communication must have the worst effect; it not only affords an indulgence to which no person in the situation of a convict is entitled, but it allows the most dangerous and improper intercourse to be kept up with old companions, from whom it is most important to disconnect them. The most assiduous attention on the part of the ministers of religion would be insufficient to stem the torrent of corruption flowing from these various and abundant sources; but, unless the evidence of these witnesses is utterly unworthy of belief, it appears that but little attention is paid to the promotion of religious feelings, or to the improvement of the morals of the convicts, and that, except for a short time on Sunday morning, the chaplains have no communication whatever with them.

III. The Origins of the Prison System in America

1. *General Historical Background of Penal and Juristic Reform*

There are two sets of influences which constitute the chief phases of the historical background of the reform of the criminal law in America, namely those general forces making for reform and progress of all kinds in the eighteenth century, and those specific attempts to reform criminal jurisprudence and penal administration during the same period, which center mainly about the writings and activities of Beccaria and Howard and the Pennsylvania reformers, such as Bradford, Rush, Vaux, Lownes, and others.

The ignorance, crudities, and barbarism of the "old régime" in Europe were effectively attacked in the writings of the French *Philosophes,* such as Montesquieu, Voltaire, Diderot, Turgot and Condorcet and of their English sympathizers and associates like David Hume, Adam Smith, Tom Paine and Jeremy Bentham. The assault on the old order in the work of these publicists was given complete and objective form in the French Revolution, and its effect upon the other states of Europe. Probably the most important of the doctrines of these writers and of the Revolutionary period was the introduction of Rationalism into social and political philosophy and the firm conviction that social progress and the resulting "greatest happiness for the greatest number" were possible of attainment through sweeping social reforms carried out according to the dictates of "pure reason." It is obvious that so barbarous and archaic a part of the old order as the current criminal jurisprudence and penal administration of the time could not long remain immune from the growing spirit of progress and enlightenment.

America, in general, and Philadelphia, in particular, were well situated to feel the effect of these new forces. A large number of Frenchmen had been in America during the Revolutionary War, had brought with them many of the ideas of their publicists and had stimulated an American interest in French thought. In addition, many of the more important and influential Americans had been in Europe during the period of the American Revolution and the years immediately following. Philadelphia, as the real center of American civilization and political life during the last quarter of the eighteenth century, was particularly affected by these progressive European developments. Benjamin Franklin had long been a resident of France and was well acquainted with radical French thought. The political leaders who assembled in Philadelphia during the period were all more or less familiar with the advanced political thought of England and France. No other foreign philosopher so influenced the

American Constitutional Convention of 1787 as did Montesquieu, and his exponents must have been nearly as
familiar with his doctrines on the reform of criminal jurisprudence as with his theory of the separation of governmental
powers. As the capital of the country during much of the
period, Philadelphia received many distinguished foreign visitors, bringing with them the doctrines of their countrymen.
Brissot, the Girondist leader in the French Revolution, was
among these. Finally, it was to Philadelphia that Jefferson
came shortly after his return from France, where he had
become very familiar with French revolutionary ideas and
leaders. Then Philadelphia had the colonial precedents of
Penn in prison reform to recur to as an inspiration and guide
in juristic and penal reform. All of these conditions combined to make Philadelphia particularly well adapted to the
carrying into execution of some of the more radical European
and colonial programs of social reform.

2. John Howard and the European Origins of Prison Reform

The first clear anticipations of the modern prison system
were the papal prison of San Michele, erected in Rome by
Pope Clement XI about 1704, and the prison at Ghent in
Belgium, established by Hippolyte Vilain XIII in 1773. In
both of these there was provided some sort of classification
and cellular separation of inmates. Labor by the inmates was
the rule, and reformation was stated to be a chief aim of
incarceration. Neither of these prisons, however, attracted
much general attention in England or America until their
virtues were discovered and reported by the distinguished
English prison reformer, John Howard (1726-90). In his
travels of inspection between 1773 and 1790 he visited these
institutions several times and his writings contain vivid descriptions of their construction and administration. It was
through his writings, well known to Philadelphians, that

America gained a knowledge of these advanced institutions and caught the spirit of Howard's labors in behalf of prison reform.

There is little or no evidence, however, that these institutions in Rome and Ghent directly influenced Pennsylvania penology to an appreciable degree. Their effect seems to have been indirect. Howard's recommendation of their system of administration, as a part of penal philosophy, induced a number of enterprising and sympathetic English reformers to adopt these principles in English jails and prisons, and the latter became the models followed by the Philadelphia reformers. In 1790, the members of the *Philadelphia Society for Alleviating the Miseries of Public Prisons* desired to educate and inform the legislature of the state in order to secure the adoption of an advanced system of prison administration. Their list of successful experiments in the new penology did not include any important reference to Rome or Ghent, but was confined almost entirely to the reforms in new English county prisons, particularly that at Wymondham in Norfolk, erected about 1784 by Sir Thomas Beevor, as a result of the enthusiasm generated by a reading of Howard's writings. In this prison there were provided a separation of sexes and of hardened criminals from first and petty offenders, separate cells for all prisoners at night and for incorrigible prisoners at all times, and a well-equipped workshop for the employment of the able-bodied prisoners.

Beyond this indirect influence of Howard's work upon Philadelphia prison reform, ample evidence exists that the Philadelphia reformers were thoroughly conversant with the printed accounts of his travels in the inspection of jails, prisons and hulks and with his recommendations of reform based upon these trips. The above-mentioned pamphlet of 1790 contains long extracts from Howard's works which were in accord with the changes urged upon the legislature.

Two years earlier, in fact, the society had sent Howard the following letter:*

Philadelphia, January 14, 1788.

To John Howard.

The Society for Alleviating the Miseries of Public Prisons, in the city of Philadelphia, beg leave to forward to you a copy of their constitution, and to request, at the same time, such communications from you upon the subject of their institution, as may favour their designs.

The Society heartily concur with the friends of humanity in Europe, in expressing their obligations to you for having rendered the miserable tenants of prisons the objects of more general attention and compassion, and for having pointed out some of the means of not only alleviating their miseries, but of preventing those crimes and misfortunes which are the causes of them.

With sincere wishes that your useful life may be prolonged, and that you may enjoy the pleasure of seeing the success of your labours in the cause of humanity, in every part of the globe, we are with great respect and esteem, your sincere friends and well wishers.

Signed by order of the Society,
WILLIAM WHITE, *President.*

This letter, written less than a year after the formation of the society, would seem to indicate that even in its origin it was powerfully stimulated by Howard's work. Indeed, we know that at the fourth meeting of the society the members listened to a letter from Dr. Lettsom of London describing Howard's journeys on the Continent in carrying on his investigation of prison conditions. That Howard evinced similar interest in progressive movements in this country is shown by the words of the following memorandum which he dictated:†

Should the plan take place during my life of establishing a permanent charity under some such title as that at Phila-

*Roberts Vaux, *Notices of the Original and Successive Attempts to Improve the Discipline of the Prison at Philadelphia and to Reform the Criminal Code of Pennsylvania,* Philadelphia, 1810, pp. 24-5.

†*Ibid.,* p. 25, note. *The London Society for the Improvement of Prison Discipline was not established until 1815.*

delphia, viz.: "A Society for Alleviating the Miseries of Public Prisons," and annuities be engrafted thereupon, for the above-mentioned purpose, I would most readily stand at the bottom of a page for five hundred pounds; or if such society shall be instituted within three years after my death, this sum shall be paid out of my estate.

Along with the influence of Howard's work, it is evident that Jeremy Bentham's *Panopticon* and its voluminous appendices, published following 1787, had some effect upon prison reform in Pennsylvania. The Western Penitentiary of Pennsylvania, authorized by the law of 1818, is one of the few institutions which were modeled to some degree after Bentham's ingenious plan for a perfect prison structure. Finally, in concluding this summary of the historical background of early prison reform in Philadelphia, the fact must not be forgotten that Pennsylvania, alone of all the states, was fortunate enough to have had its very origins linked up with the cause of judicial and penal reform. While the laws passed in Pennsylvania from 1718 to 1775 were usually about as divergent as possible from Penn's actual program, the memory of his purposes was kept alive in the enacting clauses. Therefore, when a reform of the criminal code and penal administration became necessary, the movement was rendered respectable and "safe" through its association with the venerable and esteemed name of the founder of the province.

3. The Pennsylvania System of Prison Discipline as the Model for Imitation by New York State

Inasmuch as it is undeniable that the advances in criminal jurisprudence and penology in New York State between 1796 and 1830 were primarily the result of New York's imitation of the Pennsylvania precedent, it will be necessary to review briefly the progress made in this adjoining state during the same general period. The beginnings of prison reform in Pennsylvania are generally associated with the name of Richard Wistar, a member of the Society of Friends, who, just prior to the outbreak of the Revolutionary War, was attracted by the abject misery of the inmates of the provincial jail in Philadelphia, some of whom had in fact recently starved to death. Wistar had soup prepared at his own house which was then taken and distributed among the inmates of the jail. Others became interested in the situation and, on February 7, 1776, there was formed *The Philadelphia Society for Assisting Distressed Prisoners.* The reform of the criminal code and the introduction of the prison system might have begun at that date instead of a decade later had not the British occupation of the city put an end to the activities of the society.

Immediately after the peace of 1783 a number of prominent citizens of Philadelphia, led by Benjamin Franklin, Benjamin Rush, William Bradford and Caleb Lownes, organized a movement for the reform of the barbarous criminal code of 1718, which was still in force. All were agreed that the number of capital crimes should be greatly reduced and Dr. Rush went as far as to advocate the total abolition of the death penalty. Their efforts resulted in the above mentioned law of September 15, 1786, which substituted for the death penalty as a punishment for some of the lesser felonies "continuous hard labor, publicly and disgracefully imposed." The results of the new law were not as satisfactory as had been anticipated, while the public exposure of the convicts in their labor brought their distressing condition before the attention of a larger number of persons than could have been the case when they were secluded in the gloomy jail at High and Walnut streets.

The continued evils of the penal administration, together with the added publicity given to these deplorable conditions, promoted the formation of *The Philadelphia Society for Alleviating the Miseries of Public Prisons,* on the 8th of May, 1787, in the German School House on Cherry Street. This organization, the first of the great modern prison reform societies, set forth its fundamental impulses, conceptions and purposes in the preamble to the constitution of the society:*

"I was in prison and ye came unto me.

". . . and the King shall answer, and say unto them, verily I say unto you, inasmuch as ye have done it unto one of the least of these my brethren, ye have done it unto me" (Matthew, xxv: 36, 40).

When we consider that the obligations of benevolence, which are founded on the precepts and example of the Author of Christianity, are not cancelled by the follies and crimes of our fellow-creatures; and when we reflect upon the miseries which penury, hunger, cold, unnecessary severity, unwholesome apartments, and guilt (the usual attendants of prisons), involve with them; it becomes us to extend our compassion to that part of mankind, who are subject to these miseries. By the aids of humanity, their undue and illegal sufferings may be prevented; the links which should bind the whole family of mankind together, under all circumstances, be preserved unbroken; and such degrees and modes of punishment may be discovered and suggested, as may, instead of continuing habits of vice, become the means of restoring our fellow-creatures to virtue and happiness. From a conviction of the truth and obligation of these principles, the Subscribers have associated themselves under the Title of *The Philadelphia Society for Alleviating the Miseries of Public Prisons.*

While not more than one-half of the members of the Society can be identified as also belonging to the Society of Friends, it is well known that the most active element in the prison reform organization was made up of the Friends, and the leading exponents of the Pennsylvania system of prison discipline during over a half century, Roberts Vaux and his son Richard, were members of the Society of Friends. Of course, one must recognize the important part played in the reform activity by non-Quaker members of the society, such as Bishop White of the Episcopal Church, and the generous coöperation with the Prison society on the part of those who were not members of the newly formed society, such as

---

*Caleb Lownes, *An Account of the Alteration and Present State of the Penal Laws of Pennsylvania,* pp. 5-6; *Report of the Commissioners on the Penal Code,* 1828, p. 13.

Benjamin Franklin and William Bradford. The work accomplished by the reform society fell into three related parts: (1) the relief of the physical suffering of prisoners; (2) the reform of the criminal code by reducing the number of capital crimes and by introducing imprisonment as the typical method of punishment in the place of corporal punishment; and (3) the development of a great historic system of prison discipline—the Pennsylvania or *separate* system of confinement and discipline.

It has already been pointed out that the activities in Europe of Howard and Bentham were intimately related to the development of the reform of prison administration in Pennsylvania; it is equally certain that the reform of the criminal code of the state was based upon a sympathetic reception of the juristic principles of Beccaria and Montesquieu. Writing in 1793, William Bradford, the author of the improved Pennsylvania codes from 1790-94, indicated, as we pointed out above, the indebtedness of himself and his associates to these European reformers.

The legal beginnings of the reform of the Pennsylvania criminal code date back to the state constitution of 1776, which directed a reform of the criminal law, to the end that imprisonment at hard and productive labor might be substituted for the barbarous existing methods of corporal punishment. The stress of the Revolutionary War postponed action for a decade, but the law of September 15, 1786, marked a notable step in advance by reducing the number of capital crimes, substituting imprisonment for corporal punishment in the case of a number of lesser felonies, and by abolishing for most purposes branding, mutilation, the pillory, whipping and the other conventional barbarities of the colonial period. The progressive policy was sustained and somewhat extended in the acts of 1788, 1789, 1790 and 1791, but the systematic revision of the criminal code appeared in the act of April 22, 1794, which abolished the death penalty for all crimes except murder in the first degree, and substituted imprisonment or fines for all other crimes in the place of corporal punishment of any type. This code marked the first permanent American break with contemporary juristic savagery, was the forerunner of the reform codes of other American states, and was the essential basis of Pennsylvania criminal jurisprudence until the next systematic revisions in 1829 and 1860.

This reform of the criminal code making imprisonment the normal method of punishing crime necessitated the establishment of a prison system in the place of the crude arrangement of the colonial jails and workhouses. By acts of 1789, 1790 and 1794 the Walnut Street Jail was converted into a state prison, and an addition was constructed so as to allow the trial of what became the Pennsylvania system of prison discipline, namely, the confinement of the worst type of felons in separate cells. Of these important laws the act of April 5, 1790, is conventionally regarded as the legal origin of the Pennsylvania system. In spite of promising beginnings in the years immediately following 1790, the attempt to apply the new penology in the Walnut Street Jail proved a well-nigh complete failure. The cells erected for the solitary confinement of the "more hardened and atrocious offenders," according to the act of 1790, were never numerous enough to accommodate all the convicts of this class, and the large congregate cells or rooms which housed the remainder became so overcrowded as to nullify completely all attempts to administer the institution in a scientific or effective manner.

The failure of the law of 1790 to secure the solitary confinement of those so sentenced and the general administrative and disciplinary demoralization of the Walnut Street Jail, due to overcrowding, were remedied from a legal point of view by the acts of March 3, 1818, and March 20, 1821, which provided for the erection of the Western and the Eastern State penitentiaries. It was here definitely stipulated that both penitentiaries should be constructed according to the principle of solitary confinement, but no provision was made for the employment of the convicts. It was only after a series of controversies from 1826 to 1829 that the completed Pennsylvania system was finally established. By taking advantage of conflicting recommendations made by public authorities, *The Philadelphia Society for Alleviating the Miseries of Public Prisons* was able to induce the legislature to enact into law its fundamental program in penal administration—solitary confinement at hard labor. This was finally and definitely prescribed in the law of April 23, 1829.

The classical eulogy of the Pennsylvania system is to be found in the report of the inspectors of the Western Penitentiary for 1854. Here they worked themselves into an almost neo-Platonic ecstasy in their effort to set forth the many and numerous points of supreme excellence in the Pennsylvania system of Prison discipline and administration. This is probably the most extreme and exaggerated praise that the system ever received from its advocates:*

Pennsylvania, the precursor of all her sister states in the present system of prison discipline, has justified its wisdom before the world in the practical results of its successful administration in this institution. Anticipated evils, existing more in speculative humanity and morbid philanthropy than in substantive fact, have failed in their realization. Disease and mental imbecility so confidently predicted as necessarily incident to separate confinement, have resulted in health and intellectual improvement. Depraved tendencies, characteristic of the convict, have been restrained by the absence of vicious association, and in the mild teaching of Christianity, the unhappy criminal finds a solace for an involuntary exile from the comforts of social life. If hungry, he is fed; if naked, he is clothed; if destitute of the first rudiments of education, he is taught to read and write; and if he has never been blessed with a means of livelihood, he is schooled in a mechanical art, which in after life may be to him the source of profit and respectability. Employment is not toil nor labor, weariness. He embraces them with alacrity, as contributing to his moral and mental elevation. They help to fill the zodiac of his time,

*Report of the Inspectors of the Western Penitentiary, 1854. Legislative Documents, 1854, p. 271.

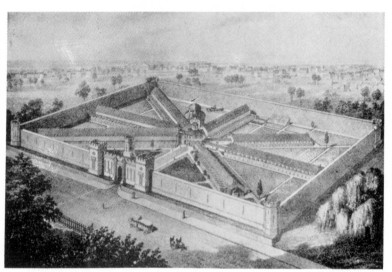

THE EASTERN STATE PENITENTIARY OF PENNSYLVANIA

THE STATE PRISON AT AUBURN, NEW YORK

which would otherwise be spent in unavailing complaint, and fruitless importunity for release. Shut out from a tumultuous world, and separated from those equally guilty with himself, he can indulge his remorse unseen, and find ample opportunity for reflection and reformation. His daily intercourse is with good men, who in administering to his necessities, animate his crushed hopes, and pour into his ear the oil of joy and consolation. He has abundance of light, air, and warmth; he has good and wholesome food; he has seasonable and comfortable clothing; he has the best of medical attendance; he has books to read, and ink and paper to communicate with his friends at stated periods; and weekly he enjoys the privilege of hearing God's holy word expounded by a faithful and zealous Christian minister.

Thus provided, and anxiously cared for by the officers of the prison, he is in a better condition than many beyond its walls guiltless of crime. He labors, but it is for his subsistence, like any other member of the community, and by his industry he relieves that community of the burden of his support.

It is a fact worthy to be remembered by the Legislature, that for the last ten years, not one county sending convicts to the Western Penitentiary has been called upon to contribute a solitary dollar towards their subsistence. Such being the domestic economy of this institution, and such its happy results, we are not required to enter into an elaborate vindication of the principle upon which it is based. The system has disappointed the anticipation of its enemies and surpassed the confident expectations of its friends, and there, for the present we leave it.

IV. The Beginnings of Prison Reform in New York State and the Origins of the Auburn System

The situation after the Revolution in New York State with respect to criminal jurisprudence and penology was much the same as that which existed in Pennsylvania. The list of capital crimes was extensive and corporal punishment was the normal mode of inflicting the revenge of society upon the offender. Imprisonment as a method of punishing crime scarcely existed and no state prison had been provided. Yet progressive and enlightened individuals were not lacking who were gravely shocked by existing conditions and were keenly interested in all proposals for improving the situation. Among the leaders of enlightened sentiment in this respect in New York were Ambrose Spencer (1765-1848), legislator and jurist; Philip John Schuyler (1733-1804), soldier and statesman; Thomas Eddy (1758-1827), financier and philanthropist; De Witt Clinton (1769-1828), political leader and social reformer; John Jay (1745-1829), statesman, jurist and diplomat; and John Griscom (1774-1852), scholar and philanthropist.

It was but natural that their attention would be attracted by previous and contemporary progress in Philadelphia. The Philadelphia group had not only taken the lead in this movement in America, but had also spared no pains in advertising its program. Roberts Vaux notes that as early as 1794 the prison society resolved to make its effect felt outside of the local municipality and state, and maintains that "an extensive correspondence was opened and carried on between the society and the executives of several of the states of the union, which tended to diffuse much information relative to its labors, and led to the adoption of reform in the penal laws in other parts of the continent." It may have been as a direct result of this communication from Philadelphia that, in his first message to the Legislature, Governor John Jay recommended the reform of the criminal code. Again, Thomas Eddy, one of the most energetic of the New York reform group, had been born in Philadelphia and had remained in intimate touch with the Society of Friends in that city. Professor Griscom was also a member of the Society of Friends.

In 1794 Mr. Eddy and General Schuyler visited Philadelphia, were received by *The Philadelphia Society for Alleviating the Miseries of Public Prisons*, were told more of the reforms which had just been achieved in the criminal code and prison administration of Pennsylvania, and were shown what then seemed the highly successful new system in operation in the Walnut Street Jail. Study and further reflection convinced them that Pennsylvania had provided the desirable reform pattern for New York to emulate. Aided by the legal sagacity of Spencer and the political support of Governor Jay, they introduced a bill into the New York Legislature designed to reduce the list of capital crimes to murder and treason, to substitute imprisonment for corporal punishment for non-capital crimes, and to provide for the erection of two state penitentiaries, one at Albany and one in New York City. This became law as the act of March 26, 1796. Only one of the two prisons contemplated in the law was erected, the so-called Newgate Prison, which was built in Greenwich Village under the direction of a commission consisting of Matthew Clarkson, John Murray, Jr., John Watt, Thomas Eddy and Isaac Stoutenburgh, and was opened for the reception of inmates on November 28, 1797.

There were, however, two fatal initial defects in this institution which led to its speedy abandonment. It was erected according to the unscientific congregate method of confinement, as practiced in the greater part of the Walnut Street Jail at Philadelphia, which made effective classification and discipline impossible. Moreover, it was so small that it very rapidly became overcrowded. The demoralizing practice arose of pardoning each year nearly as many convicts as were admitted, in order to keep the prison population down to a number which it was possible to house even under crowded conditions. According to statistics gathered by Senator Hopkins in 1824, 198 prisoners were received in 1813 and 134 were pardoned, and in 1814, 213 were received and 176 pardoned. Mr. Sullivan reports contemporary evidence as stating that between 1797 and 1822, 5,069 convicts were admitted and 2,819 pardoned.

The situation became so intolerable that on April 12, 1816, a law was passed authorizing the erection of a new state prison at Auburn in Cayuga County, and a commission consisting of Elijah Miller, James Glover and John H. Beach was appointed to direct operations. They were authorized "to build a state prison similar to the one now in use in the city of New York with such variations as they think will best promote the interests of such institution." The immediate control of building operations was handed over to William Brittin, a carpenter by trade and the first warden of the institution. The evils of the congregate system of confinement do not appear to have been fully grasped in New York State as late as 1816, for the first wing of the new structure at Auburn, the south wing, was erected with both double cells and large rooms or apartments capable of receiving ten or more convicts in each.

By 1819 the influence of the sentiment for solitary confinement had become dominant, and an act was passed on April 2 of that year directing the inspectors to confine certain classes of prisoners in separate cells and to construct the north wing according to the principle of solitary confinement of each prisoner. The outside cell construction, later adopted in the Eastern Penitentiary of Pennsylvania, was not employed, but rather what came to be known as the Auburn, or inside cell, method of construction. After consultation with the Pennsylvania exponents of the system of solitary confinement, the New York reformers succeeded in securing the act of April 2, 1821, directing the prison inspectors to select a number of the "oldest and most heinous offenders" and put them in solitary confinement, with the end in view of observing its disciplinary effects. A second class was to be put in separate cells for three days each week, while the younger offenders were to be allowed to work in the shops six days each week. Eighty convicts were awarded as a Christmas present, in 1821, the privilege of furnishing the material for this experiment in prison discipline and administration.

The method employed was not what became a few years later the developed Pennsylvania system of solitary confinement at hard labor in two large roomy cells and a small outside yard, but solitary confinement in a single small inside cell without any labor or other adequate provisions for physical exercise. The experiment continued during the year 1822 and

1823, and it is not surprising that it proved a hopeless failure and led to a marked prevalence of sickness and insanity on the part of the convicts in solitary confinement. It should be remembered, however, that this crude experiment throws no light upon the disciplinary and reformative potentialities of the perfected Pennsylvania system.

The collapse of the experiment with solitary confinement at Auburn led to the complete abandonment of this type of discipline. In 1823 and 1824 Governor Yates pardoned most of those remaining in solitary confinement. A majority of the legislative committee of investigation, appointed by the act of April 12, 1824, and consisting of Stephen Allen, Samuel M. Hopkins and George Tibbits, reported that nothing more could be hoped for from this type of procedure. The committee summarized their opinion as follows:*

A majority of the Board respectfully recommend to the Legislature the repeal of the laws for solitary confinement, in connection with the full adoption of an effectual government and discipline; and a majority of us would not recommend the same as a separate measure, nor in any case except in connection with such effective system of government and discipline.

In the meantime the local prison authorities at Auburn had been working out a disciplinary and administrative scheme which was destined to become one of great historic significance —the Auburn system of congregate work by day and separation by night, with enforced silence at all times. Warden Brittin died in 1821 and his place was taken by Captain Elam Lynds, who, with the aid of his deputy and architect, John Cray, and with the encouragement of Gershom Powers, of the Board of Inspectors, worked out the new plan. The weight of evidence seems to warrant assigning the credit for originating and applying the new system of discipline to Mr. Cray.

---

*Journal of the Assembly of the State of New York, 48th Session, Albany, 1825, pp. 91-133. See especially pp. 121-26. For a statistical summary of the scandalous prevalence of pardoning in the Newgate Prison, see pp. 126-27 of this report. This report is the best documentary source relative to the status of New York penology at the close of the first quarter of the last century.

The old system of congregate confinement having proved a failure and the alternative procedure of solitary confinement as applied at Auburn appearing likewise to promise nothing better, a compromise was reached between the two plans. The prisoners were allowed to work in groups in the prison shops and yards during the day, and were then locked singly in separate cells by night. Silence was enforced at all times, and the discipline was further extended by such devices as the lockstep, special regulations in the dining-hall, and the undeniable cruelty of Warden Lynds in his employment of whipping as a means of preserving order and securing obedience. Louis Dwight, the most powerful champion that the Auburn system ever had, describes in the following manner the operation of the new system. It is both an eloquent defense of this type of discipline and an excellent proof of the great transformation of disciplinary and administrative ideals held by prison reformers between 1826 and 1920:*

At Auburn we have a more beautiful example still of what may be done by proper discipline, in a prison well constructed. It is not possible to describe the pleasure which we feel in contemplating this noble institution, after wading through the fraud, and the material and moral filth of many prisons. We regard it as a model worthy of the world's imitation. We do not mean that there is nothing in this institution which admits of improvement; for there have been a few cases of unjustifiable severity in punishments; but, upon the whole, the institution is immensely elevated above the old penitentiaries.

The whole establishment, from the gate to the sewer, is a specimen of neatness. The unremitted industry, the entire subordination and subdued feeling of the convicts, has probably no parallel among an equal number of criminals. In their solitary cells they spend the night, with no other book but the Bible, and at sunrise they proceed, in military order, under the eye of the turnkeys, in solid columns, with the lock march, to their workshops; thence, in the same order, at the hour of

---

*It was the emphasis on silence at Auburn which led to the frequent designation of the Auburn system as the "silent system." For the best analysis of the Auburn system at an early date, see Gershom Powers, *A Brief Account of the Construction, Management and Discipline of the New York State Prison at Auburn*, Auburn, 1826.

breakfast, to the common hall, where they partake of their wholesome and frugal meal in silence. Not even a whisper is heard; though the silence is such that a whisper might be heard through the whole apartment. The convicts are seated, in single file, at narrow tables, with their backs towards the center, so that there can be no interchange of signs. If one has more food than he wants, he raises his left hand; and if another has less, he raises his right hand, and the waiter changes it. When they have done eating, at the ringing of a little bell, of the softest sound, they rise from the table, form the solid columns, and return, under the eye of the turnkeys, to the workshops. From one end of the shops to the other, it is the testimony of many witnesses, that they have passed more than three hundred convicts, without seeing one leave his work, or turn his head to gaze at them. There is the most perfect attention to business from morning till night, interrupted only by the time necessary to dine, and never by the fact that the whole body of prisoners have done their tasks, and the time is now their own, and they can do as they please. At the close of the day, a little before sunset, the work is all laid aside at once, and the convicts return, in military order, to the solitary cells, where they partake of the frugal meal, which they were permitted to take from the kitchen, where it was furnished for them as they returned from the shops. After supper, they can, if they choose, read Scripture undisturbed and then reflect in silence on the errors of their lives. They must not disturb their fellow prisoners by even a whisper.

About the time that the Auburn system was emerging into practice the Legislature, by an act of March 7, 1825, authorized the erection of another state prison near New York City to displace finally the Newgate Prison in Greenwich Village. The building commission was composed of Stephen Allen, George Tibbits and Samuel M. Hopkins, who had recommended the erection of an additional prison in their famous report of 1825 on the state prison system in New York. This new state prison was built in the three years following under the direction of Captain Lynds, and in May, 1828, was ready for occupancy. Christened at first the Mount Pleasant Prison, it has come to be known in our day as the Sing Sing institution. From the beginning it operated according to the Auburn system.

The dietary conditions in the early prisons is well indicated by the following description of the food allowance in early Pennsylvania prisons:

> Sunday—One pound of bread, and one pound of coarse meat made into broth.
> Monday—One pound of bread and one quart of potatoes.
> Tuesday—One quart of Indian meal made into mush.
> Wednesday—One pound of bread and one quart of potatoes.
> Thursday—One quart of Indian meal made into mush.
> Friday—One pound of bread and one quart of potatoes.
> Saturday—One quart of Indian meal made into mush.

A half pint of molasses to every four prisoners on Tuesday, Thursday and Saturday.

No provisions are allowed besides the prison allowance, except the more laborious part, while orderlies, who are allowed to get some of the heads of sheep from the butchers, at their own expense: this is esteemed an indulgence, and is attended with great effects, both physical and moral. Molasses are experienced to be very salutary to the health of the prisoners as well as useful in gratifying them with a small luxury. The orderly women are sometimes indulged with tea.

V. The Struggle Between the Auburn and Pennsylvania Systems

The series of advances in New York State penology which led to the complete Auburn system should be regarded as primarily an adaptation and imitation of the Pennsylvania reforms, and the Auburn system was really a variant of the Pennsylvania system. Yet, once the Auburn type of discipline had assumed an independent position, a vigorous competition sprang up between the two systems and a bitter controversy was waged between the partisans of the two methods. While the Pennsylvania system was temporarily adopted by a number of eastern states, it was speedily abandoned by all except New Jersey, which persisted in the experiment until 1858. The following data indicate the essential facts concerning the adoption and abandonment of the Pennsylvania system in the United States. Maryland introduced solitary confinement in 1809 and abolished it in 1838. Massachusetts authorized solitary confinement in 1811 and did away with it in 1829. Maine experimented with solitary confinement from 1824 to 1827. New Jersey introduced solitary confinement in 1820, abolished it in 1828, reintroduced it in 1833 and finally abolished it in 1858. Virginia introduced solitary confinement in 1824 and practically abolished it in 1833. Rhode Island introduced solitary confinement in 1838 and abolished it in 1844. Except for these instances of brief experimentation with the Pennsylvania system, the Auburn system prevailed in the early state prisons of this country.

Owing to the economic advantages of the Auburn system, and, above all, to the tireless propaganda of Louis Dwight of the *Prison Discipline Society of Boston* in the interest of the Auburn system, it triumphed almost completely over its rival in this country. On the other hand, most of the official European investigators of the two systems of prison discipline reported to their respective governments in favor of the Pennsylvania system of solitary confinement and the Pennsylvania system was much more widely adopted in Europe from 1830 to 1860 than the Auburn.

An adequate account of the bitter controversy that was waged from 1825 to 1860 between the exponents of the rival Pennsylvania and Auburn systems would occupy a large volume in itself and can only be briefly touched upon in this place. The struggle began before either system was thoroughly established. As early as 1826-27 the commissioners who were appointed to devise the system of administration for the new state penitentiaries in Pennsylvania were approached by advocates of the Auburn system and were converted to an advocacy of its adoption. The main conflict was waged between the *Prison Discipline Society of Boston,* for the Auburn system, and the *Philadelphia Society for Alleviating the Miseries of Public Prisons,* for the Pennsylvania system. After its organization in 1845, the *Prison Society of New York* supported the Boston society in urging the adoption of the Auburn system.

The *Prison Discipline Society of Boston* was organized by Louis Dwight (1793-1854). Dwight had originally prepared for the ministry, but was prevented from preaching by an injury to his lungs in an accident in a chemical laboratory. In 1824 he rode on horseback throughout the eastern part of the country distributing Bibles to prisoners. He was horrified by the appalling abuses in the contemporary penal institutions and he determined to devote his life to an improvement of their condition. He organized and directed the *Prison Discipline Society of Boston* from 1825 to his death in 1854. As Secretary of the Society he wrote its reports, which are much the best single source for the study of American penology during this period, though they are disfigured by a violent opposition to the Pennsylvania system.

Dwight was repeatedly accused of unfairness and dishonesty by members of the *Philadelphia Society for Alleviating the Miseries of Public Prisons,* but a careful examination of the polemic pamphlets of both parties to the conflict cannot fail to impress an impartial reader with the fact that neither was qualified to "cast the first stone." Both were fiercely partisan and both were disgracefully unscrupulous in their use of statistics designed to support their cause or damage that of their opponents. The only gratifying feature of the controversy was that both systems were so greatly superior to the unspeakable congregate system which they displaced that their competition inevitably worked for the betterment of penal conditions.

That Dwight and the Auburn system triumphed was not as much due to superior ability on his part as to the undoubted advantages of his position. The Pennsylvania system had been unfairly discredited by the failure of its imperfect application before 1829, and the Auburn system was free from this initial handicap. Further, the Auburn type of administration required less expenditure for introduction and the economic arguments in its favor were at least superficially, much more attractive than for the Pennsylvania system. Added to these advantages was the superior and more widespread organization of the Boston Society throughout the country.

In addition to the conflict between these prison reform societies, most of the leaders in the improvement of criminal jurisprudence and penal administration in this country took a decided stand on one side or the other of the controversy. The Pennsylvania system was defended by Roberts Vaux, Edward Livingston, Francis Lieber, Dorothea Lynde Dix, William Parker Foulke and Richard Vaux. The Auburn plan of administration was warmly favored by De Witt Clinton, Gershom Powers, Amos Pillsbury, William H. Seward, E. C. Wines, Theodore W. Dwight, Frank Sanborn and Gideon Haynes. The controversy gradually died out after 1860. With an introduction of a knowledge of the Irish system into the United States, through the efforts of Frank Sanborn and others, about 1865, and its later development into the Elmira Reformatory system by 1875, the advocates of both older types of administration soon came to see that they had been supporting a hopelessly crude and elementary penal system and few possessed the audacity or stupidity to prolong the dispute.

If the Pennsylvania system did not meet with the hearty approval of penologists in this country, the originators and promoters of the system could take keen satisfaction in the admiration which it received from the most distinguished penologists of Europe.

The interchange of ideas between penal reformers in London and Philadelphia from 1787 to 1820 has already been referred to. The French were scarcely less interested in the movement for the improvement of criminal jurisprudence and penal administration which centered in Philadelphia. As early as 1794, the Duke of Rochefoucauld-Liancourt published a pamphlet in which he praised the reforms effected in Pennsylvania between 1786 and 1793. In 1828, J. M. Charles Lucas, writing on the penitentiary systems of Europe and America, called attention to the significant reform movement which had been initiated in Philadelphia. A more signal honor came when France, in 1831, sent two of her most distinguished citizens to make a study of American penal institutions. They were the publicist, Gustave Auguste de Beaumont and the Versailles judge, Alexis de Tocqueville. It was on this visit that De Tocqueville gathered the material for his *Democracy in America,* a work which brought him world-wide fame, while the report on American penitentiaries, mainly the work of De Beaumont, is known only to the few students interested in the historical aspects of penology.

Their report on the American prison system is limited mainly to a careful survey and analysis of the rival systems in operation at Auburn and Philadelphia. It is a most calm and judicious document and is not at all marred by partisanship. The Pennsylvania system was held to be more expensive to construct and put in operation, but was regarded as more easily and economically administered. The Auburn system was believed to be cheaper to introduce and better adapted to productive labor, but less readily and successfully administered by the generally mediocre type of officials connected with prison administration. As to the relative efficacy of the two systems in securing the reformation of inmates the authors resort to the following rather curious but keen and subtle bit of penal and social philosophy:*

The Philadelphia system, being that which produces the deepest impressions on the soul of the convict, must effect more reformation than that of Auburn. The latter, however, is perhaps more conformable to the habits of men in society, and on this account effects a greater number of reformations, which might be called "legal," inasmuch as they produce the external fulfilment of social obligations.

---

*G. de Beaumont and A. de Tocqueville, *On the Penitentiary System in the United States and Its Application in France,* translated from the French with an Introduction, Notes and Additions, by Francis Lieber, Philadelphia, 1833, pp. 59-60.

If this be so, the Philadelphia system produces more honest men, and that of New York more obedient citizens.

Both systems were regarded as severe:*

To sum up the whole on this point, it must be acknowledged that the penitentiary system in America is severe. While society in the United States gives the example of the most extended liberty, the prisons of the same country offer the spectacle of the most complete despotism.

While the French commissioners were fully appreciative of the admirable advantages of the Pennsylvania system, they inclined to favor the Auburn plan:†

Yet the Auburn system, whose merit in theory is not less incontestable, is, as we have shown above, much cheaper in its execution; it is therefore this system which we should wish to see applied to our prisons, if the question were only to choose between the two.

If the first noted European commissioners to the United States were disposed to recommend the Auburn system, such was not the case with their successors. In 1832 England appointed Mr. William Crawford, of the *London Society for the Improvement of Prison Discipline*, as a commissioner to study the systems of penal administration in the United States. His report, submitted in the summer of 1834, was a glowing eulogy of the Pennsylvania system and it led to the erection of the great Pentonville Prison, modeled after the Eastern Penitentiary. This penal institution is important in the history of penology, as it was operated in connection with the Australian transportation system where Captain Alexander Maconochie first put into operation the parole and commutation system, which was later improved by Sir Walter Crofton in Ireland and ultimately became the basis of the Elmira reformatory system.

The Scotch philosopher and psychologist, George Combe (1788-1858), who visited the United States some six years

*Ibid., p. 47.
†Ibid., p. 90.

after Mr. Crawford, differed radically from his predecessor and gave his hearty approval to the Auburn system.

The fame of the new American penitentiary system spread beyond France and England, and in 1834 Prussia followed their example by sending Doctor Nicolaus Heinrich Julius (1783-1862), to this country to study its penal institutions. He remained two years and upon his return was a thorough convert to the Pennsylvania system, which, with the aid of German reformers, he succeeded in introducing into Prussia and many other German states.

France was apparently dissatisfied with the results of the investigation of De Beaumont and De Tocqueville, and in 1836 she sent two more commissioners, Frédéric Auguste Demetz and Guillaume Blouet, to make a further study of the problem. While more critical and cautious than Crawford or Julius, they were, however, inclined to favor the Pennsylvania system in a much more decided manner than De Beaumont and De Tocqueville had been disposed to recommend the Auburn plan of administration.

These recommendations of the Pennsylvania system by so many distinguished authorities led to its very general adoption in Europe. England adopted it in 1835; Belgium, in 1838; Sweden, in 1840; Denmark, in 1846; Norway, in 1851; Holland, in the same year; while in 1875 France provided for a more extended application of the system through the effect of the investigations of Haussonville from 1872 to 1875. It is true, of course, that in few countries was the adoption as complete as that in Pennsylvania in 1829, but in every case it was sufficient to leave the impress of the "separate" system upon the administration of the penal institutions, and down to the present day the Pennsylvania system dominates the penitentiary system of continental Europe.

VI. THE ORIGIN AND DEVELOPMENT OF THE ELMIRA
REFORMATORY SYSTEM

In his two works, *The Penitentiary Systems of Europe and*

America (1828) and *The Theory of Imprisonment* (1836), that wise and progressive French penologist, M. Charles Lucas, had clearly taken the advanced position that a curative reformatory type of prison discipline ought to be substituted for the contemporary repressive prison system. It was a long time, however, before this aspiration was adequately realized. It was only achieved, and then imperfectly in the Elmira Reformatory system introduced into New York State following 1870.

A number of significant currents of reform in penology converged in producing this system. An important element was contributed by the new methods of prison discipline introduced in the British penal colony in Australia. Captain Alexander Maconochie came to Norfolk Island, in the Pacific east of Australia in 1840, and was able to suggest a tremendous improvement in penal methods by eliminating the old flat-time sentence and introducing the beginnings of commutation of sentence for good behavior. Every convict, according to the seriousness of his offense, instead of being sentenced to a given term of years, had a certain number of marks set against him which he had to redeem before he was liberated. These marks were to be earned by deportment, labor and study, and the more rapidly they were acquired the more speedy the release. While Maconochie's reforms received slight support in Australasia, they were hailed by the reformers in Great Britain and were taken up specifically by Walter Crofton when he came to formulate the procedure in the Irish prison system.

At about the same time the notion of an indeterminate time sentence was originated and given popularity through the writings of Archbishop Whately of Dublin, the Scotchman George Combe, and especially the English reformers, Frederick and Matthew Davenport Hill. Its supplement, the famous parole system, while anticipated by a number of other reformers, was most systematically and effectively advocated by the French publicist, Bonneville de Marsangy. Maconochie's sys-

tem of determining the period of incarceration upon the basis
of the behavior of the convict was combined with the notion
of the indeterminate sentence and parole in the famous Irish
system of prison administration, which was introduced by Sir
Walter Crofton in the decade following 1853. To these
earlier progressive innovations he added the practice of classifying convicts in graded groups, through which each convict
had to pass before obtaining his freedom on parole, his advancement being determined by his conduct.

The notion of productive and instructive prison labor,
which goes back to the Pennsylvania Quakers, was also developed by a number of progressive penologists during the second
quarter of the nineteenth century, especially by Montesinos in
Spain and Obermaier in Bavaria.

These liberal and progressive innovations, which have been
all too briefly and casually mentioned above, attracted the
attention of the leading American reformers, most notably
Theodore W. Dwight and E. C. Wines of the New York
Prison Association, F. B. Sanborn of Concord, Massachusetts,
Z. R. Brockway, Superintendent of the Detroit House of
Correction, and Gaylord Hubbell, Warden of Sing Sing
Prison. These men prepared able, vigorous and widely read
public reports or private monographs, urging the adoption of
these advanced methods in the American prison system, but
they were only able to secure the introduction of these innovations for the treatment of younger first offenders. A law
authorizing the creation of an institution for these types at
Elmira, New York, was passed in 1869, and the institution
was opened in 1877, with Mr. Brockway as its first superintendent. A decent preliminary approximation to the principle
of the indeterminate sentences was secured, and the inmates
were divided into classes or grades through which they might
advance to ultimate parole by virtue of good conduct if they
did not desire to remain in the institution for the maximum
sentence.

The great advance which the Irish and Elmira systems

mark over Pennsylvania and Auburn systems was the fact that in these later types of penal discipline the term of incarceration was at least roughly made to depend upon the observable progress made by the prisoner on the road to ultimate reformation. It was, thus, a system which chiefly stressed reformation rather than either retaliation or deterrence.

As far as its application in the United States is concerned, however, even this method of discipline possessed serious and grave defects. In the first place, it was scarcely at all introduced into the prisons which confined the adult offenders, thus not being applied to the great bulk of the prison population. In the second place, while it was based primarily upon the idea of effecting the reformation of the convicts, it failed signally to provide the right sort of psychological surroundings to expedite this process. The whole system of discipline was repressive, and varied from benevolent despotism, in the best instances, to tyrannical cruelty in the worst. There was little, if anything, done to introduce into the mind of the individual convict, or into the groups of the convicts generally, any sense of individual or collective responsibility for the conduct of the prison community, nor was any significant attempt made to provide any education in the elements of group conduct and the responsibilities of the citizen.

There was little, if any, grasp of that fundamental fact which is basic in the newer penology, namely, that a prisoner can be fitted for a life of freedom only by some training in a social environment which bears some fair resemblance in point of liberty and responsibility to that into which he must enter upon obtaining release. There was no wide acceptance of the present position that the general body of delinquents cannot be treated as a single unified group. There was no general recognition that criminals must be dealt with as individuals or as a number of classes of individuals of different psychological and biological types. It was not admitted that they must be scientifically differentiated through a careful psychiatric study, as well as a detailed sociological study of their environment, preliminary to the major part of their treatment while incarcerated. These last conditions have only been very recently and very incompletely realized in systems of convict self-government, such as those which Mr. Thomas Mott Osborne introduced, and in such careful psychiatric studies of the criminal class as were attempted in the psychiatric clinic introduced in the Sing Sing Prison by Dr. Thomas W. Salmon and Bernard Glueck, were extended in legislation in Massachusetts following 1921, and have been more extensively employed in connection with juvenile courts and probation.

The Elmira system was unquestionably a real step forward a half century ago, but later on it became in many institutions almost as out of date as the Auburn and Pennsylvania systems. In Elmira itself the humane and reformative influences which led to the installation of the system well-nigh disappeared. A prominent officer in the institution boasted to the present writer in 1928 that young criminals begged the judges to send them to the Auburn state penitentiary instead of to the Elmira Reformatory. He apparently thought this was a reason for pride and satisfaction.

SELECTED REFERENCES

Barnes, Harry Elmer. *The Evolution of Penology in Pennsylvania.* 1927: Reprinted Montclair, N. J., 1968.

Barnes, Harry Elmer. *A History of the Penal, Reformatory and Correctional Institutions of the State of New Jersey, Analytical and Documentary.* Trenton, 1918.

Bernaldo De Quirós, Constancio. *Modern Theories of Criminality.* Boston, 1911.

Branch-Johnson, William. *The English Prison Hulks.* London, 1957.

De Beaumont, Gustave, and De Tocqueville, Alexis. *On the Penitentiary System in the United States and Its Application in France.* Carbondale, Ill., 1964.

Howard, Derek L. *John Howard: Prison Reformer.* New York, 1963.

Ives, George. *A History of Penal Methods.* 1914: Reprinted Montclair, N. J., 1970.

Klein, Philip. *Prison Methods in New York State.* New York, 1920.

Lewis, Orlando F. *The Development of American Prisons and Prison Customs, 1776-1845.* 1922; Reprinted Montclair, N. J., 1967.

Lewis, Walter David. *From Newgate to Dannemora.* Ithaca, N. Y., 1965.

Lindsley, John B. *On Prison Discipline and Penal Legislation.* Nashville, 1874.

McKelvey, Blake. *American Prisons.* 1936; Reprinted Montclair, N. J., 1968.

Phillipson, Coleman. *Three Criminal Law Reformers: Beccaria, Bentham, Romilly.* 1923; Reprinted Montclair, N. J., 1970.

Robinson, Louis N. *Penology in the United States.* Philadelphia, 1921.

Sellin, Thorsten. *Pioneering in Penology: The Amsterdam House of Correction in the 16th and 17th Centuries.* Philadelphia, 1944.

Teeters, Negley K. *The Cradle of the Penitentiary.* Philadelphia, 1955.

Teeters, Negley K., and Shearer, John D. *The Prison at Philadelphia: Cherry Hill.* New York, 1957.

Vaux, Richard. *Brief Sketch of the Origin and History of the State Penitentiary for the Eastern District of Pennsylvania.* Philadelphia, 1872.

Webb, Sidney, and Webb, Beatrice. *English Prisons under Local Government.* New York, 1922.

Wines, Enoch C. *The State of Prisons and of Child Saving Institutions in the Civilized World.* 1880; Reprinted Montclair, N. J., 1968.

Wines, Frederick H. *Punishment and Reformation.* Rev. ed. New York, 1919.

CHAPTER VII

The Nature and Evils of Imprisonment

I. PERSISTENCE OF CORPORAL PUNISHMENT IN CONJUNCTION WITH IMPRISONMENT

WE have already noted that the Pennsylvania Quakers and others responsible for the origins of the modern prison system were motivated primarily by a desire to put an end to the bloody and revolting types of corporal punishment then in vogue for the punishment of criminal acts. Imprisonment, in imposing artificial confinement on the convict, was regarded as a new and sufficient method of punishment which would do away with the necessity of flogging, mutilation and the like. According to the Quaker theory and practice of solitary confinement there would be little possibility for the convict to injure himself or his associates, and therefore little reason to inflict any other form of punishment except that of confinement.

It is necessary to observe, however, that, as usual, the hopes of the reformers were not realized. With the exception of overt mutilation, almost every form of corporal punishment known to the pre-prison days was brought over into the prison system as a method of enforcing prison discipline. Floggings of the most brutal sort have been continued in conjunction with imprisonment right down to our own time, and deaths through over-severe whippings are not uncommon in our southern prisons and chain-gangs today. Tying prisoners up by their hands and allowing to hang thus suspended with their toes barely touching the floor has been a very common method of enforcing prison discipline. The stretcher, akin in principle to the medieval rack, was frequently employed in American prisons in the nineteenth century. The prisoner's feet were fastened to the floor, while his hands were attached to a rope running through a pulley fastened to the ceiling. Prison guards pulled on the rope and carried out the stretching process. As late as 1878 a prisoner, Jacob Snook by name, died while being stretched in the state penitentiary of New Jersey at Trenton. The strapping of prisoners on wooden benches and beds of bars was widely practiced throughout the nineteenth century. The Prison Investigating Committee of 1829 discovered that in the state penitentiary at Trenton, New Jersey, men had been strapped on their backs on planks in unheated cells for as long as twenty days at a time. The Committee revealed the fact that in the preceding twenty years at least ten prisoners had died from the direct and immediate effects of this and other types of punishment administered in the institution.

Sweat boxes were frequently used as a method of punishment. These were relatively unventilated cells located on either side of a fireplace. There are occasionally reported cases of suffocation of prisoners while being punished in these sweat boxes. At times fire has been applied to prisoners for various disciplinary purposes. In 1878 the Investigating Committee discovered that the authorities in the New Jersey state prison had been in the habit of pouring alcohol on epileptics and then setting fire to the alcohol in order to detect possible shamming or faking in an epileptic convulsion. Cold baths and the pouring of cold water upon prisoners from a considerable height have been common methods of prison punishment. In the prison investigation of 1834 and 1835 in Pennsylvania the authorities referred to the following punishment of a convict named Seneca Plumley, incarcerated in the Eastern Penitentiary: "In the depth of winter, he was tied up against the wall attached to his cell by the wrists, while buckets of extremely cold water were thrown upon him from a height which partly froze on his head and person, and he was shortly after discharged as incurably insane."

Unruly prisoners have often been condemned to wear an

iron yoke or something of the sort. The New Jersey investigators in 1829 called attention to a striking example of barbarism in the treatment of a fourteen-year-old boy who was confined in prison in free association with the most hardened criminals. The boy, being undersized, was small enough to crawl through the grating in the prison doors. Therefore the prison officials put on him an iron yoke into which his head was placed and to which his arms were fastened in such a way as to keep his arms extended some twenty inches apart on a level with his shoulders. The straight-jacket was well-nigh universal in the last century and the iron cage is still in use. The use of thumb-screws and the gag has not been unknown in prison discipline. The above-mentioned Pennsylvania investigation of 1834-35 referred to the case of another prisoner in the Eastern Penitentiary, Matthias Maccumsey, "in whose mouth an iron bar or gag was so forcibly fastened, that his blood collected and suffused up into his brain and he suddenly died under the treatment."

One of the more famous of American criminals was Pat Crowe. He gained international notoriety as the kidnapper of the son of the beef magnate, Cudahy, some thirty years ago. Now long since reformed and a decent citizen, Crowe wrote a series of articles on crime and punishment for the Scripps-Howard newspapers in the autumn of 1929. The following excerpt describes the nature of corporal punishment as it went on in the Missouri State Penitentiary a generation ago:

When I was railroaded into the Missouri State Prison at Jefferson City on a trumped-up charge of train robbery, I was assigned to work in the shoe shop under the state contract system that prevailed there, the favorite contractor paying 45 cents a day to the state for the labor of each convict. Of course, the prisoners received no compensation for their work. There were 1000 convicts employed in this shoe factory. Because I had been shot through both my hands in a gun battle I was not fit to work on the regular shoe-making tasks and was given a job to distribute the work among the other prisoners, who were compelled to turn out so much work at a given time or take the consequences in the hall of punishment. It was the most brutal system that I have ever witnessed.

I have known men to be whipped to death simply because it was a physical impossibility for them to do the tasks assigned to them under this outrageous contract labor system. I worked on the job of dispensing materials to these prisoners and often they would beg me to bring them easy shoes so that they could perform their task and thus avoid the whipping post.

Of course, it was impossible for me to play any favorites in this matter and I was continually fearful that I would be stuck in the back with a knife for putting the amount of work on a prisoner's bench that he was compelled to do. Finally the situation got on my nerves to such an extent that I requested the foreman to transfer me to some other job so that I might avoid any trouble with prisoners who failed to complete the work that I carried to them and were beaten unmercifully at the whipping post for not being able to do.

Every night as we came out of the work shop, from 10 to 60 of these poor fellows would be lined up with their arms folded before the hall of punishment and we all knew what that meant. In this torture chamber they had two posts into which had been driven iron pegs. If it was a prisoner's first offense he would be handcuffed around the post all night. There was no whipping for the first offense.

In the morning he would be let down in order to go to the dining hall where he would get a breakfast of black coffee and corn bread. Then he would return to the workshop and was given ten days' grace in which to speed up to a point where he could complete his task. If he failed at the end of that time he was certain to go again to the hall of punishment and be introduced to "Betsy's sister," and believe me, she was a tough old girl.

This was another pillar extending from the floor to the ceiling and the prisoner would be handcuffed and be lifted up and hooked on one of the pegs so that his toes would just touch the floor. His back would then be bared and the rawhide would lay his flesh open. To make his hurts more painful the welts and cuts would be sponged with salt water. You could hear the cries of pain of these poor devils for half a mile. All the other prisoners could hear their moans and screams of torture and we all knew that in many cases it was the rankest kind of injustice against men who were punished because they were unable to do what was impossible.

I knew several prisoners in the Missouri penitentiary who died from the effects of the whipping post just as a 16-year-old boy did who left his North Dakota home not so long ago, was arrested in Florida for riding a box car, and was given six months in one of the prison lumber camps. That case, of course, attracted national attention, but I know of hundreds of cases just like it out of my experiences in prisons in this country. This brutal and inhuman treatment of prisoners is one of the most potent factors in making hardened criminals.

The use of the dark cell and the diet of bread and water has been probably the most universally utilized method of prison punishment in the whole history of American penology. The dark cell has usually been an underground dungeon and while confined here the prisoner is normally allowed only a glass of water and a slice of coarse bread daily. Sometimes even this allowance has not been permitted. These dark cells or dungeons have usually been infested with rats and other vermin. Therefore, this punishment was not unlike that of confinement in the dungeon of a medieval castle. The brutal straight-jacket is still used in many prisons.

It will be seen from this very brief and hasty catalogue of the more common methods of corporal punishment which have been employed to enforce prison discipline that we have had a hangover of the more usual types of corporal punishment, from which imprisonment was originally intended to provide an escape. An individual who had been intrusted with punishment at the close of the Middle Ages would not have felt strangely out of place had he returned and taken up duties as a prison deputy in the United States in the middle of the nineteenth century.

Many who cannot escape from the testimony of historic documents relative to the existence of such punishments as these in the past century frequently contend that such shocking brutalities are entirely a thing of the past and that today corporal punishment is absent from our prisons. Indeed there

is a considerable school who hold that we have now gone to
the opposite extreme and are coddling our prisoners, making
the life of the average convict more pleasant than that of individuals of a comparable economic and social status outside prison walls. Not infrequently we read of New York City
jurists of the old school complaining that Sing Sing prison has
become the best country club in the Hudson River highlands.
A little study of the actual facts will serve to dissipate this
illusion. In 1920 a trained prison investigator, Mr. Frank
Tannenbaum, made a transcontinental tour investigating
prison conditions in the United States. We may quote herewith some of his more cogent discoveries as to the treatment
of prisoners in representative prisons throughout the
country:*

This story brings me straight to the question of prison discipline in the United States. There has been so much agitation
about this particular question—and it is a crucial question—
that a survey of how things stand at present is bound to be
of interest as well as significant. I must begin by saying that
the agitation has mainly been outside of prison—that those
affected by it were mostly people who have little or nothing
to do with the prison situation. There are a few exceptions, a
few indications that all the agitation has not been entirely in
vain: a few changes in method, a possible reduction in the
number of men punished, a relaxing of the rules a little in regard to talking and the lock-step, the abolition of such things
as the straight-jacket (I am not so sure about this: rumors of
its existence reached me in more than one place, but I did not
actually see it), and the abolition of what was once a common
practice of hanging men up by their wrists and swinging their
body off the floor.

Let me introduce into this discussion of the situation the
following quotation from the Detroit *News* of January 27,
1920:

"Harry L. Hulburt, warden of the prison, explained to
the committee how the flogging apparatus is worked. The
man to be flogged is blindfolded, handcuffed, and shackled at
the ankles. Then he is stretched out on a long ladder, which
is made to fit snugly over a barrel. The prisoner is blind-

---

*Tannenbaum, *Wall Shadows*, pp. 105-15.

folded, the warden said, so that he will not see who is flogging him. (The warden told me, when I visited the institution, that he did it himself, as he thought that no one else should be allowed to do it.) His back is bared and a piece of stout linen cloth is placed over the bare spot. The instrument used in the paddling is a heavy strap about four inches in width, punched with small holes about an inch apart and fastened to a handle. The strap is soaked in water, according to the warden, till it becomes pliable; Dr. Robert McGregor (one of the best and most conscientious prison doctors that I met on the trip), prison physician, holds the pulse of the man being flogged and gives the signal for the flogger to stop."

The article then goes on to detail three different cases of flogging. We will quote only the first.

"Thomas Shultz, boy of twenty-one years old, seven months after being sent from the insane asylum, was given 181 lashes and kept in the dungeon during the period of the flogging for nine days and fed on bread and water. . . . November 3d, assaulted guard. For this and other minor offenses, none of them serious, he was sentenced to receive 181 lashes. November 3, he received 40 lashes. . . . November 5th, he received 35 lashes. November 6, he received 26 lashes. November 9th, he received 40 lashes. November 13th, he received 40 lashes. Total, 181 lashes."

Now Jackson, to which this refers, is a comparatively decent prison (I had started to use the word good; but there are no good prisons, no more than there are good diseases). If I were asked to pick the least objectionable prisons in the United States, after seeing something like seventy, I should have to include Jackson among the first ten, or possibly even among the first half-dozen. The warden is unusually intelligent, interested in his job, an advocate of the honor system, who also practises it on a large scale. He is certainly among the most humane of the wardens in the country; and, by and large, his prisoners have more freedom inside the walls than is common. I do not repeat this quotation to give it extra publicity. I repeat it to show what happens even in those prisons which are least antiquarian and hide-bound. This does not mean that all prisons have whipping. A large number still do,—more than I expected,—but old methods of punishment are still prevalent in practically all prisons.

There is hardly a prison where solitary confinement is not practiced. In some cases solitary confinement is for a few months, in some cases for a few years; and in not a few there is such a thing as permanent solitary. Some prisons have a few men put away; some have as many as twenty; and in one case there are about fifty men placed in solitary for shorter or longer periods.

Why do the wardens do it? Well, they do not know what else to do. They run to the end of their ingenuity, and do that as a last resort—that is, the best of them. Some do it as a matter of common policy. I recall climbing a flight of stairs with a good-natured warden in a western prison, and being shown a specially built courtyard with some dozen solitary cells. There were four men put away there permanently—one had been there some three years. They were not even allowed to exercise. They were not allowed to talk, they had no reading matter, they could not smoke. There had at one time been only one man in the place, and the warden permitted him to smoke; but when the others were put in, he told him not to pass any tobacco to them. This is, of course, an impossible demand. The insistence for a share of that mighty joy in solitary—a smoke—is irresistible. He did what was inevitable, —passed his tobacco, and a "puff," to the other fellows,— and the warden deprived him of the privilege. "He should have obeyed what I told him if he wanted to hold on to his privilege," was the reason given.

What is true of solitary confinement is true also of the dark cell. Practically all prisons have and use dark cells. It is common to find from one to a dozen men stuck away in the dark cells, kept on bread and water—that means a little bread and about a gill of water every twenty-four hours. In most prisons—about ninety per cent—this punishment is added to by handcuffing the man to the wall or the bars of the door during the day,—that is, for a period of ten to twelve hours each day he is in punishment,—the time varying from a few days to more than two weeks. In some institutions the handcuffs have been abolished and replaced by an iron cage made to fit the human form, which, in some cases, can be extended or contracted by the turning of a handle. A man put in the dark cell has this cage placed about him and made to fit his particular form—and it is usually made so "snug" that he has to stand straight up in the cage. He cannot bend his knees, he cannot lean against the bars, he cannot turn round; his hands are held tight against the sides of his body, and he stands straight, like a post, for a full day, on a little bread and water

—and for as many days as the warden or the deputy sees fit. I was always asked to observe that they did not use handcuffs: this was the reform. Remember, a dark, pitch-black cell, with your hands pinned against your sides, your feet straight all day, unable to move or shift your ground, for ten and twelve hours a day, on bread and water, is the reform!

In one or two institutions where the cage is used,—but it is not adjustable, the man having to squeeze into the flat space as best he can,—they added the handcuffs. In one institution, —a commendable institution, as such things go, in some ways, in one of the states that has always prided itself on being progressive, I found that they added to the dark cell the handcuffing of the man while he slept. In the particular institution I have in mind the arrangement was as follows. A bar was attached to one of the walls, and slanted down until it reached within about three inches of the floor. On this bar was a ring. At night, the board on which the man slept was placed near this slanting bar; one pair of handcuffs was put on the prisoner's wrists, another pair connected with his hands was attached to the ring on the slanting iron bar. This means that he had to lie on one side all night long, handcuffed and pressing on this board which served him as a bed.

This does not complete the list of prison punishments as they are now practiced. The underground cell is still in existence—probably not in many prisons, but I saw it in at least two different institutions. In one state prison,—an old prison, dark and damp inside,—I found a punishment cell in the cell-block. It was built underground. In the center of the hall there is an iron door flat on the ground, which one lifts sideways—like an old-type country cellar-door. It creaks on its rusty iron hinges. I climbed down a narrow flight of rickety stairs. When I got to the bottom, I had to bend double to creep into a long narrow passage. It was walled about with stone, covered with a rusty tin covering. It was not high enough to stand up in, hardly high enough for a good-sized man to sit up in. The warden above closed the door on me. I was in an absolutely pitch-black hole—long, narrow, damp, unventilated, dirty (there must be rats and vermin in it); and one has to keep a bucket for toilet purposes in that little black hole. As I came out, the warden said, naïvely, "When I put a man in here, I keep him thirty days." Let the reader imagine what that means to human flesh and blood.

I do not want to make this a chapter of horrors. Just one

more case. On my way back I stopped off at a certain very well-known prison that I had heard about since childhood. For the last ten years it has been famous as one of the great reform prisons of the country. I remember seeing pictures of the warden with prisoners out on a road-gang. The article in which these pictures appeared gave a glowing account of the freedom these men had—they guarded themselves away from the prison proper, out in the hills, building roads. The state in which this prison is situated has constructed many miles of prison-built road—and, in fact, it was one of the first in the country to undertake to build roads with convict labor, without guards. When I knocked on its gates, I thrilled with expectancy. Here, at least, would I find a model prison, unique, exceptional, a pride to the state and an honor to the man who was responsible for it. In fact, I had heard that the warden was being considered for political advancement to the office of governor because of his remarkable prison record. I found a remarkable institution—remarkable for its backwardness and brutality.

The first thing that I saw as I entered the prison yard was a strange and unbelievable thing. Nine men kept going round in a circle, wheeling wheelbarrows, while a heavy chain dangled from each man's ankle. As I came nearer, I noticed in each wheelbarrow a heavy iron ball attached to the chain. In the center stood a guard; and the men kept circling about him all day long, wheeling the iron ball in their barrows, their bodies bent over, their faces sullen, their feet dragging. They did that for ninety days each, I was told by my guide. At night they carried the ball to their cells, and in the morning they carried it to the dining-room. For three months this iron ball and chain stayed riveted about their ankles—a constant companion and, I suppose, from the warden's point of view, a stimulus to better things—one of the ways of making "bad" men "good."

A few years later Mr. Tannenbaum made a careful study of southern prisons and revealed even more deplorable conditions in these institutions. The situation in the southern prisons is rendered worse by the fact that many of the prisoners are negroes and are therefore treated with even less consideration than white prisoners in the North. While the southern prisons are bad enough in themselves the worst conditions are found among the chain gangs. Tannenbaum thus describes conditions in these chain gangs which are common throughout the South:*

The chain gang is a peculiar institution. It is made up of chained men—that is men upon whose ankles chains are riveted, ranging in length from 12 to 24 inches. As soon as a man comes to a chain camp he is shackled. That shackle generally stays put as long as he is there—and that may be a lifetime. Each camp has a few trusties. Not very many. Out of forty or fifty men there may be six, sometimes ten. Ten would be unusual. The chain riveted to both ankles tends to drag on the ground and interferes with the working energy of the prisoner. There is therefore another—a longer chain—a kind of cross chain linked at the center of the one that is riveted to the ankles. That chain serves two main purposes. It is used to lift the chain off the ground when the men are working. This is done by sticking the loose end through the belt and raising the riveted chain off the ground. Its other use is to chain the men together at night. A dozen men and more will be chained to each other when they are asleep in their beds. There will be a long chain running from one end of the cage to the other. To this chain all the men will be locked by slipping one end of the long chain through the loose end of the cross chain which each prisoner has, in addition to the one riveted about his ankles. This limits the movement of the men to the length of their cross chain. Thus they sleep. Thus they lie in their beds on Sundays. Frequently they are compelled to lie that way when it rains and that may be for two weeks together. The typical cages are small. They stand on wheels. They range from 7x7x16 to 9x9x20. The typical cage has some 18 beds. There are nine beds each side of the cage. Three beds lengthwise and three in height, one above the other. That makes the space between the beds very narrow. If the men were free to move about they would have little room—but they are shackled. They have chains about their ankles and are often, even in the daytime, locked to each other. That means that the men have no freedom of movement. They lie on their beds, their faces almost touching the bed above them. The cage frequently has a tin roofing. On hot days—Sundays, Saturday afternoons, holidays—the sun streams down on the cage and makes an oven of the place, and the human beings in

*Tannenbaum, *Darker Phases of the South,* pp. 84-89.

it roast. These cages are not clean. Under this crowding it would be impossible to keep them sanitary. . . .

"The prisoners slept in a steel road-cage similar to those used for circus animals, excepting that they did not have the privacy which would be given to a respectable lion, tiger, or bear." "At night the prisoners are fastened to a beam with a short chain and a heavy shackle . . . men should not be compelled to wear three shackles in daylight (Sunday) and be unable to gather near the stove in winter or to avoid the direct rays of the sun in the summer." "The men are often confined in the cages on rainy days and Sundays, without exercise and with scarcely enough room to do anything except lie in their bunks." "The walls of these cages are practically solid (that is not generally the case) and allow little fresh air to enter in. In one of them twelve men were sleeping in a space about 8x8x15. It must have caused suffocating heat in warm weather." "At the time of this visit 22 men were sleeping in a cage only 8x8x20. This cage contains but 18 bunks so that eight of the men were sleeping double in a bunk of about two feet." (The reader ought to be reminded here that they were also shackled to each other.) "The night before this visit was made, 19 men slept in a cage only 7x7x16 feet. The bedding is badly torn and has not been washed in months. Flies are breeding in the sewage pit where the soil buckets are emptied." (This official language is very dull. I could say that I have seen bedding of creeping straw and torn shreds—but really I have no words to describe the conditions.) "At the time of this visit fifteen men were locked in a steel cage in the direct rays of the sun. An idea of the discomfort that the men experienced can be gained by considering the effect of confining fifteen men in very hot weather in a small room with a sheet-iron roof." "At the time of this visit 18 men were sleeping in a cage 7x7x14, intended originally for only 8 single bunks. The trusties were sleeping in a tent that was full of holes. In time of rain the men have to crouch under the cage of the kitchen car. Of course when they return to their beds they are wet through and through."

The tent camps are probably a little better—but that depends on the camp. It is frequently bad enough. Here is a camp that may be used to describe a goodly number of tent camps in the South. "None of the tents have flies or second covers and must leak like sieves in rainy weather . . . the provisions are kept on the ground in a leaky tent and consequently are often damaged by rain and surface water; the bedding is very soiled and is in disrepair; and a number of prisoners have neither beds nor cots; but sleep on boards laid on the ground. The method of disposing of the sewage is most unsanitary. The night buckets are emptied just behind the tent in which the prisoners sleep. This practice exposes men to the unpleasant odors and the danger of contracting disease."

Mr. Tannenbaum thus characterizes the type of guard employed in the southern prisons and prison camps:*

All guards, under the law, are employed at a salary of forty dollars per month. Some of the guards are not desirable at any price, or even though they should work entirely without compensation; they are temperamentally, and from lack of ordinary intelligence, unfitted for this line of service. This is true of the convict chain gangs scattered throughout the South, but the prison farms are no better. "The guards on these farms were hardened against human sympathy and of a rather shiftless nature," and in another place, "we find that the guards in charge of prisoners' work in fields and on the farms, frequently beat them with ropes, quirts, bridle reins, and pistols, without necessity or authority, and that in some instances the guards have ridden over the prisoners with their horses and have set the dogs on them, inflicting serious and painful injuries."

The guard's efforts to amuse himself run to the grotesque and the barbarous. One guard takes a picture of himself with his foot planted on a convict sprawling in the dust. In another place officers surround a poor prisoner who is being whipped. The prisoner has to count the number of licks he is receiving. The rules prescribe ten licks at one time—and the guards stand about and amuse themselves by disturbing and upsetting the poor fellow. He makes a mistake and then has to begin the count over again. All of this is done in a hilarious, good-natured fashion. The guard must be sure of his authority—at least he must feel that the prisoner is sure of it, and so in many—all too many—convict road camps a new prisoner is initiated so as to impress him with due reverence for his superiors. He is whipped as soon as he arrives at the camp and before he has had a chance to prove his pliancy. An official

---

*Tannenbaum, *Darker Phases of the South*, pp. 78-80.

comment upon this is, "This form of humiliation often causes resentment among the men and is an unwarranted addition to the sentence of the court. The prisoners are punished by beating them, sometimes on the naked flesh with a piece of belting attached to a handle." This temper is not confined to the guards. The wardens are occasionally affected by it.

The brutalities which result are those which we might expect from this grade of supervision:*

I have so far described the guards, the sanitation, the food, and the treatment of the sick—a description that covers practically all of the southern prisons. I now am to describe the disciplinary methods. Frankly I hesitate to subject the reader to the tale of horror that is involved. I will only cite a few instances—and those of the milder type. A prison investigator writes that, "Within the last year I have personally visited a good many convict camps in the State and found straps weighing from five to nine pounds." When such straps are applied to the naked flesh of a man who may be drawn across a wheelbarrow, with one man sitting on his head, one man sitting on his feet, and one stuffing a dirty rag in his mouth, while the fourth man does the whipping, you get this: "In several places the skin had been beaten from his body, leaving abraded surfaces that were raw and discharging." Here is another instance of the same type. "There is evidence of brutal treatment on his wrists and legs that will remain for all time in the form of scars. On each wrist at the outer base of the thumb deep holes were worn in the flesh by the handcuffs, as a result of the hanging." One State farm is described as showing that "they had been lacerated by dog bites and testimony was developed that said lacerations had been inflicted under the direction of the sergeant after the escaped convict had been caught." "We have seen white men who have suffered all these acts of cruelty and men who have suffered even more than this." A guard had told me that when they killed an escaping prisoner he was allowed to lie in his tracks till midnight and then drawn into the prison camp, the sleeping inmates awakened and made to shake hands with the dead body. It ought to be added that these things frequently happen where there is specific legal provision against them, where there is constitutional provision against corporal punishment. And

*Tannenbaum, *op. cit.*, pp. 99-102.

one might add that the investigations which have repeatedly taken place in various southern states have almost invariably brought with their recommendations one to the effect "that we recommend that the prison commission abide by the law of the state."

The whipping of prisoners is still very common in the southern states. Sometimes, as in Alabama, its brutality defies belief. Within the last six months a veteran reporter told the writer that he had covered more than sixty murders without flinching—at times being spattered with blood. Invited to see two convicts whipped, he was compelled to turn away positively ill before the lashing of the first man had been completed. They are whipped with a heavy strap, set with parallel ridges of brass brads. It usually takes from two to three weeks in the prison hospital for the beaten man to recover.

The Southerners have acquired a deserved reputation for gallantry in dealing with womankind, but the following passages from Tannenbaum will make it clear that this does not extend to their treatment of women in the southern prisons:*

The condition of the women prisoners is most deplorable. They are usually placed in the oldest part of the prison structure. They are almost always in the direct charge of men guards. They are treated and disciplined as men are. In some of the prisons children are born in prison—either from the male prisoners or just "others." In one institution the women are living in a fire-trap with the doors locked on the outside and the key in the hands of a young man. One county warden who had state prisoners, amongst them women both white and colored, told me in confidence, "That I neah kill that woman yesterday." She had lost her temper and cursed one of the guards. One of the most reliable women officials in the South told me that in her state at the state farm for women the dining-room contains a sweat-box for the women who are punished by being locked up in a narrow place with insufficient room to sit down, and near enough to the table so as to be able to smell the food. Over the table there is an iron bar

*Tannenbaum, *op. cit.*, pp. 104-6.

to which women are handcuffed when they are strapped, and on the wall there is the sign, "Christ died to save sinners." The woman prisoner who smuggled out a letter writes, "It (the prison) is built in the order of a zoo, having cells on each side of a passage ending up with a bull ring. We are in the sole charge of a man and subjected to every humiliation it is possible to conceive. The only exception being he does not force himself upon us, but he has forced women in nude state to bathe before him, comes into the bathroom at all times, he compels us to keep our cell doors open all day. We have absolutely no exercise. The mode of punishment is flogging with a split hose containing holes so that each lash raises and at the same time breaks the blister. . . . Last week the woman over my cell was flogged 35 lashes I counted." An official report in one of the states indicates that "We also found in the female ward sweat-boxes just large enough for a person of normal size to be confined, said sweat-boxes contained chains for the purpose of preventing the prisoners incarcerated therein from assuming a squatting position. The sweat-boxes had no ventilators."

That the conditions which Tannenbaum describes among the women in southern prisons is in no sense unique may be discerned from Mrs. Kate O'Hare's description of the conditions she met with during her incarceration in the woman's ward of the state penitentiary of Missouri at Jefferson City. We may present first her reaction to general living and sanitary conditions in the prison:*

The first thing that struck me was the dead, rancid odour, the typical institution smell, much intensified. It was the concentrated odour of dead air, venerable hash, ancient stews, senile "wienies," and cabbage soup, mingled with the musty odour of decaying wood saturated with rancid grease and home-made soap.

The benches and tables were very old, having done service for more than half a century. Many generations of prisoners had scrubbed them; they creaked and groaned with the infirmities of age, and every crack and crevice was inhabited with old and well-established cockroach families. They were very hungry roaches, who insisted on sharing our meals with

*O'Hare, *In Prison*, pp. 64-5.

us; so we ate with one hand and picked roaches out of our food with the other. I was not adept at one-handed eating and could not develop a taste for roaches to garnish my food. I made enough fuss about the matter to induce the management to have the dining-room cleaned and painted, and to provide tables, chairs, white table cloths, and real dishes. The dining-room is now quite civilized, except for the missing spoons. . . .

Rats, flies, and cockroaches, not to mention other vermin unmentionable in polite society, were plagues of our prison life. The rats were perhaps worst of all. They overran the place in swarms, scampered over the dining tables, nibbled our bread, played in our dishes, crept into bed with us, chewed up our shoes, and carried off everything not nailed down or hung far above their reach. I have not the instinctive fear of rats and mice that many women have, but for weeks I spent sleepless nights routing them out of my bed and chasing them out of my cell. Not until my young son visited the prison and had the ingenuity to think of covering the front bars with screen wire did I ever know a night's rest.

The most robust and buxom cockroaches I have ever known were ever present and fought with the rats for the food which we were permitted to buy. There were no screens, and the flies swarmed about the cellhouse in clouds. One of the most terrible things which I had to endure was that an Indian woman in the last stages of syphilis, her body covered with open lesions and dripping pus, occupied the cell directly below me. Her open sores were never properly dressed, the stench was frightful, and the flies swarmed over her and then awakened us in the morning by crawling over our faces. The effect of these unnecessary pests upon human nerves can readily be imagined. The sleepless nights caused by them were a very large factor in the punishments administered for "bad work" and failure to make the "task."

Mrs. O'Hare proceeds further to describe the bathing facilities and hygienic conditions in this institution, particularly her experience with compulsory bathing in the wake of a person in the terminal stages of syphilis:*

As Alice stepped out of the bathroom she was one of the most terrible creatures I have ever seen. From her throat to

---

*O'Hare, op. cit., pp. 67-8.

her feet she was one mass of open sores dripping pus. I have seen her with her clothes so stiff with dried pus that they rattled when she walked, and I have seen live maggots working out of the filthy bandages about her neck.

Alice had used the bathtub, and I was ordered to use it also. I asked the matron if it were necessary that I use the same tub that Alice had used, and she said it was. I then asked who cleaned the tub, and she replied that Alice was too ill and that I was to do it. I then asked what disinfectants were used. "Disinfectants!" she snarled; "whatdaya mean?"

"I mean what prophylactic measures do you use to keep the clean women from becoming infected with venereal disease?" I replied.

She screeched: "Hell, we ain't got none of them highfalutin' things here. This ain't no swell hotel—this is the pen!"

I protested: "But Miss Smith, you know what disease Alice has, you know how communicable it is, you know that if I use that tub I may become infected. You know I am a married woman with a husband and four children. You know I travel a great deal and sleep in Pullman cars and use public facilities. Does the United States Department of Justice expect me to become infected with syphilis and go back to civilized life and infect others who are certainly innocent of wronggoing?"

Sputtering and snarling with rage, the matron cried: "I don't know a thing about that, and care a damn sight less. You are a convict; this is what there is here for you to use. Now get ter hell outa here and take yer bath."

"But I refuse. To do so would be a social crime!" I replied.

Shrieking and cursing, the matron told me that I would bathe in the infected tub or she would send me to the "black hole" and "break" me. I knew she had the power and the temperament to do it. She had broken Minnie Eddy in the black hole a few weeks previous—and Minnie had been carried out in a pine box. So I stepped into the bathroom and turned on the taps—but I did not bathe.

That night I got a letter out "underground" to my husband. He reproduced the letter and sent it to a thousand influential people. It was published in newspapers and magazines, and a storm of protest arose all over the country. In less than three weeks we had shower baths installed in the females' wing of the prison, and that horror was abated.

I was able to rout the common bathtub, but I was never able to prevent the diseased women from handling the food. The women who were too ill to work in the shop were used in the dining-room. I think all of them were tubercular and syphilitic. I have seen the food which the women were forced to eat handled by women with pus oozing from open sores on their arms and dripping into the dishes, and it was a common sight to see our food sprayed with tuberculosis germs from the lips of coughing convicts.

There is nothing in my prison life that I remember with so much loathing as the inexcusable methods used in dealing with communicable diseases.

In devoting considerable attention to the persistence of corporal punishment in connection with prison discipline we must not forget that physical beatings and the like were not the only form of torture to which the imprisoned were subjected. It is quite possible that even greater suffering was induced by the enforced solitude of the Pennsylvania system of prison discipline, even when free from all special punishment. In spite of the ardent defense of the system by many of its protagonists, Governor Johnston of Pennsylvania, in his annual message in 1850, called attention to the large number of pardons which the governor of the state was compelled to issue on the ground of insanity:*

The Eastern and Western penitentiaries have been conducted with skill and prudence, and in the reformation and security of offenders, society has derived important advantages. It is, however, worthy of serious consideration whether in the adoption of a system of solitary confinement the severity of the punishment authorized by law does not injuriously affect the mental and physical vigor of the prisoner. The frequent recommendations to the Executive for the pardon of convicts afflicted with ill health and mental imbecility, would appear to require a modification of the penal laws.

One of the best summaries of the nature and influence of the solitary system of prison discipline was set forth in the an-

*H. E. Barnes, *The Evolution of Penology in Pennsylvania*, p. 296.

nual report of the Board of Inspectors of the Western Penitentiary of Pennsylvania in 1866:*

In looking over the annual reports made of the officers of this institution to the State Legislature for more than thirty years, we find that they have rarely ever omitted to express their entire satisfaction with the workings of the separate system of confinement which Pennsylvania has adopted as her own.

We are not at this time disposed to controvert the self-complaisant arguments so profusely lavished upon the Legislature from both extremities of the state, in their annual reports, as to our "humane and reformatory" system of prison discipline.

We think, however, that it might be well for the Legislature to look at the other side of this question and inquire, whether, in the onward progress of events and in the constant and interesting changes that are always being developed in the world, there might not be a more excellent plan adopted or worked out for the improvement and reformation of this unfortunate people than the one which we have adopted. As we have made from time to time our frequent visitations to the convict's cell, and have engaged him in conversation and studied his situation, we have often been oppressed with the feeling of despair that seemed to settle upon his face as he would look forward (sometimes through a quarter of a century) to a hopeless future. In his loneliness he broods over his condition, walking his dreary cell in the quiet hours of the night, and during the unemployed moments of the day. No human face visible save that of the officers and his keepers, he feels that "his hand is against every man and every man's hand is against him," and having no object or interest beyond his own walls to attract his attention or arrest his thoughts, he falls back upon himself and his fancied wrongs, and in sullen anguish preys upon his own vitals!

Man is formed for society. He cannot well live without it. Ostracize him from the world and his fellow men, and he soon loses his own self-respect, because he feels that he has forfeited that of others.

The rioting in the New York state prisons at Dannemora and Auburn in the summer of 1929 were indications of the

*Ibid., pp. 307-8.

anachronistic nature of contemporary prison discipline. Auburn prison was well administered for a conventional institution for adult criminals. Yet, it took but a brief flash to ignite the tinder of deep-seated convict resentment at the whole system of discipline. A commentator stated the case cogently when he observed that the Dannemora and Auburn incidents were proof that the old prison system, under which we have labored for a century, is "at its breaking-point."

A number of factors undoubtedly contributed to the riots in New York State, in Colorado and at the Federal Prison at Leavenworth. Overcrowding and lack of work appear to have been the most important inciting causes. Poor food and archaic cells contributed their share. In New York State there was a special factor at work, namely, the habitual criminal act, known as the Baumes Law. Under this a man convicted of a fourth felony is arbitrarily given a life sentence. In addition, the New York judges indulged in an orgy of long sentences in an hysterical effort to stem the so-called crime wave. These long sentences developed a sense of hopelessness and desperation on the part of the convicts. Their prison future was utterly without hope, while there was one chance in a hundred of freedom through a jail delivery. Hence, they were willing to look death in the face through reckless rebellion.

II. How Prisons Demoralize the Convict Personality

In spite of the brutalities of prison administration and the perpetuation of corporal punishment in the modern system of prison discipline, the most deplorable aspect of modern prison life is not the sporadic cruelty or the revolving filth of prisons. The most serious social liability inherent in the prison system is its forwarding the disintegration of the personality of those committed to its confines. We assume that imprisonment, which, by the opening of the nineteenth century, had become the usual method of handling convicted criminals, represents the enormous advance over corporal punishment. If one examines, however, the actual nature of the penal institutions and prison discipline of the last century he may be led to doubt whether the contemporary prison is really any improvement over the whipping-post or the stocks. The whipping-post, whether or not it exerted any deterrent influence, did not to any notable extent contribute to the degradation and disintegration of the personality of the individual punished. The present penal and "reformatory" institutions almost invariably tend to make the individual much more of a menace to society than he was before incarceration.

Theoretically, a prison may be an excellent institution for the reformation of the criminal, but in the light of its practical methods and actual operation it is doubtful if anything more ineffective or vicious could be devised as a method of protecting society from the depredations of the anti-social classes. Almost everything which could possibly contribute to the debasing and demoralization of the human personality characterizes present day prisons and the contemporary methods of penal administration. If one sat down and calmly endeavored to construct with unbridled imagination the sort of place which would either increase the already anti-social proclivities of a criminal or create anti-social attitudes and methods on the part of a hitherto normal individual, he would arrive at an institution bearing a very close resemblance to the modern prison.

The basic issue is, of course, whether we desire to establish and operate an institution to punish convicts or one to reform them and to train decent citizens. The two things cannot be done together. Punishment and reformation cannot be made twins in any system. We must choose clearly between the ends we desire to reach. The present prison is an admirable place in which to inflict brutal punishment. It is the last place in the world in which to expect reformative influences to be created and applied. In their *Five Hundred Criminal Careers* Sheldon and Eleanor Glueck found that out of five hundred prisoners released from the Massachusetts State Reformatory eighty per cent were not reformed five to fifteen years later. The percentage of reformation in state penitentiaries is even less.

Our penal institutions represent a veritable hierarchy in the scheme of criminal pedagogy. A youngster is relegated to a state reform school where he obtains his elementary instruction in criminal methods and tendencies. His secondary school work and his undergraduate collegiate career are passed in the state reformatory. Having thus obtained what may be regarded as his Bachelor of Arts degree in crime, he goes forth as a journeyman criminal. If highly successful he avoids arrest and continues his career with no important setback. If he is lacking in intelligence and adroitness, or a victim of ill-luck, he comes to the state prison to initiate his graduate work in this field in the seminars of the greatest specialists available for his instruction inside prison walls. He leaves prison not only a more competent criminal but a more embittered man.

Our prisons are equally fatal in their effect on those who have not passed through reform schools and reformatories. An adult first offender, while awaiting trial, may be thrown into a miserable county jail where he is compelled to associate with hardened criminals awaiting trial like himself, or with the degraded scum of the delinquent and pauper groups who make up that portion of the jail population that is actually serving time under a jail sentence. Convicted and sentenced to state prison, the first offender proceeds with the process of adjusting himself to association with crooks and to existence within a society characterized by corruption and intrigue.

We may now outline in a brief and general way the effect of contemporary imprisonment on the mind of the prisoner, the prison officials and the public at large. The key to the defects, abuses and cruelties of the present system is to be found in the fact that, whatever the pretense, the actual purpose of imprisonment is not reformation but punishment. If this were not so we would design our institutions and their administration so that they might more intelligently and directly promote the various methods and processes of reformation. Of course, the older attitude of conventional penology was that punishment itself necessarily produces reformation, but we know that in most cases the opposite result is produced.

The modern prison system brings into play a large number of disastrous influences constituting a vicious circle. The present prison system would put the most severe strains upon even a thoroughly normal person, but its savagery actually operates in most cases upon those who are physically or mentally abnormal or subnormal upon commitment. These emotionally unstable persons are upon entry into prison denied the assertion or enjoyment of the more important and basic human urges and impulses. Normal sociability is severely curtailed; self-assertion is practically denied; interesting work is rarely provided; play and recreation, if existent at all, are grotesquely inadequate. The natural outlet for the sex instinct is totally denied in the average prison, though the sex urge is rendered abnormally active due to the blocking of the other forms of emotional and intellectual expression which might otherwise drain off or sublimate sex desires.

The effects of all these abnormalities and abuses are greatly intensified by the regimentation and cruelty inevitable in the conventional prison administration of today. Hence, it is but natural that prison life should result in various types of explosion such as psychoses, neuroses, sex perversions, general physical and moral disintegration and sporadic insurrection. No understanding can be expected from the average warden, as his function is primarily that of a jailer who must keep a certain number of human animals safely herded within the prison walls. Nor can any sympathy be hoped for from the majority of those outside the walls, as the prison supplies the herd's machinery for collective vengeance, through which the individual gets a vicarious satisfaction as well as experiencing a pleasant indirect and symbolic release of the cruel and sadistic impulses which most citizens could scarcely apply in direct personal contact with another individual. This perverse emotional motivation of the average citizen renders him unfavorably disposed toward any proposal for an improvement of the situation, thus making it very difficult to break into the vicious circle and bring about any significant and permanent advances and reforms.

We can now take up the specific disastrous effects of imprisonment upon the individual convict. First and foremost should be placed the denial of one of the most basic human motives and impulses, namely, normal human sociability. The fact is that the association and communication of criminals is looked upon as mutually degrading. This, along with the greater supposed ease and simplicity of administration with the relative isolation of prisoners, leads the average prison warden markedly to curtail the opportunities for normal sociability between the inmates of his institution. We have now in most places abandoned the unmitigated savagery of the old Pennsylvania system of solitary confinement, but almost never is there any adequate provision for healthy social intercourse among the inmates of modern prisons. Along with the blocking of sociability goes the impossibility of normal self-assertion. The whole psychology of prison administration is based chiefly upon the desire to repress and intimidate the prisoner, in order that he may in this way feel very directly and certainly the displeasure of society over his violation of its rules and his threat to its safety. Rarely is there any interesting work provided for the prisoner which might allow the development of some sense of craftsmanship and some absorption in a definite task. More and more, modern mental hygiene is coming to emphasize the fundamental integrating function of a definite job or task in which the individual may become interested. This salutary and dynamic motive is obviously almost entirely absent in the case of the majority of the inhabitants of our present-day penal institutions. Then there is the notorious lack of adequate physical exercise, which is accompanied by unfortunate results both physical and psychological.

One of the most indefensible and demoralizing items in our

prison administration today is this prevalence of complete idleness or of mere make-believe occupations on the part of prisoners. Sanford Bates, Superintendent of Federal Prisons, points out that in Atlanta work is provided for only 800 convicts out of the 3,400 in the institution. In Leavenworth around 2,000 inmates live in complete idleness.

Nothing is more depressing to even the best of wardens than to be compelled to witness his convicts loafing in idle groups in the prison yards or rotting in their cells. Stanley Ashe, of the Western Penitentiary in Pittsburgh, is one of the best wardens this country has produced, but his efforts at reformation are well-nigh paralyzed by the fact that he can employ but 200 out of the 1,100 convicts in the institution. The best of us cannot endure prolonged idleness without personal demoralization. This is even more true of convicts, with their already warped personalities and their lack of means of diversion.

To put all convicts at work would accomplish at one stroke a number of highly desirable results. It would reduce restlessness, improve contentment, reduce the financial burden of prisons on the State, provide some financial remuneration for the convicts, make possible industrial training, and notably promote the probability of ultimate reformation.

The chief obstacles to sensible employment of convicts have been public inertia, administrative apathy and the opposition of union labor. The rioting may help to remove the two former, and the slightest examination of the facts will be sufficient to explode the competition bogey of labor. Even at the height of the prosperity of prison labor under the contract system in the late '80's the volume of prison-made products amounted to less than one per cent of what was being produced by free labor. This Volsteadian percentage could constitute no real competition with free labor. The hue and cry on this point was a man of straw compounded by short-sighted and selfish unionites and political agitators.

A resolute attack upon the problem of prison labor will do

more to eliminate those conditions which sprout riots than any amount of strong-arm methods.

The inferior food, the unattractive methods of serving it and the exclusion of conviviality from the convict meal remove practically all of the desirable psychic exuberance which is supposed to accompany the most successful execution of the process of nutrition. There is little opportunity for any considerable degree of emotional outlet in recreation, games, contests, music or sex. Particularly serious, though almost uniformly overlooked, is the total denial of any sex life to any of the inmates of penal institutions, in spite of the fact that many prisoners are of a hyper-sexed type who have been leading an unusually free sex life before incarceration.

This human animal, the convict, thus denied practically every phase of a normal expression of his personality, is still further rendered "safe and secure" through an elaborate scheme of regimentation and rules which are designed to simplify the task of the warden as a successful jailer. There is no attempt to understand or minister to the specific needs of a prisoner or to meet him on any ground of sympathetic human contacts. Rather, he is faced with a bewilderingly complete and rigid set of rules, any violation of which is punished either by physical pain or a decrease in his already slight body of privileges.

In the light of the above atrocious situation it is not surprising that many and diverse types of psychic abnormality are either intensified or generated by prison life. First, one must remember the general attitude of hopelessness and despair which dominates the majority of convicts when they reach these living tombs. The "Mark Twain Burglar" thus describes his feelings on arriving at the Wisconsin State Prison:*

I shall never forget the bleak November day during which the train passed through the barren country on its way north. I sat handcuffed to the sheriff and absorbed in my own

*In the Clutch of Circumstance, pp. 84-5.

thoughts, watching through the window of the car for the prison walls which were to receive me and shut me away from the world for six years.

At last it appeared in the distance, the tall water tower and smokestack, then the group of gray buildings with their parapets and the watch towers on the high walls. A sickening feeling took hold of me, and a lump rose in my throat. Any other place in the world, I thought, except that awful prison! The loud voice of the brakeman announcing our arrival at Waupun roused me from my reverie. The sheriff took me by the arm, and we dropped off the train to the platform. When we arrived at the prison and the numerous iron-barred gates closed behind me, I felt as though some great cavern had swallowed me up and I would never see the light of the free outside world again. Society had fed another individual into the great iron jaws of the prison hopper.

In addition to the general atmosphere of fear, isolation and hopelessness which is produced by the architecture and punitive psychology of the modern prison, there is the even worse situation generated by the usual method of handing over the practical control and operation of the prison to certain selected prisoners or "trusties" with the resulting cliques, favoritism, corruption and cruelty which this system produces. There is a popular tradition that the "trusties" are invariably the best type of convicts—those who have given the most evident promise of reformation. More often than not they are the worst criminals in the institution—clever crooks who outwit the officers, know how to play the game, and have no scruples about treason towards either their superiors or their fellow-convicts. By various means they gain the friendship of officers and guards and maintain their position through coöperation with them in whatever duties and intrigues are involved in this relationship. The results are bound to be evil in any event. If the prisoner "plays the game" and aligns himself with one or another of these inner gangs based on special favoritism and on "snitching" and "squealing" on his fellow-prisoners, he may get along fairly well while in prison. But, instead of being trained to become a decent citizen, he is

getting a most effective education in fundamentally anti-
social, and contemptible—even criminal—conduct, not even
matched by employment in the Prohibition enforcement
service. On the other hand, if he remains a decent and honest
man and refuses to coöperate with the scheme of prisons politics he is hopeless, unprotected, and the legitimate prey of any
who desire to secure special favors by passing on false stories
about him to the prison authorities. The latter are usually
themselves involved in the system of intrigue and conspiracy
which honeycombs the whole institution.

One of the worst manifestations of prison favoritism and
the resulting convict rule is the so-called "Kangaroo Court."
This is a court maintained by the convicts with the con-
nivance of the prison authorities. It formulates rules, decrees
penalties, and enforces discipline. Those convicts who are in
ill-favor with those who dominate the kangaroo court are
likely to be dealt with severely and their lives made permanently miserable while they remain in prison. Failure to
carry out the orders of the kangaroo court is frequently
punished with severity, sometimes with beatings and mutilations. Occasionally a kangaroo court may be used for
the benefit of the convicts, when able and fair-minded convicts control its operation and offset cruel and unfair rule
by the prison officials, but for the most part this institution
is a method of manifesting favoritism and oppression.

The decent convict is thus without friends inside the walls,
and unable to communicate with those outside except through
letters read and censored by the selected representatives of this
same group of official-convict intriguers, from whose persecution and machinations the individual is seeking relief. There
is thus developed in the mind of the convict a feeling of utter
hopelessness and helplessness, which not only promotes mental and personal disintegration, but also in many cases physical disease. The administrative system of the average prison,
then, far from promoting efforts at reformation and personal
rehabilitation, results either in most efficient training in crook-

edness, corruption and intrigue or in the gradual but certain breakdown of the body and mind of the convict.

If sufficient space were afforded we could describe in detail the numerous and varied psychoses and neuroses which modern psychiatrists have demonstrated to be the result of the abnormal modes of life forced upon inmates by the contemporary prison system. Suffice it to say that an extremely broad range of psycho-neuroses are thus produced. Particularly should there be emphasized the inevitable development of the greatest variety of sex perversions, the pathogenesis of which has been so well described by Alexander Berkman. The sex situation in prisons is even worse than in abnormal modes of existence outside, for, in addition to the blocking of normal sexual manifestations, there is no opportunity whatever for sublimation through professional, cultural or recreational outlets. Hence, the sex urge necessarily finds expression in all sorts of pathological conduct. If one were consciously to plan an institution perfectly designed to promote sexual degeneracy he would create the modern prison. The wide prevalence of masturbation and homosexuality among men prisoners is a commonplace to all prison administrators and investigators, but Mrs. O'Hare thus describes an almost unbelievable condition existing in the women's department of one of the leading contemporary state penitentiaries:*

Whether or not we agree fully with Dr. Sigmund Freud and the psychoanalytic school that sex is the dominating force of human life, we must admit that it is a powerful factor. Prison life, by denying the normal expression of sex, breeds and fosters sex perversions and all the degenerating vices that these perversions include. . . . It is a stark ugly fact that homosexuality exists in every prison and must ever be one of the sinister facts of our penal system. In the Missouri State Penitentiary it is, next to the "task," the dominating feature of prison life and a regular source of revenue to favored stool pigeons. . . . In fact, homosexuality was not only permitted, but indulgence was actively fostered, and in the cases of

*K. D. O'Hare, *In Prison*, pp. 112, 159-60.

young, helpless, and unprotected women actually demanded and enforced.

The vile and degrading conditions which are thus brought about are, after all, the least serious aspect of this abnormal situation. The most deplorable result is the fact that these sex perversions are normally correlated with the parallel or subsequent pathogenesis of many types of psychic abnormality and emotional instability, many of which emerge in definite criminal compulsions. The sexual results of prison life, which have been practically ignored by both conventional criminologists and reformers, would, therefore, by themselves alone suffice to create or train up a veritable crop of degenerates and potential criminals. Not only is the sex situation in the modern prison one of the most challenging of the social, psychological and administrative problems existing in penal institutions; it is also one of those most impossible to deal with in a direct or efficient fashion. With society still medieval in its attitude towards the sexual problem in the general social world outside the prison, there is even less hope that it will be able to handle the sexual problem within prisons in an intelligent or expeditious manner. This constitutes an additional argument for the abolition of the prison.

Along with these various emotional defects and disorders, emerging chiefly on an unconscious level, should be mentioned the conscious resentment of the prisoners at the general complex of cruelty and dissatisfaction in which they find themselves. This results in the unfortunate desire not to reform but to devise better and more efficient methods of avenging themselves upon society. The net result of modern imprisonment upon the average criminal is, thus, not only to produce an emotional situation which bears with it the high probability of creating or intensifying criminal compulsions, but also to produce a conscious desire to commit crime in order to get even with society for its cruelties to the individual convict. We are not, of course, contending that society can afford to ignore criminal conduct, but are rather endeavoring to make it clear that it is a strangely ineffective method of dealing with criminal conduct which inevitably and uniformly results in the creation of a more serious and determined potential criminal as the chief product of the expensive machinery of the modern prison system. Pat Crowe well summarizes how the barbarism of prison life tends to make the convict more desperate and more determined to carry on his depredations against society:*

I had ample time to study the effects of this system on prisoners and I will never efface from my memory the picture of these men pacing back and forth in their cells like caged lions as they listened to the cries of pain that came nightly from the hall of punishment. Bitterness against this inhuman system, against the law, against society in general, is a mild word to express the attitude of the average prisoner.

Every man who went through this terrible ordeal came out of this penitentiary more vicious than when he entered it. I know positively that is the way it affected me. After my release from the Jefferson City penitentiary I took a diabolical delight in holding up trains and dynamiting the express safe. I was a real, hard-boiled outlaw and glad of it, because I felt that anything I did was mild compared with the wrongs that society was inflicting on the men in its prisons.

III. PRISON DISCIPLINE AND PRISON OFFICERS

In describing the psychological effects of the contemporary prison system upon prison officials it is necessary, in the first place, to recognize the relatively low types of individuals who are normally chosen for positions in prison administration, particularly for those posts beneath the office of warden. Such appointments normally fall to a rather inferior grade of human being, usually as a part of the spoils system, and the salaries paid them are not sufficient to act as an incentive to any competent person to seek the appointment. Mrs. O'Hare has thus admirably described these important, if regrettable, facts:†

---

*Crowe, loc. cit.
†K. D. O'Hare, In Prison, p. 161.

Because public opinion concerns itself less with prisons than with any other sort of public institution except, perhaps, almshouses, prison management has for the most part fallen into the hands of the most ignorant and corrupt type of politicians, and prison jobs have become the dumping ground for the inefficient and unfit relatives and political hangers-on of the professional politicians. These human misfits and failures are thrust into prison jobs because, as a rule, they are too worthless for other employment. So far as I have been able to study them, I have found court bailiffs, jail turnkeys, prison guards, and prison matrons industrially unfit and generally illiterate human scrubs, mentally defective, morally perverted, and very often of much lower type than the prisoners whom they handle.

Beginning all too often with non-professional and untrained individuals as the basis of the personnel of prison administration, we have to add to this the inevitably degrading and brutalizing effects of the details of contemporary prison administration.   The primary function of the prison warden is to act as an efficient jailer.   It is not usually regarded as a part of his duty to bring about the reformation of the convict, except insofar as it is believed that this may be produced by the miseries inflicted through imprisonment.   He is supposed, above all, to keep his subjects safely incarcerated during the period of their sentence, and his success as warden is measured very largely by the degree to which he is able to insure the minimum number of escapes and the lowest amount of friction and scandal irrespective of the record as to reformation.

To achieve this result he naturally turns to the most rudimentary conceptions of discipline and regimentation. He relies almost entirely upon rules and coercive administrative procedure. This prevents practically all possibility of sympathetic human contact with the inmates of the prison, and the system thus creates a purely mechanical spirit which brutalizes both the prison officials and the prisoners, and creates a fatal antipathy between these two groups. This severe prison regimentation, being widely different from the life of freedom to which the prisoner will ultimately be restored, constitutes the worst type of training, if indeed it can be called any training at all, for the responsibilities of citizenship. Frank Tannenbaum, in his interesting book, *Wall Shadows*, has well summarized the effect of this mechanical attitude, inseparable from the conception of a warden as a jailer, upon the development of prison cruelty, as well as the unfortunate results of the system upon the prison population:[*]

The function of the prison is to keep the men confined. The function of the warden is to make sure that the purpose of the prison is fulfilled. He is primarily a jailer. That is *his* business. Reform, punishment, expiation for sin—these are social policies determined by social motives of which he, as jailer, becomes the agent. He is a jailer first; a reformer, a guardian, a disciplinarian, or anything else, second. Anyone who has been in prison, or who knows the prison régime, through personal contact, will corroborate this fact. The whole administrative organization of the jail is centered on keeping the men inside the walls. Men in prison are always counted. They are counted morning, noon, and night. They are counted when they rise, when they eat, when they work, and when they sleep. Like a miser hovering over his jingling coins, the warden and the keepers are constantly on edge about the safety of their charges—a safety of numbers first, of well-being afterwards.

This leads to some very important consequences. It is the core of the development of prison brutality. It is the feeding basis upon which a number of other important elements tending in the direction of brutality depend. The warden is human. Being human, he is strongly inclined to follow the path of least resistance. And the path of least resistance, in the light of the ordinary understanding of a prison warden, is to make jail-breaking hard by making the individual prisoner helpless.

Punishment takes the form of a greater isolation, of more suppression, and for the prisoner has the result of greater discontent, more bitterness, and the greater need for friendship, for communication, and the very pleasures of attempted association, in spite of opposition. This simply means that the more rules there are, the more violations there are bound to be,

---

[*]Tannenbaum, *op. cit.*, pp. 11-24.

and the greater the number of violations the more numerous the rules. The greater the number of violations, the more brutal the punishments; for variety of the punishments and their intensification become, in the mind of the warden, the sole means of achieving the intimidation of the prisoner by which he rules.

Brutality leads to brutality. It hardens official and inmate alike, and makes it the ordinary and habitual method of dealing with the criminal. It adds hatred to the prisoner's reaction against the individual official, and makes the individual official more fearful, more suspicious, more constantly alert, and develops in him a reaction of hatred against the prisoner, making the need for brutality greater and its use more natural. The general consequence holds true for the whole prison. The punishment of the individual prisoner develops within the whole prison a feeling of discontent and hatred because of the natural sympathy which the prisoners feel for one whom they know to be no more guilty than themselves; and particularly because solidarity of feeling is in proportion to individual physical helplessness. This adds to the tensity of the situation in the prison, adds fuel to the discontent, and makes the need for isolation in the light of the warden's disciplinary measures more justified, brutality more normal, hatred on the part of the prison group more constant, and irritation more general. . . .

The harshness, silence, twilight, discipline, hold true, not only for the prisoner, but also for the keeper. The keeper, too, is a prisoner. He is all day long in this atmosphere of tense emotional suppression and military discipline, and, in addition, he is generally there at least two nights a week when on special duty. He is a prisoner. For him there is little beyond the exercise of power. This exercise is a means of escape and outlet, but it is not a sufficient means. It does not make the keeper a happy person. It makes him a harsh and brutal one.

The brutality and grossness of male prison guards have long been recognized, but many have frequently supposed that matrons in the women's wards are of an altogether different type characterized by kindliness, sympathy, and insight. The following comments by Mrs. O'Hare on the nature of the matrons of the Missouri State Penitentiary are very illuminating on this point:*

The matrons were required to live in the prison and were never, except on rare leaves of absence, out of the sights and sounds and smells of prison. They were prisoners to almost the same degree that we were, and they all staggered under a load of responsibility far too great for their limited intelligence and untrained powers. They handled human beings at their worst, and under the worst possible conditions, and saw nothing day or night but sordid, ugly things ungilded by the glow of hope or love.

These women who were our keepers had missed love and wifehood; they had nothing to look back upon or forward to. There is a sort of stigma attached to their work that makes the possibilities of love and mating for them very limited indeed. The ordinary social relations of normal life were impossible for them, and they lived in a very inferno of loneliness and isolation. . . .

The conditions under which these prison matrons lived and did their work would have made harpies and shrews out of the finest types of women—and these certainly had never been fine types. For the conditions that place women of their attainments and character in such positions, the public is incontrovertibly responsible.

Properly planned and administered a prison might be a good thing, but it would not be the institution which has passed under the name of prison up to the present time. Hospitals are extremely humane and therapeutic institutions as at present conducted, but they would scarcely be so regarded if they followed the practice of throwing a recently received patient suffering from double pneumonia into an ice-cold bath and then leaving him half-clothed on an exposed balcony in zero weather. The administrative and disciplinary system of the modern prison acts in a wholly comparable fashion upon the inmates of penal institutions. They inevitably render more unfit for civilized social existence those unfortunates committed to their custody, ostensibly for reformation and rehabilitation.

*Op. cit., pp. 162-63.

IV. PUNISHMENT AND THE PUBLIC MIND

Though it is usually overlooked in discussions of the psychological effects of prison administration, it is probable that the most serious and disastrous aspects of modern prison cruelty are not those which affect the prisoners or the prison officials but rather the results of this system upon the public mind. In the first place, imprisonment supplies the present method of carrying out the revengeful spirit of outraged society, which thus secures satisfaction for the wrongs, real or alleged, that are brought upon it by the convict. In an earlier period of criminal justice culprits were punished by mob vengeance, and imprisonment is the present substitute for this more primitive technique. Along with this element of social protection expressed in a crude psychological form, there must be taken into consideration the fundamentally sadistic and cruel tendencies of human groups, well analyzed by S. Sighele, E. D. Martin and others. The savagery of contemporary imprisonment offers a vicarious release of these sadistic traits under respectable and approved circumstances, whereas relatively few individuals would personally and individually find themselves able to carry out, or to admit themselves subject to, such obviously sadistic impulses. These points have been very well expressed by Bernard Shaw:*

It is said, and it is in a certain degree true, that if the Government does not lawfully organize and regulate popular vengeance, the populace will rise up and execute this vengeance lawlessly for itself. The standard defense of the Inquisition is that without it no heretic's life would have been safe. In Texas today the people are not satisfied with the prospect of knowing that a murderer and ravisher will be electrocuted inside a jail if a jury can resist the defense put up by his lawyer. They tear him from the hands of the sheriff, pour lamp oil over him, and burn him alive. Now the burning of human beings is not only an expression of outraged public morality: it is also a sport for which a taste can be acquired much more easily and rapidly than a taste for coursing hares, just as a

---

*Preface to S. and B. Webb, *English Prisons Under Local Government*, pp. xxiv-xxv.

taste for drink can be acquired from brandy and cocktails more easily and rapidly than from beer or sauterne. Lynching mobs begin with Negro ravishers and murderers; but they presently go on to any sort of delinquent, provided he is black. Later on, as a white man will burn as amusingly as a black one, and a white woman react to tarring and feathering as thrillingly as a Negress, the color line is effaced by what professes to be a rising wave of virtuous indignation, but is in fact an epidemic of Sadism. The defenders of our penal system take advantage of it to assure us that if they did not torment and ruin a boy guilty of sleeping in the open air, the British public would rise and tear that boy limb from limb.

Along with the function of imprisonment as a means of manifesting social revenge and securing social protection, and as an "elegant" method of expressing collective sadism, there should be added the powerful factor of social catharsis which rests upon the age-old notion and symbol of the scapegoat. Our individual sense of guilt is drained off, and we inevitably feel a certain vicarious release and satisfaction at the conviction and imprisonment of an alleged culprit, who symbolically bears to the prison the sins of his social group. The insistence of those who wreck railroads, corporations and banks, leaving a train of poverty-stricken widows and orphans in their wake, upon the necessity of solemn severity in the punishment of a man who has stolen a few dollars' worth of bread or cloth or failed to pay his debts admirably illustrates the operation of this mechanism.

Beyond all of these aspects of the function and effect of imprisonment upon the public mind must be mentioned the fact that at the present time crime and punishment have in them a high degree of publicity appeal, curiosity, and exhibitionism which arouse the more sordid emotions of the public and prevent citizens from developing any intelligent insight into the basic questions and problems involved. Then, our system of justice is not free from being exploited in the interests of the political and personal careers of those in charge of it. These factors have been admirably summarized by Mr. Mencken:*

If the criminal's art is irrational, then society's instinctive reaction to it is equally irrational. This fact blew up the work of the old-time criminologists. They accepted the current scheme of punishments, but tried to purge it of revenge. They found very quickly that revenge was an essential part of it— that no criminal would ever be brought to justice if there were not somebody in the background, full of strong feeling against him. When the crime that is proceeded against is one that seems to offer a menace to the general security—that is, when every citizen feels that he is himself in danger unless something is done about it—then that feeling is generally dispensed, and we have a spectacle such as was witnessed during the Leopold-Loeb trial, with a district attorney applying all the arts of forensics to the undoing of the accused, the press full of inflammatory stuff about them, and even the ambassadors of Christ snorting and bawling from the pulpit against them. It is idle to say that such a process is rational. It is as full of pure emotion as a necking match. Its aim is to discharge emotions, to achieve a communal orgasm, not to establish and enforce a scientific fact.

There is even more to it than this. Criminal trials, if they are gory and obscene enough, make capital shows—perhaps the best shows that the average human being can imagine. They offer hunting in the grand manner; the quarry is man. They thus take on something of the character of war, and are just as powerful in their emotional appeal. To convert them into scientific investigations, entirely calm and impersonal, would be as grave an offense against the public happiness as to enforce Prohibition. Thus even when *mobile vulgus* is not enraged against the criminal, and hence eager to see him barbarously used, it is delighted by the battle that goes on over him. Such battles make heroes. The district attorney, if he wins, is sure to be elected to higher office; some of our most eminent statesmen got their starts that way: the names of Hughes, Folk and Brandeis come to mind at once. And if the district attorney loses, then the counsel for the defense is the hero.

*American Mercury, January, 1925, pp. 122-23.

V. The Solution

These psychological characteristics of society's attitude toward crime and punishment thus quite apparently create attitudes which obstruct, if they do not entirely prevent, any true appreciation of the real problems involved in the detection, conviction, and treatment of the criminal. The psychological attitudes which prevail are in their core identical with the reactions of primitive man to those who violated the taboos and mores of tribal society. Society's reactions are almost entirely emotional and scarcely at all intellectual. Joined to this is the fact that the cruelties of present-day imprisonment are for the most part screened from the concrete and specific knowledge of the public. The individual can endure, can even get satisfaction out of contemplating punishment in the abstract when he would tend to recoil in the face of concrete and specific pain and suffering, except when a member of a mob or when in personal danger. It is for this reason that we have outbursts of public indignation against prison officials following every sporadic revelation of unusual cruelty in a particular penal institution. As Shaw well suggests, much of the hideous nature of present-day penal institutions is due, not so much to our specific intent as to the fact that they have grown up unconsciously in piecemeal fashion without our full knowledge:*

We must, however, be on our guard against ascribing all the villainy of our system to our cruelty and selfish terrors. That would be inconsistent with the fact that, as I have pointed out, the operation of the criminal law is made very uncertain, and therefore loses the deterrence it aims at, by the reluctance of the sympathetic people to hand over offenders to the police. Vindictive and frivolous as we are, we are not downright fiends, as we should be if our modern prison system had been deliberately invented and constructed by us all in one piece. It has grown upon us, and grown evilly, having evil roots; but its worst developments have been well

---

*Preface to S. and B. Webb, *English Prisons Under Local Government*, p. lviii.

meant; for the road to hell is paved with good intentions, not with bad ones.

This being the case, it is quite obvious that one of the most direct methods of assaulting and alleviating the cruelties of the present system of prison administration will be found in making more frequent and more specific and concrete the revelations of contemporary abuses. It is here that books like Tannenbaum's *Wall Shadows*, Mrs. O'Hare's *In Prison*, and Fishman's *Crucibles of Crime* perform a useful educational function. This would need to be supplemented, of course, by emphasizing day in and day out the necessity of abolishing punishment and introducing rational treatment of convicted criminals. Once the treatment program is accepted prisons will inevitably and speedily disappear.

Another practical proposal of real merit in abating the prison nuisance would be to enact by law that all prosecuting attorneys and all judges sitting in criminal courts should be compelled to spend at least two weeks out of each year in the state penitentiaries with no privileges whatsoever. One week should be served in mid-summer and one in mid-winter. This would enable both of these types of officials to realize what juristic savagery really implies and involves with respect to the human victims. Certainly, Mr. Baumes and his associates should be sentenced to at least six months of penal observation. Indeed, it should be prescribed that no commission on the reform of the criminal law or prison administration should be allowed to begin deliberations until all its members had spent at least a fortnight in a state penitentiary. Further, each time any public official or private citizen alleges that prisoners are being coddled he should be compelled to specify the institution in which the coddling is going on and thereupon he should be committed to this institution for a minimum of two weeks.

This suggestion, if followed out literally, would bring about more extensive progress in the reform of criminal jurisprudence and prison discipline in a year than we have witnessed in the last generation. One of the first things which would disappear would be the arrogant and arbitrary nonchalance of many judges in abusing the sentencing power. We should get rid of a condition where a judge who has won well at poker and slept well afterwards sentences a man to five years, and two days later, on the basis of indigestion and a bad hang-over, sends a man to prison for twenty years for the same crime committed under less atrocious conditions. We might also be able to free ourselves from medieval nuisances like Mr. Baumes.

VI. The Nuisance of the County Jail

In the preceding portion of this chapter we have been dealing with state penitentiaries and reformatories, to which are sent, for the most part, those adults who have been convicted of felonies. No account of contemporary punishment would be at all complete which overlooked the population of the county jails. Of those committed to penal institutions in the United States over ninety per cent are sent to jails and workhouses. In general, the jails are markedly inferior to the state penitentiaries as regards architecture, discipline, hygiene and comforts. The only mitigating circumstance is to be found in the fact that the sentences to the jails are much shorter than those to the state penitentiaries and reformatories.

Down to the close of the eighteenth century the jails were used primarily as institutions for detaining those accused of crime pending their trial. As imprisonment was not the usual method of punishment at this time, very few persons convicted of crime remained in jail, the exception being those who were sentenced to death and were awaiting execution. In addition to those awaiting trial, the other large class in the county jails at this time were the debtors, who were confined until they or their friends could raise the money to meet the debts. To the accused, the debtors and those awaiting execution were added material witnesses who were held pending the trial at which their testimony was desired.

The grossest inequalities prevailed in the treatment of those confined in the county jails. In general, the public did not pretend to feed and clothe the inmates, but the latter were compelled to provide for their own maintenance. Wealthy inmates might live very well, while it was not uncommon for those with no resources whatever to die of starvation. Indeed, in some states the sheriff was permitted to allow wealthy defendants to take lodging in an inn under the general surveillance of the sheriff. Discipline scarcely existed in these institutions. Complete promiscuity prevailed. The following description of the county jail at the end of the colonial period by Roberts Vaux is a reasonably accurate portrayal of the county jail in the pre-prison era.*

What a spectacle must this abode of guilt and wretchedness have presented, when in one common herd were kept by day and night prisoners of all ages, colors and sexes! No separation was made of the most flagrant offender and convict, from the prisoner who might, perhaps, be falsely suspected of some trifling misdemeanor; none of the old and hardened culprits from the youthful, trembling novice in crime; none even of the fraudulent swindler from the unfortunate and possibly the most estimable debtor; and when intermingled with all these, in one corrupt and corrupting assemblage were to be found the disgusting object of popular contempt, besmeared with filth from the pillory—the unhappy victim of the lash, streaming with blood from the whipping post—the half-naked vagrant—the loathsome drunkard—the sick, suffering from various bodily pains, and too often the unaneled malefactor whose precious hours of probation had been numbered by his earthly judge.

In the nineteenth century notable changes took place in the nature of the jail population, even though there was lamentably slight progress made in the way of improving the administration of living conditions in the jails. The jails

---

*Notices of the Original and Successive Attempts to Improve the Discipline of the Prison at Philadelphia.

now had to house not only those detained awaiting trial
but also those who had been convicted of lesser offences. On
the other hand, one class which had figured prominently in
the jail population of the colonial period, namely, the debtors,
finally disappeared from the jails. The average layman who
has read about the colony of Georgia being founded as an
asylum for British debtors may have developed the notion
that imprisonment for debt has never existed in the United
States. As an actual matter of fact it was universal in the
colonial period and was still widely practiced throughout the
first quarter of the nineteenth century. It was generally
abolished in the decade following 1828, partly as a result of
the agitation of the *Boston Prison Discipline Society* and
partly as a product of the democratic tendencies associated
with the Jacksonian régime. Since the opening of the nineteenth century the jails have thus performed a dual function
of receiving both those accused of crime and those convicted
of the lesser crimes. There has rarely been any differentiation
between the treatment of those accused and those convicted.

The condition of the county jails was a subject for general complaint and the most vigorous condemnation in the
writings of all the leading American criminologists and penologists throughout the nineteenth century, but we shall
limit our discussion to the condition of the jails at the present time. We shall base our discussion upon the most competent and trustworthy description of the American jail system
ever prepared, namely, Joseph F. Fishman's *Crucibles of
Crime*. Mr. Fishman is a talented prison investigator of the
highest probity and reliability, and of unrivaled experience in
first hand study of American jail conditions. He thus describes the experiences from which he has drawn the material
for his book:*

During the past sixteen years I have visited approximately
1,500 jails in the United States, many of them over and over
again, from Boston to San Francisco, and from Brownsville,

*Fishman, *op. cit.*, pp. 18-19.

Texas, to Seattle, Washington; as well as Porto Rico and Alaska, in addition to a very large number of prisons, reformatories, reform schools, houses of correction and asylums for the criminal insane. I have, I suppose, talked to forty or fifty thousand prisoners of every age and description, and of every degree of criminality, degradation and viciousness; listened to their stories; investigated every phase of the conditions under which they live, and employed them in various capacities.

From the standpoint of architecture the jails present the greatest diversity of conditions. In some places we have old structures which were erected a century or more ago, while in others we have new and relatively efficient cage-like structures. In almost no case is modernity of architecture combined with humanitarian sentiment and scientific insight in the design of the jail. The old promiscuity which was a scandal of the colonial period still continues with slight abatement. Almost nowhere is there any thoroughgoing separation of the accused from the convicted. Those awaiting trial and regarded before the law as still innocent are treated exactly as are those who have been convicted of a misdemeanor. In some of the jails the women are not even separated from the male population, though this elementary form of differentiation and segregation exists in the majority of places.

There is almost never any such thing as expert control. The average prison warden is certainly far enough removed from the status of a scientific criminologist, but at least he has usually had considerable experience in dealing with criminals, and sticks to his post for some time. The sheriff, who is, in the majority of states, in control of American jails, is a purely political officer, usually holding office for not more than one elective term at a time. The county jail is looked upon as one of the largest sources of legitimate political graft, and the sheriff is supposed to make his office chiefly worth while upon the basis of the profits he can make out of the maintenance of the county jail. Many states still maintain the notorious fee system of compensating the sheriff, the operation of which in Pennsylvania is thus well described by Mr. Fishman:*

But the worst feature of all in Pennsylvania is the fee system of compensating jailers. Instead of paying them a salary, many of the jailers are given a certain sum a day to feed the prisoners in their charge, the jailer retaining as part of his compensation such portion of his allowance as is not paid out in food for the prisoners. For instance, if a jailer receives 50 cents per day per prisoner, and has a daily average of 50 prisoners in his jail, he will get $25 to pay for food. Every cent which he does not pay out for food goes into his own pocket. A more vicious system it would be impossible to conceive; that of one man lining his pockets in the same degree as he may withhold food from another.

In short, every deplorable by-product of corruption and non-professionalism in the treatment of crime emerges from the record of the administration of the county jails in the United States.

We may now proceed to present certain concrete descriptions which will indicate the actual state of life in American jails today. Mr. Fishman offers the following preliminary definition of the jail as a composite picture of the impressions he has drawn from the fifteen hundred or more jails which he has visited:†

JAIL: An unbelievably filthy institution in which are confined men and women serving sentence for misdemeanors and crimes, and *men and women not under sentence who are simply awaiting trial.* With few exceptions, having no segregation of the unconvicted from the convicted, the well from the diseased, the youngest and most impressionable from the most degraded and hardened. Usually swarming with bedbugs, roaches, lice, and other vermin; has an odor of disinfectant and filth which is appalling; supports in complete idleness countless thousands of able bodied men and women, and generally affords ample time and opportunity to assure inmates a complete course in every kind of viciousness and crime. A melting pot in which the worst elements of the

*Fishman, p. 68.
†*Op. cit.,* p. 13.

raw material in the criminal world are brought forth blended and turned out in absolute perfection.

The following description of the county jail in Albany, New York, given by Mr. Fishman early in his book, might be deemed by the reader an unusual case were he not to discover from a perusal of the complete volume that the Albany institution ranks somewhat above the average American jail as to equipment and administration:*

The institution was built in 1847,—just 76 years ago,—and the antiquated, uncivilized design of that day is still retained.

The cells are entirely without light, even of the artificial kind. When in some emergency the officials must have light in the cells, a candle is used. The cells are only eight feet long, and they are so dark that even in the day time, standing directly in front of the closed barred door, it is impossible to see to the rear of the cell. I had a photographer attempt to take a picture of the interior of one of these cells, but although he took a long time exposure, the best picture he could obtain showed only two feet into the cell.

All the cells are exactly alike. They each are eight feet long, four feet wide, and seven feet high, with a barred door two feet wide. Each contains a cot two feet wide, allowing but a two foot width for the prisoner to move in, and a bucket for toilet purposes which is cleaned, supposedly, every morning.

Now draw out on the floor of your home a space eight by four feet—the size of a small rug—imagine that over it is a ceiling seven feet high, that just half of the width of your space is given up to a cot, that in one corner stands a reeking bucket, and that out of this totally dark, evil-smelling space, with its enclosing walls, you cannot move for forty-three hours at a time.

For this is exactly what happens to the prisoners at the Albany County Penitentiary and Albany County Jail. Each Saturday at noon they are locked in their cells, not to come out until Monday morning at 7.30, except for a voluntary chapel attendance on Sunday. During the remainder of the week they are similarly locked in about twelve hours of each day. In the 103 hours spent this way each week a prisoner

—————
*Fishman, pp. 28-30.

can do absolutely nothing, can read absolutely nothing, and has for sole inspiration an odoriferous bucket, a most edifying companion and one indeed calculated to make him reflect on the error of his ways and lead him to a better life.

The odor throughout the entire jail would sicken an animal. The bedding is dirty beyond belief. The place is so full of vermin that the deputy Mr. Fish, cautioned me not to brush against walls, pipes or anything else. The institution has no "delousing" facilities for newly-arrived prisoners, and Mr. Fish frankly admitted his helplessness in combating this plague.

The Maryland Free State is regarded by many, not without some justification, as the chief outpost of civilization in the United States. It will be obvious from Mr. Fishman's description of the Maryland jails that this advanced condition does not extend to the jails:*

And the jails of Maryland! Who can adequately describe their bestiality—their utterly frigid, filthy desolation? With two or three exceptions the cells are of stone, and in the winter stone cold; there is no light; there is no fresh air, and the atmosphere of decades poisoned by the exhalations of countless prisoners sick and well, is rendered still more foul by the loathsome night bucket; bathing is usually unknown; bedding is considered plentiful when a mere mattress and a blanket are supplied, and often one or both of these are omitted; there is no segregation of sex, or age, or anything else; there is no exercise, no work, no occupation or diversion of any kind—it is impossible even to see in most places because of the darkness. The only positive qualities that obtain, and these they have in abundance, are dirt, vermin and the execrable fee system of feeding. Life here is indeed not only debased and stripped of every sign of civilization; it is a living death in cold, dark tombs.

The following description by Mr. Fishman of the South Carolina jails will, however, lead one to a more tolerant judgment of the Albany jail and the Maryland jails described above:†

---

*Ibid., p. 239.
†Ibid., pp. 164-65.

My first visit to many of the jails in South Carolina was made fifteen or sixteen years ago. Although I have visited these jails many times since and have, I suppose, grown somewhat callous from constant inspections, never will I forget the impression made upon me by that first visit.

The jails of thirty-five of the forty-four counties of the State would be abandoned as living quarters by the most tolerant pig. Some of them are a hundred years old, others not quite so ancient. But old or new, with the few exceptions mentioned, they are reeking holes of pestilence. To describe them is to give a monotonous repetition of rotten plumbing, horrible overcrowding, damp, dark, and indescribably dirty caverns, and other conditions the description of which are not printable, all bespeaking a callous and brutal disregard of the most elementary rules of hygiene and sanitation.

The treatment of women in the jails is in harmony with the vulgarity and brutality characteristic of jail discipline as a whole. Mr. Fishman offers the following observations on the state of women in the county jails in the United States:*

Not ten percent of the jails in the United States employ matrons to care for the female prisoners. In a very few of the smaller places the wife of the jailer will look after them, but I repeat that, including this small number, not ten percent have any women attendants whatsoever.

In the remaining ninety percent, the male jailers have at all times free and unrestrained access to the women's quarters, and I have not once, nor a dozen times, but actually upon hundreds of occasions seen jailers walk through the women's quarters without even the formality of announcing their presence, taking it quite as a matter of course whether the women were fully dressed, half dressed, or scarcely dressed at all. I have on many occasions seen them walk through unconcernedly while the women were even engaged in performing their toilet. In such jails the women are absolutely at the mercy of the officials who can, if they desire, work their will upon them, be they submissive, reluctant or defiant. I do not say that the majority of jailers take advantage of this situation. To my knowledge some of them do. Only recently a case came to my attention in which a jailer hastily resigned

---

*Fishman, pp. 92-5.

following disclosures of undue familiarity with the female prisoners in his charge. But whether they take advantage of the situation or not, the fact remains that all jailers where no matrons are employed are in a position to do so and that the women in these places have no one at all to whom they can turn for protection. This is not mentioned in the judge's sentence, either.

In the jail at Gainesville, Georgia, during the war, I saw eight or ten girls who walked around the jail with no clothing whatever except a very thin skirt. They were barefoot, and wore nothing at all above the waist. Not only the jailer, but also any of the town loafers who happened to wander in could easily see into the women's quarters, and the jailer walked in and out in pursuance of his duties in the same matter of fact way in which he walked around the quarters of the men. Both were indescribably filthy.

The desirable reforms in the jail system of the United States are clear and obvious enough. In the first place, the jails should be made over into exclusively detention stations for the safe custody of those accused of crime and not admitted or admissible to bail. Such inmates, still being adjudged legally innocent, should not in any sense be treated as convicts or punished in any manner. They should be kept in comfortable quarters and provided with adequate and healthful food. The jails of the future should be primarily places where those accused of crime may be thoroughly studied as to their career and personality prior to their trial. In other words, the jails should be exclusively a place of detention and examination.

The great majority of those who are today confined in jails as convicts should be dealt with through probation and the suspended sentence and should not be subjected to any form of confinement. Those who require temporary segregation should be placed in county institutions exclusively for convicts. Such institutions should be of modern construction and labor should be provided for all inmates. County farms have proved satisfactory in this respect where experimented with in any sane and reasonable fashion. In addition to farm work, the inmates of such institutions could be employed at the simpler forms of mechanical effort and on road work. It is obvious that the fee system should be abolished root and branch, and the superintendent of such institutions should be a salaried officer, entirely divorced from politics, and well trained in dealing with the criminal classes. The bums and other degenerates who make up a considerable portion of the seasonal population of the jail should be segregated in the proper institutions, such as the feeble-minded colonies, homes for the inebriates, state hospitals for the insane, and institutions for incurables. Unfortunately, the logic and simplicity of the reforms needed are probably exceeded only by the difficulty of securing their practical adoption.

SELECTED REFERENCES

Alexander, Myrl E. *Jail Administration.* Springfield, Ill., 1957.

Bryan, Helen. *Inside.* New York, 1954.

Chessman, Carl. *Cell 2455: Death Row.* New York, 1954.

Clemmer, Donald. *The Prison Community.* New York, 1958.

Fishman, Joseph F., and Perlman, Vee. *Crucibles of Crime.* 1923; Reprinted Montclair, N. J., 1969.

Gaddis, Thomas E. *The Birdman of Alcatraz.* New York, 1955.

Lawes, Lewis E. *20,000 Years in Sing Sing.* New York, 1932.

Mattick, H., ed. *The Future of Imprisonment in a Free Society.* Chicago, 1965.

Nelson, Victor. *Prison Days and Nights.* Boston, 1933.

Nitsche, Paul H., and Wilmanns, Karl. *The History of the Prison Psychoses.* Washington, D. C., 1912.

O'Hare, Kate R. *In Prison.* New York, 1923.

Powell, J. C. *The American Siberia; Or, Fourteen Years' Experience in a Southern Convict Camp.* 1891; Reprinted Montclair, N. J., 1970.

Reiwald, Paul. *Society and Its Criminals.* New York, 1950.

Robinson, Louis N. *Penology in the United States.* Philadelphia, 1921.

Shaw, George Bernard. Preface to *English Prisons under Local Government,* by Sidney and Beatrice Webb. London, 1922.

Tannenbaum, Frank. *Wall Shadows.* New York, 1922.

Viereck, George S. *Men into Beasts.* New York, 1952.

Winning, James M. *Behind These Walls.* New York, 1933.

CHAPTER VIII

The Progress of Penology

I. The Development of Differentiation in Institutions for the Treatment of the Criminal Classes

ONE of the most conspicuous and significant phases of the progress of prison administration in the last century has been the development of a scientific differentiation in the institutions designed to treat the criminal classes. In the early modern prisons which prevailed before the Pennsylvania and Auburn prisons came into existence, all alleged and real delinquents were herded together in one enclosure, generally in one room or group of rooms, containing accused and convicted, debtors and criminals, male and female, young and old, insane, idiotic and those of normal mentality, first offenders and hardened recidivists. The reformation of the offender was rendered hopeless at the outset under such conditions.

The rise of the Pennsylvania and Auburn systems marked a great step in the way of progress. The accused were separated from convicted felons, and distinct portions of the prison were assigned to the male and female prisoners. The next step came in the erection of Houses of Refuge for young offenders, their condition in the prisons of the time naturally giving rise to much sympathy on the part of reformers. The historical background of their development is a long one. The origins of institutions for juvenile delinquents must be sought in the juvenile departments of the English workhouses of the sixteenth and seventeenth centuries. The movement reached its highest early development in Holland, where, by the seventeenth century, a famous system of such institutions for the neglected and delinquent youth had developed. From an observation of their operation William Penn is said to have derived in part his notion of imprisonment as a method of treating the criminal.

The beginning of the modern movement is normally taken to date from the building of the House of Refuge at Danzig, in 1813, under the direction of one John Falk. In London, also, similar institutions were developing in part out of earlier progress there and in part from imitation of continental methods. The introduction of such institutions into the United States was due to the work of Professor John Griscom, a Quaker who traveled extensively in Europe in the early 'twenties and was struck with the importance of these "child-saving institutions." He brought back his impressions to New York City and Philadelphia, where they were appropriated by the reforming groups. The first House of Refuge for juvenile delinquents in this country was opened at Madison Square in New York City on January 25, 1825. It was built far north of the center of the city, in the futile hope that a century of municipal expansion would not disturb it. The second institution of the kind was opened in Boston in 1826, and the third in Philadelphia in 1828. But these were private institutions, though in part open to the use of the commonwealth. The first state institution for juvenile delinquents was opened at Westboro, Massachusetts, in 1847.

These early Houses of Refuge, however, were nothing more than prisons for young offenders. In neither architecture nor administration did they differ from the conventional prison, though an exception must be made in the case of the Boston House of Refuge, where, as early as 1831, De Beaumont and De Tocqueville discovered the existence of a crude but real system of classification, promotion and inmate self-government. The origination of the more modern and humane method of handling juvenile delinquents in the cottage or family arrangement was due to the work of the French publicist and reformer, Frédéric Auguste Demetz. Looking upon the problem as a French judge, Demetz was shocked by the conventional method of handling juvenile delinquents. Aided by the Vicomte de Courteilles, a wealthy Touraine landholder, who gave Demetz the necessary farming land, the latter, in 1840, opened at Mettray his first agricultural colony for juvenile delinquents administered according to the "Family system."

His system spread rapidly, being first introduced into this country at the state reform school in Lancaster, Ohio, in 1855. But the family system of housing and administration, initiated by Demetz, was only a beginning in the right direction. Long hours and heavy work were prescribed for the inmates, with the avowed aim of making them too tired to desire to play or engage in mischief. The progress has been a long and gradual one from these early "cottage institutions" to such a system as that of the George Junior Republic or that now practiced in such a reform school as the girls' institution at Sleighton Farms in Pennsylvania, where inmate self-government and an extremely close approximation to normal family life prevail.

The remaining step which has thus far been taken in differentiating penal institutions was introduced in the Elmira Reformatory system. Here provision was made for a class of first offenders midway in age between the juvenile and adult offenders. This specialization embodied in separating the younger prisoners marked a double differentiation, being not only one based on age, but also one which was founded upon the primary aim of reformation of inmates rather than chiefly incarceration and punishment, as in the prevailing type of prison.

The other major type of differentiation in institutions for treating the groups that were once incarcerated in the older prisons has consisted in removing from prison those classes that admittedly have no place in a prison system. Perhaps the first step was the removal of the debtors. To those who have read of Oglethorpe's foundation of an American colony to furnish a refuge for European debtors it may seem strange that as late as 1830 Louis Dwight could find a wide prevalence of imprisonment for debt in this country, being carried out under atrocious conditions. It was not terminated until the decade of the thirties, when humanitarian agitation and the democratic wave that brought Jackson to the presidency succeeded in abolishing this archaic and oppressive practice.

II. PSYCHIATRY AND CRIME

In no phase of penology has the progress been greater in the last century than in the growing recognition of the intimate relationship between mental abnormalities and criminal conduct. This advance has, of course, been primarily a result of the unparalleled progress of psychiatry or medical psychology during this period. As long as insanity was regarded the product of demoniacal possession, and idiocy was believed to be a divine curse on the individual due to ancestral indiscretions, it was no more possible to entertain a rational conception of abnormal mental states than it was to hold a valid notion of criminality when all types of criminals were indiscriminately viewed as "perverse free moral agents"—the victims of their own self-willed folly.

Two influences, which had a somewhat parallel development, tended to destroy this barbarous theological heritage and make possible the present-day attitude on these questions. Both sprang from the contributions of the English *Deists* and the French *Philosophes* of the seventeenth and eighteenth centuries. These writers shattered the theological epic that had restrained scientific progress for more than a thousand years, asserted the amenability of man to scientific study and investigation, and declared for that healthy confidence in man's inherent decency and worth which was the indispensable prerequisite to humanitarian efforts to improve the earthly lot of mankind.

The beginning of a really scientific insight into the nature and problems of insanity is usually associated with the work of the Frenchman, Pinel (1745-1826), and there is no more notable chapter in the history of medical and social science than the progress of psychiatry from Pinel to Charcot, Janet, Freud and White. The humanitarian current was continued in the work of reformers, such as John Howard and Elizabeth Fry, and in the multifarious activities of the Quakers in social and penal reform. In the introduction of the humanitarian impulse into the treatment of the insane the name of an American woman, Dorothea Lynde Dix (1802-1887), stands out beyond all others in this country or Europe. To her prodigious labors and untiring devotion to the cause of more rational and humane treatment of this class of unfortunates is mainly due the establishment of hospitals for the insane in the United States during the first half of the last century.

But the mechanism for effecting the transfer was faulty, and it was not until long after her death that, at the very close of the nineteenth century, some progress was made in providing separate hospitals for the criminal insane. Only within the last decade, chiefly as the result of the work of H. H. Goddard and his associates, has there appeared any general recognition of the necessity of creating separate places for the care and treatment of the feeble-minded who have been guilty of a violation of the law. Finally, even the little that has been done in the way of a psychiatric study and classification of the criminal population, has, as Dr. Bernard Glueck has so convincingly demonstrated, proved the futility of hoping to treat even the classes which now remain in the conventional prison as a single group to be handled in a uniform type of penal institutions. Instead, the present adult convict population requires a very careful psychological, biological and sociological classification, differentiation and treatment in a specialized set of institutions equally well diversified. There is little doubt that in the scientific prison administration of the future the agencies for dealing with the socially sick, or the criminal class, will be as varied and scientifically adapted to their work as are the institutions which are now provided to deal with the physically and mentally sick.

The most progressive step yet taken by any state in this respect was embodied in the Massachusetts law of 1921 which provided for a psychiatric examination of: (1) those indicted for a capital offense; (2) those indicted for any other offence more than once; (3) those previously convicted of a felony. The law has subsequently been extended and strengthened. Dr. L. Vernon Briggs was chiefly responsible for its passage. One of the most notable features of the act is that it allows the psychiatrist to examine the accused prior to trial and to present his report in complete and orderly fashion instead of having the facts distorted or obscured through the conventional courtroom examination of alienists by lawyers. In *Mental Hygiene* for October, 1928, Dr. Winfred Overholser of the Department of Mental Diseases in the State of Massachusetts presents a scholarly summary of the development of psychiatric service in the penal institutions and criminal courts of the United States. We reproduce herewith his major conclusions:

Questionnaires giving information concerning their use of psychiatry were returned by 259 public penal and correctional institutions of the United States. Ten non-public institutions replied, these replies being considered separately.

Of the 259 public institutions, 93, or 35.9 per cent, employ psychiatrists on either a full-time or a part-time basis.

Eighty-five, or 32.8 per cent, so employ psychologists.

The practice in 130, or 50 per cent, of the institutions is to refer cases suspected of mental abnormality to private physicians for examination.

A favorable opinion as to the value of ascertaining the mental, nervous, and physical condition of prisoners as an aid to their classification and disposition was expressed by 129, or 50 per cent, of the institutions.

In general, psychiatry and psychology appear to be used less in penal and correctional institutions in the South and Far West than elsewhere in the country.

Of the various groups of public institutions, the reformatories report the largest proportion of psychiatrists and psychologists.

The smallest proportion of psychiatrists is reported by the

juvenile institutions. This group ranks second to reformatories in proportion of psychologists.

All of the army disciplinary barracks report a full-time psychiatrist.

The state prisons and country jails differ but little in the proportions of psychiatrists and psychologists reported. More of the state prisons than of the jails have full-time psychiatrists. . . .

A preliminary survey has been made relating to the use of psychiatry in the criminal courts of the United States. Questionnaires were sent to 2,194 judges, representing a somewhat smaller, though uncertain number of courts. Replies were received from 1,168 courts, of all grades of criminal jurisdiction, and representing all the states except New Mexico. These replies form the basis of the present study.

One hundred and ten courts (9.4 per cent) report themselves to be served regularly by a psychiatrist, either employed by the court on a full-time or part-time basis, or furnished by some other public agency. These courts are distributed through thirty-one states and the District of Columbia.

The services of a psychologist are similarly utilized by 70 courts, or 6 per cent, of the total number, representing twenty-seven states and the District of Columbia.

Sixty-one courts reported as to the date of the first regular employment of a psychiatrist and psychologist. In considerably over half of these cases (39 out of 61 psychiatrists, 19 out of 35 psychologists) such services have been instituted since January, 1921.

Four hundred and seventy-three courts, representing forty-seven states, report that it is their custom to refer defendants to private physicians for mental examination before trial. This number constitutes 41.6 per cent of the 1,137 courts that answered this query definitely.

Two hundred and twenty-eight courts, representing thirty-nine states, report that they employ trained social workers in addition to the regular probation officer. This number is 20.6 per cent of the 1,106 courts that replied to this question.

Four hundred and forty-one courts, representing forty-three states and the District of Columbia, report that the probation officers assist the physicians in obtaining data for their examinations. This number is almost one-half (49.3 per cent) of the 895 definite answers given to this question.

Five hundred and eighty-four judges expressed an opinion as to the value of medical reports in the disposition of cases. Of these opinions 473 (81 per cent) were frankly favorable, and 111 (19 per cent) were counted as unfavorable. Favorable comments were received from all but four states; of these, one court only replied from each of three states, and no replies whatever were received from the fourth.

Certain states are particularly well equipped along psychiatric lines, notably California, Illinois, Massachusetts, Michigan, New York, Ohio, and Pennsylvania.

Those states which employ psychiatry the least are found chiefly in the South (6) and the West and Southwest (6).

Both of the groups enumerated in the two preceding paragraphs show a strongly favorable trend in the comment offered on the value of medical (including mental) reports as an aid in the disposition of criminal cases.

There have been a number of studies made of the mental state of convicts, summaries of the results of which are contained in such places as chapter vi of P. A. Parsons' *Crime and the Criminal*. The writer has examined most of these, and from them one could safely draw the deduction that about one-fourth of the convict class are mentally defective, another quarter psychopathic, and about one-half the victims of an unfortunate social environment producing bad or criminal habits. Yet, feeble-mindedness is far more important in crime than the above summary statement would indicate. Among the more serious forms of criminals the feeble-minded criminals are far more numerous than among the convict class as a whole. Dr. Healy holds that among the worst types of criminals the feeble-minded are from five to ten times as numerous as they are in the population at large. One point which must always be kept in mind when evaluating these psychiatric studies of criminals is that we have never been able to study the whole criminal class. We can only study those arrested and convicted, namely, the convict group. It is safe to assume that those not convicted are, on the whole, more intelligent and capable than the convicts. The convicts appear to be as intelligent as the population at large. Hence, we may safely infer that, whatever their other shortcomings, the criminal class as a group is more intelligent than the non-criminal population. Therefore, the hypothesis of mental defect cannot account for all or most crime, as was often maintained a decade or so ago.

III. The Commutation of Sentence for Good Behavior

What is probably the earliest instance of the application of the principle of the commutation of the sentence of a prisoner for good behavior appears in a law passed in 1817 in the state of New York and put into operation in the state prison at Auburn. It provided that all prisoners sentenced for five years or less might earn a reduction of one-fourth of their sentence by good behavior and the performance of a stipulated amount of "overwork." This appears, however, to have been regarded quite as much an economic measure as a disciplinary feature, and it remained purely a local enactment.

It is to the broader development of the principle as an integral factor in the improvement of prison discipline that one must look for the sources from which it came into rather common use in the United States. It is generally held that the first writer to enunciate the doctrine of the commutation of sentence for good behavior as a basic principle in the improvement of prison discipline was Archbishop Whately of Dublin. In 1829 he published a letter in the *London Review* in which he set forth his belief that the definite time sentence should be replaced by one which represented a certain amount of labor to be performed before release and would allow a convict to reduce his sentence by industrious application to assigned tasks. This suggestion was given temporary application by Captain Alexander Maconochie in his reconstruction of the penal discipline at Norfolk Island, an Australasian penal colony, in the years following 1842.

When Walter Crofton began his epoch-making work in reorganizing the Irish prisons in 1853 he adopted as a component part of his celebrated "Irish" system of prison administration the so-called "mark" or commutation system of Maconochie. From Ireland it was introduced into America by the enthusiastic admirers of Crofton's methods, among whom were E. C. Wines, Theodore Dwight, Frank Sanborn, Gaylord B. Hubbell and Z. R. Brockway. The principle of commutation was widely adopted in the United States in the last quarter of the nineteenth century, and is now universal in some form or another. Its potential reformative influence is probably largely offset by the brutalizing results of prison discipline.

It is necessary to differentiate sharply between commutation of sentence for good behavior and the indeterminate sentence. In the case of commutation the prisoner is given a designated time sentence. He may reduce this in a definite and publicly announced way by good behavior which earns a specific reduction of the original sentence. In the case of the true indeterminate sentence there is no specific time mentioned in the sentence. The prisoner is sent to the prison for an indefinite period, his release to depend upon his behavior and the judgment of this behavior by the prison officials and others on the pardon or parole boards.

IV. THE INDETERMINATE SENTENCE AND PAROLE

The principle of commutation discussed above was a step towards the indeterminate sentence. It was, however, much too rigid and definite in its provisions to constitute the true indeterminate principle. The first application of the principle of an indeterminate sentence in America, if not in the world, seems to have been in the New York House of Refuge provided by a law of 1824. A very similar condition was introduced into the government of the Philadelphia House of Refuge which was created in 1826. Here the board of managers was given large discretion in the matter of discharging or indenturing inmates.

This application of the indeterminate principle was, however, wholly limited to juvenile institutions, and few reformers possessed any idea that the principle might be beneficially extended to institutions for adult delinquents. As with the practice of commutation, one has to turn to Europe for the origins of the principle of the indeterminate sentence as applied to adult convicts. Archbishop Whately had certainly anticipated the principle in his letter of 1829. It has been held upon reputable authority that the first comprehensive statement and defense of the theory of the indeterminate sentence was contained in the *Moral Philosophy* of the brilliant if eccentric Scot, George Combe, written about 1835. In 1839 Frederick Hill, inspector of prisons for Scotland, in his report to the Secretary of State for Home Affairs, definitely recommended the introduction of the indeterminate sentence into the prisons of England and Scotland. As far as the writer is aware, it has never been fully determined whether or not Hill obtained the idea of the indeterminate sentence from Combe or as a result of his own experience. But whoever may claim the honor of having first presented the principle, it is doubted by no one that its most effective exponent was Matthew Davenport Hill, the brother of Frederick Hill, who agitated for the indeterminate sentence in the 'forties of the last century.

Almost from the first it has been agreed that the indeterminate sentence must have as a supplementary principle and practice the system of parole or "ticket-of-leave," as it is known in England. The fundamental value of the parole system in the discharge of prisoners was noted by Jeremy Bentham as early as the close of the eighteenth century. The elaboration of the principle was left, however, to Bonneville de Marsangy of France, who became its great and untiring exponent in the middle of the nineteenth century. The "twin principles" of the indeterminate sentence and parole were combined by Crofton in his Irish prison system and were introduced into American practice in the famous "Elmira system," where they were first applied in the treatment of young and relatively petty offenders, though the Cincinnati Prison Congress of 1870 recommended their immediate application in all state penitentiaries.

Though it is generally held that the parole and the indeterminate sentence are a fundamental unit in principle and successful practice, their progress and acceptance in America was more or less uneven. The parole system, being less radical in appearance, as a rule came earlier, entering the state prisons of this country rather generally in the decade of the 'nineties. The indeterminate sentence found no widespread welcome until about 1910, when a campaign for its introduction was waged by the enlightened jurists of the country and by the *American Institute of Criminal Law and Criminology*. At the present time about forty of the states have adopted some form of the indeterminate sentence, and all of them utilize the parole system in some fashion. Both the indeterminate sentence and parole are far more widely employed in the United States in dealing with juvenile delinquents than in handling adult criminals.

One reason why our sadness concerning the incomplete adoption of the indeterminate sentence may be mitigated is that its successful operation requires a high grade of technically trained prison administration. If the prison officials are to determine when the prisoner shall be released, then these officials must be men of sufficiently high ability and professional training in medicine, psychiatry and sociology to allow them to execute such a responsibilty with real competence. Until we improve the personnel and training of our prison officials it is, perhaps, just as well that the thorough-going indeterminate sentence should be delayed in its adoption.

There is no such grim satisfaction in the contemplation of the present parole system. It is already applied to tens of thousands of released prisoners, but almost everywhere it is nothing but a palpable paper parole which neither provides supervision of these prisoners nor encouragement to reform. The only good thing which can be said for the system is that it gets the men out of prison sooner, which is not an unmixed blessing for the community.

V. Inmate Self-Government and Social Reëducation

It is probable, however, that the most effective agency in advancing the cause of the reformation of the criminal has not been special rewards for good behavior, whether privileges while in prison or a shortening of the sentence, but rather the education of the prisoner for a normal life after his release.

Perhaps the earliest type of education in prison administration was in the economic field. The exponents of the Pennsylvania system back in the 'thirties of the last century laid special stress upon the adaptability of their system to the teaching of a remunerative trade to each inmate. While trade instruction in prisons for adults has made certain sporadic progress in Europe, it has advanced but slightly in this country. Little has been done along this line here except in the reformatories, and even in these there has been a tendency to carry too far the element of high productivity in the shops, as at the Rahway Reformatory in New Jersey, or to go to the other extreme and develop a great trade school with no practical application, as at the Huntingdon Reformatory in Pennsylvania.

Likewise the academic or literary education of adult prisoners, while present in some form in most American prisons since the middle of the last century, has rarely received any scientific and thoroughgoing application outside of the reformatories. In some of these, as at Rahway, it has, however, reached a level of excellence not equalled by most of the public school systems of the country. Usually it is carried on in perfunctory fashion by convicts under the direction of the chaplain or the prison teacher. For the most part these prison schools are conducted for illiterates and make no pretense to carrying on secondary or higher education. At times, however, enlightened wardens may make provisions for elaborate educational opportunities. In the new central penitentiary in Pennsylvania, for example, Warden Stutsman made it possible for a number of prisoners to take extension courses in Pennsylvania State College.

Probably more important than either economic or academic education is the social reëducation of the prisoner, namely, the attempt to readjust the personality of the convict to the necessities imposed by a normal social life through supplying him, as far as possible while in prison, with the inward motives and the external social environment which are required to meet the conditions of the life of the ordinary citizen. While some faint anticipation of this step might possibly be detected in the Irish and Elmira systems, it is probable that the first conscious and comprehensive attempt to provide an effective system of social reëducation is to be seen in the *Mutual Welfare League* and the system of convict self-government introduced by Thomas Mott Osborne at Sing Sing.

There can be little doubt that the underlying thesis upon which Mr. Osborne constructed the Mutual Welfare League is thoroughly sound. He perceived the obvious fact that convicts are not good citizens when they enter prison. He asked the inevitable question of how we could make them good citizens by the time they were discharged. The answer was clear: only by giving them training in the duties and responsibilities of citizenship while in prison. The old repressive system in no way permitted any such training. But Mr. Osborne had for many years been connected with the management of the George Junior Republic. In this model democracy juvenile delinquents managed their own affairs. They made and enforced their laws. If this system would work with child criminals, why would it not operate even better with adult convicts?

Mr. Osborne possessed the courage of his convictions. He built up the Mutual Welfare League at Auburn and then introduced it elsewhere, notably at Sing Sing. He based it upon the logical position that if a man could not execute the duties of citizenship in the simple democracy of a self-governing prison community he could hardly be expected to do so in the much more difficult conditions in the great society outside of prison walls. Mr. Osborne's reasoning would seem to be convincing and his conclusions inescapable.

The rules of discipline of the institution were chiefly left to a body of delegates of fifty convicts elected by the inmates on the basis of the representation of the several work or shop gangs. Infractions of discipline were dealt with by a board of five judges chosen by the delegates, though an appeal might be taken from their decisions to the warden. The decisions of the judges were carried out by the regular officers of the prison. No keepers or guards were allowed in the shops, discipline here being wholly in the hands of the convicts. A system of token money was introduced in the shops. A convict commissary was organized from which inmates could purchase articles of comfort. An employment bureau was maintained by the members of the League. Outdoor recreation, lectures and entertainments were provided for. The position and privileges of the inmates depend upon the degree and excellence of their adherence to the regulations of the self-governing system. It was further intended that released members of the League should make an effort to find employment for their fellow-members upon the expiration of their sentences and should attempt to sustain the efforts at reformation which have been initiated at Sing Sing. In this way it was hoped that an adequate system of social education might be provided which would restore to a normal life the great majority of convicts who had hitherto been released only to be returned for another offence after a brief period of freedom.

Mr. Osborne's scheme possessed one unnecessary weakness, namely, that he attempted to apply it to the whole prison population, while it obviously could and should be applied only to those for whom there might be some decent probability of reclamation. What is still needed is the establishment of psychiatric clinics at every prison, so as to make it possible to weed out at the beginning those hopeless defectives and degenerates whose reformation is obviously impossible and whose presence in any self-government scheme only lessens its effectiveness for those to whom it is legitimately serviceable. Yet even this is insufficient. A sociological study must be made of the social environment from which each criminal comes, with the end in view of attaining a better understanding of his past experiences and the type of treatment needed while in prison, as well as getting the proper information to aid in a thorough follow-up treatment after the prisoner has been released. Nothing could be more foolhardy than to terminate reformatory measures at the gate of the prison. It seems generally agreed that the penology of the future will demand as thorough after-care for the discharged prisoner as that which public hygiene now requires for patients discharged from the ordinary hospital or that which mental hygiene now prescribes for those returning from psychopathic hospitals.

The Mutual Welfare League and the issues involved in convict self-government have been brought sharply to the fore in connection with the rioting at Auburn prison in the summer of 1929. Beneath the dramatic externals in the crisis at Auburn prison—riots, machine guns, arson, assaults, unsanitary cells, bed-bugs, inadequate food and the like—is a far more fundamental issue. It is nothing less than the question of whether a prison shall be a place in which to punish criminals or an institution for training convicts to become decent citizens. It was once believed that punishment and reformation went hand in hand—indeed, that punishment produced reformation. Few informed students of the crime problem would defend this position today. The choice is a clear one between punishment and reformation.

Governor Roosevelt's personal investigator into conditions at the Auburn prison recommended the abolition of the Mutual Welfare League on the ground that it contributed markedly to the demoralization of discipline within the institution. The officials of the National Society for Penal Information deny the truth of this charge, condemn the report as hasty and ill-founded, and charge many of the guards with disloyalty to the warden and with a deliberate effort to discredit the League.

Most persons will be inclined to let the matter rest by taking sides with respect to the accuracy or the unreliability of the report presented to the Governor. But the important fact is not how well or how poorly the League worked at Auburn. Rather, it is the issue of whether American penology will accept or reject the principle upon which the Mutual Welfare League was conceived and operated. It is none other than the question whether American penal administration is going to pledge itself to continue the old system of cruel and repressive punishment or will boldly experiment with progressive measures which harmonize with scientific facts and elementary logic.

Conspicuous success or failure in the operation of the League in a particular prison has little bearing upon the validity of the underlying principle. Local operation of the League depends in no small degree upon such factors as plant and personnel.

Further, let the critics of the League ponder this: It is an unsettled question as yet whether the League worked badly or well at Auburn. There can be no doubt that the punitive and repressive system has always worked evil wherever it has been tried during the century and a quarter in which the modern prison has existed. Riots are not the most serious proof of the failure of a penal institution.

We may well accept the statement of the eminent criminologist, Dr. George W. Kirchwey, published in the New York *World* of January 7, 1930. Particularly worthy of note and commendation in his assertion that the Mutual Welfare League represents the only notable advance in prison administration in the last century:

The first voice of protest against Gov. Roosevelt's decision not to restore the Mutual Welfare League in Auburn Prison, twice the scene of mutiny, was raised yesterday by George W. Kirchwey, former Warden at Sing Sing and ex-Dean of the law school at Columbia University.

In a long oral statement to The World, in which he defended the Welfare League as "usually the organization on the side of law and order," Dean Kirchwey said he hoped Gov. Roosevelt would not abolish it at Auburn.

He said that the Welfare League did away with half the disciplinary problems in the prison and usually threw a spotlight on 80 per cent. of the remaining problems because of its democratic usefulness among the prisoners.

"Gov. Roosevelt, by his mandate—although I can't believe it—will shut the door hard and fast against the only great advance in prison management which has been made in 100 years," Mr. Kirchwey said.

"I can't believe that Gov. Roosevelt has the intention, as attributed to him by the Sunday newspapers, of depriving the Warden of the co-operation of the prisoners.

"The common organization of prison inmates, known as the Mutual Welfare League, has functioned since it was instituted at Auburn Prison by Thomas Mott Osborne in 1914, demonstrating its usefulness.

"Whether it works for good or evil depends on the Warden. If he is the type of man who can bring the inmates into control and whole-hearted co-operation with him, the league will avert one-half of his disciplinary problems and solve 80 per cent. of the other half without his resorting to drastic measure.

"Riots were unthinkable in Auburn, Sing Sing and the Portsmouth Naval Prison when the Osborne system was in operation, and I venture to assert that the most careful investigation of the two outbreaks at Auburn will show that the Welfare League in that prison was, on both occasions, arrayed on the side of law and order.

"From the purely administrative point of view no Warden who is capable of understanding that system should be refused the authority to avail himself of it.

"I have too much faith in Gov. Roosevelt to believe he will shut the door hard and fast against the only great advance in prison management which has been made in a hundred years."

VI. The Development of Prison Labor

The history of the economic aspects of modern prison administration has not been more inspiring than the other phases of its development. The European situation is so varied and complicated that it must be passed by with the mere mention of the fact that Montesinos in Spain and Obermaier in Bavaria share with the Quakers of Pennsylvania the honor of having been the earliest advocates of productive labor as a part of a successful prison system. In general, the industrial phases of penal administration are far more highly developed in Europe than in America.

Our prisons started at the close of the eighteenth century either with no labor at all, or else with merely the crudest forms of tasks, such as breaking stone, grinding meal, or even manipulating a treadmill. At the outset prison labor was looked upon chiefly as an aspect of the system of discipline and punishment. It was designed to make the life of the prisoner hard and laborious, thus punishing him more severely and making him repent more quickly. It was not until much later that prison labor began to be considered in relation to the economics of the situation and came to be regarded primarily from the standpoint of manufacturing productivity and financial income. With the development of the merchant capitalists in this country in the 'thirties there arose a demand for prison labor, and these men very generally contracted for the services of such convict labor as they desired, according to the "lease" system, whereby they took complete charge of the prisoners during working hours. This method became remarkably popular during the period of abnormal demand for prison labor in the Civil War. This crude lease system obviously possessed certain oppressive features, and it was gradually supplanted by the so-called "piece-price" variety of the contract system, according to which the contractor did not lease the bodies of the convicts, but agreed to pay for the product of their labor at a stipulated price per piece.

Where willing contractors did not exist or where their methods were obnoxious, the "public-account" system was introduced, and the products made by the prisoners were sold by the state agents in the public market.

After the rise of the modern labor organizations in the 'seventies, violent opposition to convict labor arose on the part of the laborers outside the prison walls. Prison labor was branded an unfair type of competition, and free labor demanded a cessation of both the contract and public-account systems. Where the labor organizations were strong they either brought about the abolition of practically all prison labor, producing great suffering on the part of the prison population, as in Pennsylvania since 1897, or forced the states to adopt the "state-use" system, in which prison-made products were not sold to the public at all, but were used in various state institutions. The contract system in one form or another persists in a number of states, but the lease system has finally been abolished throughout the country. There was a humanitarian basis for union labor opposition to the lease and contract systems, but the general opposition of this group to prison labor on economic grounds was indefensible. Convict labor has never been a serious competitor with free labor in American industry. In 1905 convict labor produced less than one-quarter of one per cent of the goods manufactured.

More recently the progress of a more liberal attitude towards the criminal has allowed him to be employed outside the prison on roads or public improvements, and in this way there has developed that variant of the state-use system known as the "public works and ways" system. Particularly significant has been the recent movement to purchase large prison farms and to put the convicts at agricultural labor. In 1923, out of about 50,000 employed convicts, eighteen per cent were employed under the contract system, twenty-six per cent under the public-account system, thirty-seven per cent under the state-use system, and nineteen per cent under the public-works-and-ways system. Some feeble beginnings have been made in certain prisons toward instituting a system of compensation or wages for convicts. Some states have a rather flourishing convict industry, for example the binding-twine and hardware industry in Minnesota and Wisconsin, the burlap bag industry in California, and the sugar plantations and factories in some southern states.

We have already pointed out the scandalous degree of idleness which prevails among the inmates of American prisons and have emphasized the fact that this is a chief cause of the demoralization of convicts and of prison riots. The most notorious and significant defect in American prison labor, however, is the fact that it has made almost no provision whatever for the teaching of a trade to convicts, so that they may earn an honest living after discharge. The prisons have not only failed, for the most part, to be self-supporting, but they have also made but slight contribution to the reformation of inmates from the economic angle.

VII. THE STERILIZATION AND SEGREGATION OF THE FEEBLE-MINDED CLASSES AND THE HABITUAL CRIMINAL

Owing to the alarming increase of the defective classes and their special menace to the community, much of the best social investigation in recent years has been devoted to a study of the defective and degenerative elements in the general population. A number of classic investigations of congenitally defective and degenerate families by Dugdale, Goddard, McCulloch and Blackmar have revealed, with a wealth of evidence, the disastrous results which attend the promiscuous and unrestricted breeding of defectives and degenerates. The general dissolution of the theological view of the causation of defective and degenerate personalities and the development of our scientific knowledge regarding the transmission of congenital defects has at last indicated the only possible method of ridding society of this small but ever-increasing degenerate element, from which a substantial proportion of the paupers, criminals and other social derelicts are recruited.

The sole manner of procedure whereby this class can be speedily eliminated, before it becomes so large as to drag down the normal population in a common destruction, is to segregate or sterilize all of its members. The former expedient, while arousing less traditional resistance and opposition, and desirable with females, is attended with great expense, and the much simpler and more humane method of sterilizing those male members of the defective class that can be safely trusted outside of an institution has of late met with great favor among biologists and physicians. If this policy were systematically pursued it would be a conservative prediction to state that in fifty years the defective and degenerate groups would greatly decline in numbers and the criminal class be reduced more than one-fourth. Most states have begun to make some pretense at custodial segregation of the worst types of the idiotic and the feeble-minded, and twenty-three, following the Indiana precedent of 1907,* have legalized the sterilization of the hopelessly defective and the habitually criminal groups, but the laws have not been applied with any thoroughness except in California. Thirteen states now have formally active sterilization laws: California, Delaware, Idaho, Maine, Minnesota, Montana, Nebraska, New Hampshire, North Dakota, Oregon, Utah, Virginia and Wisconsin. California has performed over five thousand sterilization operations. No other state has yet performed five hundred. Many of the earlier sterilization laws were set aside as unconstitutional, but this obstacle has been removed by a recent decision of the United States Supreme Court in the case of Carrie Buck vs. Virginia, upholding sterilization. The plan suggested by McKim of painlessly exterminating the idiotic, hopelessly insane and habitually criminal is probably remote from practical adoption.

The progress in psychiatry in the last decade has, however,

---

*Pennsylvania passed the first sterilization act in 1905, but it was vetoed by the governor.

indicated that we can no longer indulge in the easy generaliza-
tion that the majority of criminals are feeble-minded and that
feeble-mindedness is a simple and uniform product of invariably inherited defect. The psychiatric study of criminality, particularly in the clinics devoted to this purpose, has
shown that psychopathic criminals are more often suffering
from psychoses and neuroses than from overt mental defect.
And many of these mental disorders are purely functional
without any physical basis and, hence, quite incapable
of biological transmission. Therefore, any comprehensive
plan for the prevention of crime would call for not only segregation and sterilization of the feeble-minded but also for
the establishment of psychiatric clinics designed to discover
and treat those psychopathic disturbances which are the potential cause of even the most serious crimes, such as those of
Harry Thaw, Loeb and Leopold and Hickman. And, while
doubtless an extremist on the other side, Abraham Meyerson
has shown that we must adopt a critical attitude towards the
doctrines of Goddard and others with respect to the easy-
going assumption of the hereditary derivation and biological
causation of most types of feeble-mindedness.

VIII. PROBATION AND THE NON-INSTITUTIONAL CARE OF DELINQUENTS

The beginnings of the non-institutional care of delinquents
may be traced to the ticket-of-leave or parole system, which
originated in the middle of the nineteenth century and has
come to be a cardinal feature of advanced penological theory
and practice. This, however, merely made possible the removal of the convict from imprisonment during the latter
portion of his term and in no way attempted do away with
imprisonment altogether. There has been a gradual growth
among careful students of penology of the conviction that in
many, if not in most cases, the convict issues from prison a
worse character than he was upon entry, especially in the case
of young first offenders. There has thus arisen a determined

movement to secure the introduction of a system of suspended sentence and probation, to be applied to those first offenders and others, who, it seems reasonable to believe, can be most effectively treated outside of a penal institution.

As has been the rule with nearly all of the radical innovations in penology, this progressive practice was first applied mainly to juvenile delinquents, especially in connection with the creation of a juvenile court system in the more advanced municipalities of the country. This juvenile court movement originated in Rhode Island, Illinois and Minnesota in 1899, and Judge Benjamin B. Lindsey of Denver was a pioneer and the most picturesque figure. It should be remembered, however, that the first probation laws in Massachusetts (1878), Maryland (1894), Vermont (1898) and Rhode Island (1899) specified no age limit. Forty-seven states now have juvenile probation laws.

As has been the case with almost every progressive prison-reform practice in the past, so with probation, its application to juvenile delinquents was soon followed by its introduction into the method of treating adult delinquents not convicted of major crimes. At the present time, some thirty-three states and the District of Columbia allow probation to be applied to adult delinquents with a greater or less degree of thoroughness. Only nineteen, however, really have adult probation in operation. Massachusetts, New York, New Jersey, Michigan, Illinois and Pennsylvania have led in this practice. There can be no doubt about the soundness of the principle of the suspended sentence and probation, particularly when linked up with child guidance bureaus and psychiatric clinics. It provides a double advantage over institutional treatment in promoting reformation. It avoids demoralizing association with degenerate and hardened criminals and offers as a special incentive to improvement the prospect of keeping out of a penal institution. The chief drawback in American probation practice has been the difficulty in getting funds adequate for the support of a sufficiently large and well-trained force of probation workers and in keeping the selection of such officers out of politics. Probation can never succeed until we have the service adequately manned with trained social workers who have been professionally prepared for this kind of work. This will mean many more and better paid probation workers than are now employed in most cities.

IX. Some Desirable Changes in Criminal Jurisprudence

It is a fact well recognized by criminologists and penologists that any fulfilment of their progressive plans for reform must wait upon a radical reconstruction of our criminal law and criminal procedure. Our legal system for ascertaining guilt and dealing with the criminal is founded directly upon medieval metaphysical and theological presuppositions, which wholly antedate modern biological, psychological and social science. The criminal is proceeded against as "a perverse free moral agent" and the court is charged with wreaking upon him the vengeance of society. For the average criminal the law recognizes no biological, psychic or social fact in the causation of the crime nor any biological, psychic or social condition of the criminal, when administering the sentence. The crime and not the criminal is what is theoretically punished, and the effort has been made in a crude and unscientific way to adjust the penalty to the crime, the possibility of which modern criminology and penology utterly denies. Further, the jury system renders the scientific ascertainment of guilt difficult if not impossible. At least, one may say that it is little more scientific than the ancient ordeal or trial by battle and the element of chance involved is quite as large as in these outgrown practices. The jury system renders null and void most of the laws of evidence and other safeguards of legal procedure, and destroys the whole machinery of justice by submitting the final decision as to guilt to a group of utterly untrained and usually quite unfit men, singularly responsive to rhetorical arguments by opposing counsel. Little is needed to condemn the jury beyond an honest examination of its historical development and its obvious and palpable legal, psychological and sociological defects and absurdities.

In the place of this anachronistic scheme of criminal law and criminal procedure, the criminologist and penologist of today would introduce a permanent body of experts drawn from the law, biology, psychology, sociology and economics to examine the evidence against the accused and to determine his guilt. There would be no flat sentence, but rather a truly indeterminate sentence, which would allow the convict to be properly studied, classified and treated under the supervision of another body of administrative experts in institutions for the treatment of convicts. Only such a group is competent to determine when a convict is fitted for freedom or to prescribe the treatment which can lead to any hope of differentiating and reforming the convict. It may well be conceded that such a system of criminal procedure and jurisprudence and of penal administration is remote from enactment and popular acceptance, but this very remoteness is the measure of the time which must elapse before we can achieve anything like a scientific method of ascertaining guilt or treating and reforming those adjudged guilty of violating the basic legal rules of the social order.

It goes without saying that any scheme for the apprehension, conviction and treatment of criminals will fail to provide adequate social protection unless we see to it that the criminal code actually embodies and designates as crimes all forms of truly anti-social action. At present the criminal code is cluttered up with a vast number of offences which are archaic or else should not be branded as crimes at all. Particularly notable in this latter class are the offences involved in sumptuary legislation designed to control the private morals of citizens. At the same time, extremely serious forms of anti-social conduct involving the fraudulent impoverishment and the ruination, indeed in many cases the death, of thousands are not specified as crimes at all in our criminal code. It would avail us little to capture, convict and treat all formal criminals if the most dangerous types of anti-social individuals were not regarded as criminals before the law. This point is very well dealt with by Bernard Shaw in his famous comparison of the conventional criminal and the respectable gentleman:*

We may take it, then, that the thief who is in prison is not necessarily more dishonest than his fellows at large, but mostly one who, through ignorance or stupidity, steals in a way that is not customary. He snatches a loaf from the baker's counter and is promptly run into gaol. Another man snatches bread from the tables of hundreds of widows and orphans and simple credulous souls who do not know the ways of company promoters; and, as likely as not, he is run into Parliament. . . . We have whole classes of persons who waste, squander, and luxuriate in the hard-earned income of the nation without even a pretense of social service or contribution of any kind; and instead of sternly calling on them to justify their existence or go to the scrap heap, we encourage and honor them, and indeed conduct the whole business of the country as if its object were to produce and pamper them. How can a prison chaplain appeal with any effect to the conscience of the professional criminal who knows quite well that his illegal and impecunious modes of preying on society are no worse morally, and enormously less mischievous materially, than the self-legalized plutocratic modes practised by the chaplain's most honored friends with the chaplain's full approval? . . . How is the divine judgment, by which all mankind must finally stand or fall, to distinguish between the victims of these two bragging predatory insects, the criminal and the gentleman? The most obvious reply is "By their number." For the depredations of the criminal are negligibly small compared to the military holocausts and ravaged areas, the civic slums, the hospitals, the cemeteries crowded with prematurely dead, the labor markets in which men and women are exposed for sale for all purposes, honorable and dishonorable, which are the products of criminal ideals imposed on the whole population. . . . The gentleman really believes that he is an instrument of national honor, a defender of the faith, a pillar of society; and with this conviction to strengthen him he is utterly unscrupulous in his misplaced

---

*Introduction to S. and B. Webb, *English Prisons Under Local Government.*

pride and honor, and plays the wholesaler in evil to the criminal's petty retail enterprises.

X. ABSENCE OF SUBSTANTIAL IMPROVEMENT IN PRISON CONDITIONS

In spite of these various phases of progress in penology embodying such innovations as better differentiation and classification of inmates and improved machinery in administration, it is the painful duty of any candid historian of prison discipline to point out with some emphasis that there has been no substantial change in the essentials of prison discipline since the first few prisons were established approximately a century ago. In larger outlines the system remains precisely what it was when the Auburn and Pennsylvania systems were first offered to the admiring observation of the world in the 'twenties of the last century. Social revenge remains the motive of conventional criminal jurisprudence, and imprisonment is still looked upon as a method of inflicting the punishment wherewith this desire for revenge is satisfied. All talk about reformation is either pure hypocrisy or entirely beside the point.

The system remains essentially unchanged. Even the best wardens are for the most part benevolent despots. The whole objective is still to make prison life as hard and unpleasant as possible and as different as may be from the life of the free person outside prison walls. The punitive and penitential ideal still remains ascendant. There have been trivial improvements such as the occasional abolition of the lock-step and the elimination of striped uniforms for convicts, but the same oppressive and brutal system of discipline still persists. If new prison structures have supplanted those erected in the first half of the nineteenth century, they still remain only bigger and better cages. Almost never do we find a prison warden who is both a trained criminologist and a humanitarian in outlook. His subordinates remain the same type of semi-illiterate, hardened and brutal functionaries that guarded prisons a century ago. Even many of the brutal punishments which we find condemned by Louis Dwight and others a hundred years back are still revealed with disheartening frequency. The picture of prison life revealed in such books as Booth's *Stealing Through Life* and Tasker's *Grimhaven*, describing prison life in California in 1928, paint as depressing and discouraging a picture as one can discover in the prison literature of the year 1830. The Eastern Penitentiary was one hundred years ago a more habitable and more humanely administered prison than the Dannemora prison is today. Jack Bethea's revelations concerning the brutalities towards convicts in the prisons and convict mines of Alabama, and the exposure of conditions among the convict gangs of Florida by the New York *World* a few years back brought to light facts that almost rival the situation in Australia in the first half of the nineteenth century.

In short, the problem of really fundamental and significant prison reform is something which lies ahead of us and the historian can do little more than to call attention to trivial achievements and futile and ineffective gestures in the last century. Indeed, one may remark that, after all, the only truly relevant prison reform must consist in the complete abolition of the prison as it has existed down to the present time.

SELECTED REFERENCES

Bacon, Corinne, comp. *Prison Reform.* New York, 1917.

Barnes, Harry Elmer. *The Evolution of Penology in Pennsylvania.* 1927; Reprinted Montclair, N. J., 1968.

Barnes, Harry Elmer. *Prisons in Wartime.* Washington, D. C., 1944.

Barrows, Samuel J., ed. *The Reformatory System in the United States.* Washington, D. C., 1900.

Bramer, John Philip. *A Treatise on Parole.* New York, 1926.

Brockway, Zebulon Reed. *Fifty Years of Prison Service.* 1912; Reprinted Montclair, N. J., 1969.

Carpenter, Mary. *Reformatory Prison Discipline as Developed by the Rt. Hon. Sir Walter Crofton in the Irish Convict Prisons.* 1872; Reprinted Montclair, N. J., 1967.

Cooley, Edwin J. *Probation and Delinquency.* New York, 1927.

Ellington, John R. *Protecting Our Children from Criminal Careers.* New York, 1948.

Folks, Homer. *The Care of Destitute, Neglected and Delinquent Children.* New York, 1902.

Glaser, Daniel. *The Effectiveness of a Prison and Parole System.* Indianapolis, 1964.

Goddard, Henry H. *The Criminal Imbecile.* New York, 1915.

Goddard, Henry H. *The Kallikak Family.* New York, 1919.

Haynes, Frederick E. *The American Prison System.* New York, 1939.

Healy, William. *The Individual Delinquent.* 1915; Reprinted Montclair, N. J., 1969.

Hoag, Ernest B., and Williams, Edward Huntington. *Crime, Abnormal Minds and the Law.* Indianapolis, 1923.

Ives, George. *A History of Penal Methods.* 1914; Reprinted Montclair, N. J., 1970.

Klein, Philip. *Prison Methods in New York State.* New York, 1920.

La Roe, Wilbur. *Parole with Honor.* Princeton, 1939.

Lewis, Burdette G. *The Offender.* 2d ed. New York, 1921.

Lindsley, John B. *On Prison Discipline and Penal Legislation.* Nashville, 1874.

McKim, W. Duncan. *Heredity and Human Progress.* New York, 1900.

Monahan, F. *Women in Crime.* New York, 1941.

Murchison, C. *Criminal Intelligence.* Worcester, Mass., 1926.

Myerson, Abraham. *The Inheritance of Mental Diseases.* Baltimore, 1925.

Ohlin, Lloyd E. *Selection for Parole.* New York, 1951.

Osborne, Thomas M. *Society and Prisons.* 1916; Reprinted Montclair, N. J., 1972.

Parsons, Philip A. *Crime and the Criminal.* New York, 1926.

Pollak, Otto. *The Criminality of Women.* Philadelphia, 1950.

Robinson, Louis N. *Penology in the United States.* Philadelphia, 1921.

Robinson, Louis N. *Should Prisoners Work?* 1931; Reprinted Montclair, N. J., 1972.

Smith, M. Hamblin. *The Psychology of the Criminal.* London, 1922.

Snedden, David S. *Administrative and Educational Work of American Juvenile Reform Schools.* New York, 1907.

Stutsman, Jesse. *Curing the Criminal.* New York, 1926.

Tannenbaum, Frank. *Osborne of Sing Sing.* Chapel Hill, N. C., 1933.

Tiffany, Francis. *Life of Dorothea Lynde Dix.* Boston, 1918.

Timasheff, Nicholas S. *One Hundred Years of Probation.* 2 pts. New York, 1941-1943.

Timasheff, Nicholas S. *Probation in the Light of Criminal Statistics.* New York, 1949.

U. S. Bureau of Prisons. *Handbook of Correctional Institution Design and Construction.* Washington, D. C., 1949.

U. S. Bureau of Prisons. *Recent Prison Construction. 1950-1960; Supplement to the Handbook of Correctional Institution Design and Construction.* Washington, D. C., 1960.

White, William A. *Insanity and the Criminal Law.* New York, 1923.

Whitin, Ernest S. *The Caged Man.* New York, 1913.

Wines, Frederick H. *Punishment and Reformation.* Rev. ed. New York, 1919.

Young, Pauline W. *Social Treatment in Probation and Delinquency.* 2d ed. 1952; Reprinted Montclair, N. J., 1969.

CHAPTER IX

Capital Punishment

I. HISTORIC METHODS OF ADMINISTERING CAPITAL PUNISHMENT

IT is desirable at the outset to understand exactly what is meant by capital punishment, as the subject is to be discussed in this chapter, and to keep clearly in mind the underlying doctrines upon which the criminological theories of the exponents of capital punishment actually rest. By capital punishment we mean the involuntary termination of the life of an individual convicted of a crime, this cessation of corporal existence being the penalty imposed upon the individual as the direct consequence of the commission of a crime. At the present time the discussion is, for practical purposes, limited to the exaction of the death penalty for the commission of the act of premeditated murder.

While the methods of executing the death penalty are today confined to less than a half-dozen standard devices such as beheading, hanging, shooting and electrocution, capital punishment has been enforced in the past in a great variety of ways. We shall here endeavor very briefly to survey some of the more usual methods of inflicting the death penalty throughout the course of human history. We may begin with flaying and impaling, which was widely practiced in the ancient Orient and came down into medieval Europe. It was still employed in England in the age of Canute. This punishment meant first skinning the victim alive and then placing his body upon a sharp stake where he remained until death fortunately intervened. In the meantime the victim was left exposed to the hot rays of the sun and the depradations of insects and ravenous birds. Another method of administering

231

the death penalty in the Orient was the exposure of the individual to gradual death as the result of the work of insects. Dr. Wines recounts how this was applied to the Persian general Mithridates:*

He was encased in a coffin-like box, from which his head, hands, and feet protruded, through holes made for that purpose; he was fed with milk and honey, which he was forced to take, and his face was smeared with the same mixture; he was exposed to the sun, and in this state he remained for seventeen days, until he had been devoured alive by insects and vermin, which swarmed about him and bred within him.

The exposure to biting by poisonous serpents was commonly employed in oriental and classical times. This type of death was frequently insured by sewing the culprit in a sack in company with a poisonous reptile. The infliction of the death penalty by throwing the convicted person to lions or other ravenous beasts is well known. In other cases they were thrown before enraged elephants to be trampled under foot.

Drowning has been widely used as a way of inflicting capital punishment. In order to intensify the punishment, the victim was frequently allowed to half drown, was then revived, and subjected to this process several times before being allowed to pass out completely. Stoning to death was very popular in oriental and classical times. The stoning of the martyr Stephen is a well-known New Testament story. It was retained as a penalty for theft as late as tenth century England. Stoning was usually regarded as a peculiarly disgraceful method of meeting one's death.

Another widely used method of inflicting the death penalty in the olden times was to cast the victim from a high rock or precipice to the stones beneath. This was sometimes combined with other punishments. It is said that the Carthaginians frequently flayed prisoners before pitching them from a high rock. Poisoning was not an uncommon type of death penalty, and it has been rendered classic in history through its imposi-

---

*F. H. Wines, *Punishment and Reformation*, p. 70.

tion upon the Greek philosopher Socrates. Crucifixion was a very popular type of capital punishment in the antique period. Death might come from prolonged exposure on the cross or might be hastened by various tortures and wounds inflicted by the executioners. The burning of culprits has been employed from primitive times to contemporary lynching of negroes in the South.

Death at the stake was one of the most popular forms of administering the death penalty during the Middle Ages and was almost invariably applied when killing witches. In its most simple and humane fashion the victim was burned to death with promptness and expedition, but it was not uncommon for the victim to be snatched from the flames after being thoroughly seared, left to suffer with his burns and then be returned to the flames at a later period. Burning might also be preceded by or combined with other forms of punishment, usually divers types of mutilation. That savage ingenuity has not yet departed from the human race when inflicting the death penalty may be seen from the following passage, taken from Dr. Llewellyn Hughes' article on the Ku Klux Klan in *Humanity and Its Problems* for April, 1924:

Tom Price was a negro, married, and father of two children. While he acted as porter in the town hotel his wife did washing for a number of white families. Price had little education, and was in no way extraordinary, except that he was rather more consistent in attention to his job than is usually the case. His wife, a rather attractive negress, in August of that year was fired by one of her male employers because she insisted on remaining faithful to her legal spouse. Price, in a moment of angry bravado, threatened the white man.

On the second night after this occurrence, Price was awakened and dragged from his bed by three hooded figures. Before the small house, which was on the outskirts of the town, waited a group of fifteen or twenty more, all similarly attired, and each provided with a horse. The negro was tied to the end of a rope and then dragged behind the cavalcade to the centre of the town. Here he was wired to an upright post and straw and faggots, soaked in kerosene, were piled about his legs. To the crowd that was gathering the leader of the hooded band declared that Price was to be "executed for attacking a girl." The mob growled approval, and shouted advice to the captors.

The first step in the execution was the whipping which raised crimson gorged weals on the negro's naked body. Then a match was set to the straw and sticks—but not too many of these: the flame was not intended to kill. As the flames reached his flesh the negro writhed and screeched in agony, but only now did the real torture commence. So tightly was Price wired to the post that his tense body could not shrink when one of the white men advanced with a brace and bit. Into the muscles of the groin cut the biting tool. Time after time he fainted to be revived again as the torture was stayed. From the crowd came again and again that animal growl—lustful and cruel. The game was nearly over. A slash of knives and another form of medieval torture had been revived. The fire was now kicked out and the unconscious, but still living, negro was dragged to a tree at the side of the square. As his limbs jerked and danced at the end of a rope, his body was riddled with bullets. He had found peace at last. But Mrs. Price is no longer faithful to her husband. In one southern town there will be no insistence upon black equality.

A form of capital punishment which appears in ancient times and was very popular during the Middle Ages was what was known as drawing and quartering. A horse was hitched to each leg and arm of the individual and then the four horses were led in opposite directions thus pulling the victim in pieces. Occasionally the process was speeded up by the assistance of a knife which cut the muscles and tendons. It is stated that, in the case of an attempted assassin of Louis XV, he was so tough that after an hour's pulling the horses were unable to tear him apart and a knife had to be used to assist them in quartering him. To reveal something of the flavor of the times it is said that the observers expressed much pity for the struggling horses but none for the writhing victim.

Beheading has been one of the most universally employed

types of capital punishment, and has usually been regarded as a relatively noble and enviable type of death penalty. In the Middle Ages beheading was looked upon as an honorable method of meeting death, while hanging carried with it a definite stigma. The methods of beheading persons have called forth much inventive ingenuity. One of the earliest methods was to use a two-handed and broad-bladed sword. The culprit was ordinarily compelled to stand in a bent posture and a rope was frequently put about his neck in order to stretch it preparatory to the blow. In medieval and early modern times the block and broad axe were usually employed for beheading. The most elaborate device for beheading thus far produced is the well-known guillotine. As Mr. Andrews makes clear in his *Bygone Punishments,* the guillotine was suggested by much earlier English devices like the "Halifax Gibbet" and the "Scottish Maiden." It was given this name because it was invented by a Dr. Guillotin, a member of the French Revolutionary Assembly. It consists of a heavy steel blade held in position by grooves in a wooden frame. It gains force for the cutting process through its weight and the long fall. The guillotine is still in use in France. Decapitation has been assumed to be essentially painless, but an able physician, Dr. Frederic Gaertner, offers the following testimony to the contrary. He thus describes the behavior of a decapitated head, which was delivered into his custody after the execution:*

Immediately after the head was severed and dropped into the basket, I took charge of it. The facial expression was that of great agony, for several minutes after decapitation. He would open his eyes, also his mouth, in the process of gaping, as if he wanted to speak to me, and I am positive he could see me for several seconds after the head was severed from the body. There is no doubt that the brain was still active. . . . His decapitated body which was previously fastened by a strap upon a bench, was in continuous spasmodic and clonic

*C. Duff, *A Handbook on Hanging,* p. 98.

convulsions, lasting from five to six minutes, also an indication of great suffering.

Of all the forms of administering the death penalty there
is little doubt that hanging has been more widely utilized
than any other single mode of hurrying a victim to the Great
Beyond in expiation for his crimes. We read of hangings in
the earliest historic literature, and hanging remains today
more widely used as a method of executing the death penalty
than any other device employed in the United States. There
were veritable orgies of hanging in late medieval and early
modern times. It is estimated that in England alone during
the reign of Henry VIII there were about seventy thousand
hangings. In a similar period today in the United States there
would be about forty-five hundred executions. The United
States today has a population more than ten times that of
England in the Tudor period. Like beheading, the technique
of hanging has received much attention from ingenious experts
in the ways of capital punishment. In its simplest form, as
employed in primitive times and by the Vigilantes in the
frontier days of American society, hanging simply meant
throwing a slip noose around a man's neck, pulling him off
the ground and leaving him to die of slow strangulation. In
public executions by hanging in modern times an attempt
was made to hasten death through breaking the neck, instead
of relying upon the slower process of strangulation. What
was known as "the drop" was introduced. The prisoner was
taken up on a platform, the noose adjusted about his neck
and then the floor of the platform upon which he was standing was pulled from beneath him, allowing him to drop for
a distance supposed to be sufficient to break his neck. It is
a fine art to determine just how much of a drop is necessary
to break the neck and at the same time not sever the head from
the body. The following descriptions of hangings will indicate the effects of too short or too long a drop. The first quo-

tation describes the hanging of four negroes as reported by the official surgeon in attendance on this occasion:*

When the first pair were hanged it was my duty to determine the fact of death. As a general rule, on auscultation the heart may be heard beating for about ten minutes after the drop, and on this occasion, when the sounds had ceased, *there was nothing to suggest a vital spark.* The bodies were cut down after fifteen minutes and placed in an ante-chamber, when I was horrified to hear one of the supposed corpses give a gasp and find him making spasmodic respiratory efforts, evidently a prelude to revival. The two bodies were quickly suspended again for a quarter of an hour longer. The executioner, *who was thoroughly experienced,* had done his part without a hitch, and the drop given was the regulation one according to individual physique. Dislocation of the neck is the ideal aimed at, but, *out of all my postmortem findings, that has proved rather an exception, while in the majority of instances the cause of death was strangulation and asphyxia.*

In the following instance, in hanging of one Patrick Harnet, the drop was too great and the head was practically pulled from the body:†

As the body dropped to a standstill a heavy gurgling sound was heard, and soon the blood in torrents commenced pouring on the stone floor below. The cap was raised and it was found that decapitation was almost complete, the head hanging to the body only by a small piece of skin at the back of the neck. During the half-minute or more that the heart beat, the blood was thrown against the platform above from the exposed gash caused by the head being pulled back on the shoulder.

Mrs. Eva Dugan, the first woman to be executed in Arizona, was hanged on February 21, 1930. Her head was jerked off by the gallows noose.

An even later mode of hanging has been devised which is held to be fool-proof and inevitably to break the neck of the victim. The culprit stands on the ground and about his neck is placed a noose in a rope from which all flexibility has been removed. This rope runs through a pulley and on the opposite

*C. Duff, *op. cit.*, p. 36.
†*Ibid.*, p. 96.

end is a tremendous weight which can be released at the pleasure of the executioner. As soon as the noose is adjusted to the culprit's neck the executioner releases the weight on the other end of the rope and this jerks the condemned person from the ground with such force as ordinarily to break the neck of any man. If the neck is not broken when the victim is originally yanked from the earth it is sure to be when he falls back again taking the slack out of the rope, the falling weight having pulled the rope up to such an extent as to make it impossible for the condemned person to touch the ground upon the return fall. This ingenious device is used, for example, in the Connecticut state prison at Wethersfield, and was there employed in the "hanging" of Gerald Chapman.

In earlier days hanging was not limited to the period necessary to produce death. It was a common custom to hang the corpse in irons after death and leave it to decay and be eaten by birds. The sight and stench were regarded as valuable deterrent influences. Parts of the skeleton might hang in irons for years. This practice continued in England until 1834.

It was a common custom to allow condemned persons to make such observations as they cared to before the actual act of execution. Sometimes these took the form of elaborate philosophical and sociological disquisitions. A representative example is afforded by the remarks of one George Manley, offered just before his hanging in 1738:*

"My friends, you assemble to see—what? A man leap into the abyss of death! Look, and you will see me go with as much courage as Curtius, when he leaped into the gulf to save his country from destruction. What will you say of me? You say that no man, without virtue, can be courageous! You see · what I am—I'm a little fellow. What is the difference between running into a poor man's debt, and by the power of gold, or any other privilege, prevent him from obtaining his right, and clapping a pistol to a man's breast, and taking from him his purse? Yet the one shall thereby obtain a coach, and honour, and titles; the other, what?—a cart and a rope. Don't imagine from all this that I am hardened. I acknowl-

*W. Andrews, *Bygone Punishments*, pp. 22-3.

edge the just judgment of God has overtaken me. My Redeemer knows that murder was far from my heart, and what I did was through rage and passion, being provoked by the deceased. Take warning, my comrades; think what would I now give that I had lived another life. Courageous? You'll say I've killed a man. Marlborough killed his thousands, and Alexander his millions. Marlborough and Alexander, and many others, who have done the like, are famous in history for great men. Aye—that's the case—one solitary man. I'm a little murderer and must be hanged. Marlborough and Alexander plundered countries; they were great men. I ran in debt with the ale-wife. I must be hanged. How many men were lost in Italy, and upon the Rhine, during the last war for settling a king in Poland. Both sides could not be in the right! They are great men; but I killed a solitary man."

Strangulation has been brought about by other modes than hanging, though hanging has been much the most prevalent method of producing death through strangulation. One method of producing strangulation was to wind a rope around the defendant's neck and then have two executioners pull hard on the opposite ends. Sometimes they sawed back and forth on the rope, thus combining strangulation with complete or partial decapitation. In early times strangulation was carried out directly by the use of the hands of a powerful executioner. A much more complicated method of producing strangulation was effected by a device known as the garrote, which was very widely employed in Spain in early modern times. Here strangulation was produced by the closing in of an iron band about the neck of the culprit, while at the same time piercing the vertebrae of his neck by a sharp iron point. This method of inflicting death is still used in Spanish and Latin-American countries. The following excerpt from the American press describes a recent execution of a double-murderer in Havana:

Quesado Castillo, a Negro murderer, died today in the clutch of the medieval garrote. The long lever, which forced a steel spike into Castillo's vertebrae was turned at 6.03 a.m., and at 6.11 Castillo was pronounced dead. According to custom, the body was to remain in the Santiago jail on public view, still gripped by the garrote, for four hours, when it would be buried.

Castillo could not sleep last night, but his calm was unperturbed as he walked to the execution chair today, smoking a cigar.

"Gentlemen," exclaimed Castillo as though putting a toast, "until eternity!"

The garrote is a holdover from the Spanish occupation of Cuba. The head and body of its victim is held firmly against the back of the garrote by an iron collar, which fits tightly around the neck.

Closely related to strangulation was the execution of the death penalty by pressing the convicted person to death. Dr. Wines thus describes the sentence imposed upon one condemned to die in this fashion:*

That you be taken back to the prison whence you came, to a low dungeon into which no light can enter; that you be laid on your back on the bare floor, with a cloth around your loins, but elsewhere naked; that there be set upon your body a weight of iron as great as you can bear—and greater; that you have no sustenance, save, on the first day three morsels of the coarsest bread, on the second day three draughts of stagnant water from the pool nearest the prison door, on the third day again three morsels of bread as before, and such bread and such water alternately from day to day until you die.

In his well-known work *Bygone Punishments* Mr. William Andrews thus describes another case of pressing to death carried out in English criminal procedure in the year 1676:†

One Major Strangeways and his sister held in joint possession a farm, but the lady becoming intimate with a lawyer named Fussell, to whom the Major took a strong dislike, he threatened that if she married the lawyer he would, in his office or elsewhere, be the death of him. Surely, Fussell was one day found shot dead in his London apartments, and suspicion at once fell upon the officer, and he was arrested. At

---

*Wines, *op. cit.*, p. 67.

†Andrews, *op. cit.*, pp. 92-4.

first he was willing to be subjected to the ordeal of touch, but when placed upon trial, resolved not to allow any chance of his being found guilty, and so refused to plead, in order that his estates might go to whom he willed. Glynn was the Lord Chief Justice on this occasion, and in passing the usual sentence for *Peine forte et dure,* used instead of the word "weights," as above, the words "as much iron and stone as he can bear," doubtless to suit the prison convenience, and make the sentence perfectly legal. He was to have three morsels of barley bread every alternate day, and three draughts of "the water in the next channel to the prison door, but of no spring or fountain water," the sentence concluding, "and this shall be his punishment till he die." This was probably on the Saturday, for on the Monday morning following, it is stated, the condemned was draped in white garments, and also wore a mourning cloak, as though in mourning for his own forthcoming death. It is curious to notice that his friends were present at his death, which was so much modified from the lengthy process that his sentence conveys as to be in fact an execution, in which these same friends assisted. They stood "at the corner of the press," and when he gave them to understand that he was ready, they forthwith proceeded to pile stone and iron upon him. The amount of weight was insufficient to kill him, for although he gasped, "Lord Jesus, receive my soul," he still continued alive until his friends, to hasten his departure, stood upon the weights, a course which in about ten minutes placed him beyond the reach of the human barbarity which imposed upon friendship so horrible a task.

Suffocation has been resorted to frequently in imposing the death penalty. One method of producing this result was to throw the condemned person into a great pile of soft ashes. Even more common has been suffocation by smoke, especially smoke heavily charged with sulphur fumes. Burying alive has also been a straightforward and effective method of producing a combination of pressing and smothering to death. This was a form of punishment widely employed in primitive society as a penalty for serious types of sex crimes.

Boiling the condemned person to death has been a common method of carrying out the death penalty. It was legal in France until the French Revolution, and was employed in

England during the Tudor period as a punishment for poisoning. The boiling was frequently carried out in oil as well as in water. Public boilings of convicts are frequently recorded in medieval history. We have already pointed out that flogging one to death has been a popular method of executing the death penalty through the ages. Particularly was this the case with severe floggings with the Russian *knut*.

Breaking on the wheel was a very popular mode of execution in the Middle Ages. The prisoner's arms and legs were propped up on a wheel-like platform and were broken in several places by the use of a heavy iron bar. The mangled remains were then turned rapidly, scattering gore about until the unfortunate victim was dead. Sawing in pieces was a popular medieval execution. The victim was usually hung up by his feet and sawed in two vertically by two executioners. Another ingenious method of carrying out this mode of execution was to nail a man alive in a casket and then saw the casket in several sections. This was employed wholesale as late as the French occupation of New Orleans in the colonial period. We have also referred to the iron maiden in connection with torture. Her embraces meant certain death and were widely exploited in the medieval period. Capital punishment has also been frequently inflicted by means of starvation or death from thirst.

While several of these earlier forms of inflicting the death penalty are still popular, only hanging and beheading are widely used today. At the present time capital punishment is chiefly inflicted by beheading, hanging, shooting, electrocution and the administration of lethal gas. Shooting has been employed for centuries in administering the death penalty and is still almost invariably utilized in executing military prisoners. In addition to execution through rifle fire, prisoners have been executed by being blown from the mouths of cannon. This method was hit upon by the English at the time of the Sepoy mutiny in India in the middle of the last century, and was also often relied upon by the Russians in dealing with conspirators against the old Tsarist régime.

Modern science has provided us with new methods of execution in the form of the application of electricity and some type of asphyxiating gas. Electrocution was first introduced in New York State in 1890. After it was adopted it was defended as a humanitarian move. As an actual matter of fact, its original introduction was based upon thoroughly commercial motives and was a result of the effort of an electrical company to market its products. It has been commonly held that death by electrocution is entirely painless, but a distinguished French scientist, Professor L. G. V. Rota, writing in the London *Daily Mail* for January 14, 1928 disputes this contention:*

In every case of electrocution, in the way in which Ruth Snyder and Judd Gray were executed (they are reported to have been subjected to 2,200 volts) death inevitably supervenes but it may be very long, and, above all, excruciatingly painful . . . the space of time before death supervenes varies according to the subject. Some have greater physiological resistance than others. I do not believe that anyone killed by electrocution dies instantly, no matter how weak the subject may be. In certain cases death will not have come about even though the point of contact of the electrode with the body shows distinct burns. Thus, in particular cases, the condemned person may be alive and even conscious for several minutes without it being possible for a doctor to say whether the victim is dead or not. . . . This method of execution is a form of torture.

Another attack on the pain of death in electrocution has been made by Nicola Tesla, whose electrical discoveries made possible the construction and operation of the electric chair. He sets forth his views at length in the New York *World* of November 17, 1929:

Nicola Tesla, the seventy-two-year-old inventor whose discoveries in alternating current led to the invention of the electric chair, hopes to abolish, before he dies, "the barbarous

*Duff, *op. cit.*, pp. 99-100

machine which inflicts the most excruciating torture known to man" in favor of some humane method of capital punishment, such as an artificial bolt of lightning which kills instantaneously.

"I am opposed to capital punishment in any form," explained Mr. Tesla, the lean, keen-eyed wizard whose inventions revolutionized electrical science a generation ago. "I do not think it deters crime. But if society is determined to kill certain criminals who are, after all, human beings, we should attempt to spare them agony in death. We should prepare civilized punishment.

"The prototype of the electric chair was designed by myself and another engineer for a commercial use. Our opponents raised a cry that alternating current was deadly.

"To gain wide publicity for this they managed to have our commercial machine adapted to mete out capital punishment. It was a crime, which can be laid directly at the door of those who conducted this unscrupulous campaign. Of course, in time, they were forced to use alternating current.

"But in the meantime Legislatures had passed laws installing in the death houses of the prisons, electric chairs, completely unsuited for such work; because alternating current, due to the periodic rise and fall and reversal of direction, creates resistance to its own passage.

"The human body offers great resistance to the passage of current. If life is to be taken away, then the individual must be stunned by the application of the current and the organs must be destroyed.

"The alternating current used in the electric chair does not pass in a direct course, despite of all precautions taken. A wet sponge is established in contact with a metallic plate over the head, in expectation that the current will divide and pass uniformly through the tissue.

"The alternating current flows along a restricted path into the body, and destroys all the tissue confronted in this path. In the meantime the vital organs may be preserved; and pain, too great for us to imagine, is induced. The brain has four parts. The current may touch only one of these parts; so that the individual retains consciousness and a keen sense of the agony. For the sufferer, time stands still; and this excruciating torture seems to last for an eternity.

"With the electric chair now used for purposes of capital punishment, it is impossible to tell what will happen in each individual case. The path of the current is accidental and upon its chance direction depends the amount of agony to which the criminal is subjected.

"We call ourselves a civilized people. Yet this infliction of death by the electric chair is the most cruel form of torture ever invented by man. It is the destruction of human flesh by a process which induces the maximum amount of pain which the human mechanism is capable of feeling, to say nothing of the mental anguish caused during the lengthy process by which the electroplates, etc., are arranged.

"If capital punishment must be retained, we should use some method which instantly destroys consciousness and makes extended agony impossible. Ironically enough, the electric chair was introduced by the votes of legislators who thought themselves soft-hearted and wished to save criminals the tortures of hanging. Actually the guillotine or the hangman's noose causes less torture than the electric chair.

"It seems to me that the use of a bolt of artificial lightning is the most humane way to inflict the death penalty. These bolts are already being produced on a large scale in certain commercial processes. They could be adequately controlled by a comparatively simple machine, and would instantly destroy the criminal's consciousness so that he would be spared all agony."

The writer is unable to offer any conclusive opinion as to the accuracy of those who contend that electrocution is painless and those who maintain that it is a brief but severe form of torture. He has been informed, however, by a person present at the execution of Gray and Mrs. Snyder that, upon the application of the current to the latter, the mask fell from her face and revealed her eyes and tongue protruding in such a manner as to indicate tremendous shock and possibly severe temporary pain. Persons who have been shocked into unconsciousness by electricity but have recovered report the registration of strong sensations during the period of temporary consciousness after the shock has been received.

Lethal gas is certainly a painless, indeed, a pleasant form of meeting death, and humanitarian sentiment would indicate the desirability of making it a universal method of execution pending that time when civilization will have advanced sufficiently to do away with capital punishment entirely.

Curious and hideous practices were associated in earlier times with the execution of the death penalty. We have already referred to the practice of hanging the corpse in irons. Another procedure consisted in carrying the corpse to the door of the chief witness or the informer responsible for conviction. This would frequently result in a concerted assault upon the house and family by the friends of the deceased. Mutilation after death was often ordered. After the condemned person had been hanged or beheaded, he might be disemboweled, drawn and quartered, or otherwise torn or cut to pieces.

As a final comment upon the various methods of executing the death penalty which we have described all too briefly above, we may observe that these atrocious examples of "man's inhumanity to man" were carried out by the selfsame animal who, through certain of his spokesmen like Mr. Bryan and Dr. Straton, object to biological affiliation with the kindly, harmless and inoffensive apes. These savage acts are also the product of an animal who believed during the World War that he could effectively stigmatize others of his kind by likening them to a gorilla.

We might logically close this historical section with an indication of the status of capital punishment in the United States of America today. Six of our states make capital punishment obligatory for murder in the first degree. These states are Vermont, Massachusetts, Connecticut, North Carolina, New York and New Mexico. Eight states have abolished capital punishment, namely: Michigan (1847), Rhode Island (1852), Wisconsin (1853), Maine (1887), Kansas (1907), Minnesota (1911), North Dakota (1915), South Dakota (1915). Thirty-four states make capital punishment optional for murder in the first degree with life imprisonment as the alternative.

With respect to the methods of executing the death penalty in the United States, the conditions are as follows: twenty-four states still employ hanging as the approved method of administering the death penalty, though in Utah the condemned person may take his choice of being hanged or shot. Fifteen states have adopted electrocution. One state, Nevada, carries out capital punishment by asphyxiation through the administration of lethal gas. In 1925 there were 123 persons put to death in the United States. Eighty were electrocuted, forty-one were hanged and two were shot.

The absurdities to which we go even in contemporary times in insisting on the literal and formal execution of the death penalty is admirably illustrated from the following news item taken from the Springfield *Republican* for September 16, 1929. Desperate efforts were made to snatch a condemned prisoner from natural death, so that the state could exact his life according to due process of law and execution. It was apparently not deemed sufficient protection to society to allow the convict to die a natural death. It should further be remembered that this preposterous procedure was enacted in the institution presided over by Warden Lewis E. Lawes, one of our leading opponents of capital punishment. We reproduce herewith the account of this almost incredible performance, which is, however, nothing rare. Much more attention is given to preserving the health and life of condemned men than to improving the physical condition of prisoners serving a time sentence:

Ossining, N. Y., Sept. 15.—Three expert surgeons, sent here by the state of New York, fought tonight to save the life of Frank Plaia.

Frank Plaia's life is most valuable to the state of New York. The state of New York will electrocute Frank Plaia in Sing Sing prison after he recovers.

The sentence passed upon Plaia said he must die by the passage of a current of electricity through his body. So the state, through its Sing Sing warden and three surgeons, fought to keep Plaia from dying of appendicitis Saturday night and today.

He was taken from the deathhouse, under guard, to the new hospital a quarter of a mile away. Drs. W. H. Sweet, Robert Bloom and George McCracken performed the operation. A guard watched, and a guard is at Plaia's bedside.

He must die for the murder of Mr. and Mrs. Sorro Graziano, in Nassau county. It is charged he killed them to prevent them from testifying against him on a holdup charge.

The operation was pronounced a success. Plaia, it is said, will be healthy and strong again when it is time for him to die.

II. Capital Punishment in the Light of Scientific Criminology

The question of capital punishment is still a subject for animated debate and has taken on a renewed interest with the growing alarm over the so-called "crime" wave of the present time, with the resulting demand for a revival and intensification of the archaic modes of repressing crime. The present writer would introduce his discussion of the subject by a statement somewhat unusual for the introductory paragraph of such a treatment, namely, that he does not look upon the question of capital punishment as of any prime significance, whether viewed from the standpoint of the conventional jurist or from the point of view of the most radical scientific criminologist. It is a problem which relates to only a minute fraction of the criminal classes as a whole, and it involves a discussion of issues which are to the educated and scientifically-minded person of purely historical significance. Not a single assumption underlying the theory of capital punishment, as at present applied can be squared with the facts about human nature and social conduct which have been established through the progress of scientific and sociological thought in the last century and a half.

In fact, it is the opinion of the writer that the whole concept of capital punishment is scientifically and historically on a par with astrological medicine, the belief in witchcraft, the

Fundamentalist view of Biblical authorship and the rejection of biological evolution. In his famous *Historical Essay Concerning Witchcraft,* written in 1718, Francis Hutchinson assumed that the whole set of assumptions upon which the witchcraft epidemic rested had already become hopeless anachronisms. A similar attitude is taken toward Fundamentalism by men like H. L. Mencken, James Harvey Robinson, and Clarence Darrow. This is the approach which also may well be assumed by the criminologist in discussing the matter of capital punishment. The doctrine of human behavior, the theory of the nature of the human personality, the explanations of human conduct, and the conceptions of justice which dominate the thought of the conventional jurists and penologists who advocate the death penalty are no more valid in a scientific sense than astrology, witchcraft, the thesis of the literal and direct inspiration of the Bible, or the doctrine of a special creation of the world and its inhabitants in the six days between October 23 and October 28, 4004 B.C.

In its origins the death penalty rested primarily upon the effort to placate the gods, lest their beneficent solicitude for the group be diverted as result of apparent group indifference to the violation of the social codes supposedly revealed by the gods of the people. The complete blotting out of the culprit was looked upon as a peculiarly forceful demonstration of group disapproval of the particular type of anti-social conduct involved in the case.

Later, with the rise of the metaphysical theories of human conduct, the individual came to be looked upon as a free moral agent entirely capable of free choice in every aspect of his conduct, wholly irrespective of biological heredity or social environment. From the standpoint of these assumptions the criminal was inevitably regarded as a perverse free moral agent who had willfully chosen to do wrong and outrage his social group. The theory of capital punishment which evolved in this period was that of revenge. His life was demanded of the individual who willfully determined to carry out an act which brought some serious loss to his social group.

More recently the exponents of capital punishment have added to this underlying notion of revenge that of deterrence: namely, the thesis that the death penalty acts as a powerful form of discouragement to criminal conduct on the part of those who are aware of the existence and horrors of this mode of treating the criminal class. At the present time the exponents of capital punishment lay more stress upon the alleged deterrent influence of the death penalty than upon any other argument in its favor. They not only assume the overwhelming deterrent influence of punishment in general, but they also contend that the death penalty is a far more powerful and effective deterrent than life imprisonment. It need scarcely be added that the friends of capital punishment still hold tenaciously to the free moral agent theory of crime, contend that the criminal voluntarily and freely chooses to be guilty of anti-social action, and steadfastly maintain that the criminal or his survivors may, through the pain or example of punishment, be effectively deterred from being again willing to commit crime.

It is a significant fact that the scientifically-minded person can only approach the refutation of those assumptions of the exponents of the death penalty in an attitude of mingled amusement and impatience, much as he would if compelled to engage in a serious argument to refute the astrological theories of the pathogenesis of physical disease as expounded by Hippocrates and Galen. Modern physiological chemistry, dynamic psychology, and sociology have proved the free moral agent theory of human conduct alike preposterous in its assumptions and its implications. The human animal finds his conduct and his thoughts determined by the combined influences of his biological heredity and his social surroundings. There is not the slightest iota of choice allowed to any individual from birth to the grave. Conduct can be modified only by alterations in the organism or by the introduction of new or different social influences and forms of stimulation.

Those whose biological heredity is adequate, whose social surroundings are normal or above the normal, and whose education is sound and constructive will conduct themselves in a law-abiding manner and avoid the commission of crime, except under the most unusual and inciting circumstances. Those whose biological heritage is defective or who are subjected to a social environment which stimulates anti-social action and breeds anti-social habits will be equally naturally inclined toward anti-social or criminal action.

If one desires to eliminate crime, it is apparent that this can be achieved only by providing ever greater assurance that defective types shall not be born and that unfavorable social environments shall not exist. In the light of a strictly scientific attitude toward crime and the criminal, it is as absurd to speak of punishment for crime as to speak of punishment for physical or mental illness. Yet we cannot ignore crime. Indeed, the scientific sociologist and criminologist is much more solicitous over the matter of the repression of crime than the policeman, the detective, or the conventional jurist. The difference lies in the fact that the criminologist has a grip upon the real facts involved in the causation of crime and is interested in taking those measures which will actually protect society from the depredations of the anti-social classes.

Applying these scientific precepts to the issue of murder and the death penalty, the criminologist first logically asks the question as to why people actually murder and what types of persons commit murder. Until we know what types engage in homicide and why they do so, it is obviously futile even to discuss the proper measures that should be taken to reduce the number of murders committed. From our study of psychology, particularly abnormal and criminal psychology, we know that the vast majority of murders are committed either as the result of deep-seated subconscious criminal compulsions, which find outlet in the greatest variety of murderous acts, or in moments of intense and utterly irresponsible anger. A few individuals commit murder in what is apparently cold deliberation. Such individuals fall into three main classes: first, there are those who suffer from serious physical, mental, and cultural deficiencies which make it possible for them to contemplate murder as a more or less natural form of conduct. Their social point of view is so defective, or their sense of fellow-feeling and sympathy so ill-developed, that the compunction against taking human life which exists in the normal individual is more or less absent in their case. The second type consists of those who are relatively normal physically, mentally, and culturally, but who are subjected to intensely difficult or inciting situations which lead them to commit murder, whereas under normal circumstances they would lead a law-abiding existence. In the third place, there are the professional gunmen, who bear a close resemblance in their mental habits to members of the standing army. Their attitude toward the taking of human life is very much like that of the soldier on the battlefield: namely, it is taken as a matter of course, not involving any personal responsibility or depravity. In the environment in which they have developed, they have acquired the view that human life is of no great consequence and that it is legitimate to take life freely in order to advance their personal prestige or prosperity. Gunmen represent a sort of civilian soldiery of a perverted type who kill casually for their own advancement, whereas a member of a standing army is supposed to kill casually to increase the power and prestige of his country. It is obvious that the gunman is the victim of bad social habits which have deprived him of his sense of responsibility and his notion of the value of human life. Indeed, it would seem that at times gunmen may contract the killing habit and their lack of respect for life in the time of war. This is well brought out in the case of Frederick Burke, regarded as the most dangerous criminal in America and the best machine gunner in the underworld. He distinguished himself as a member of a machine gun detachment in France.

The next logical point at issue is as to whether the death

penalty, as at present imposed, would act as an effective deterrent to these various classes of murders. It will be apparent at the outset that those who commit murder as a result of psychopathic compulsions or in fits of rage would be entirely immune to the deterrent effect of the death penalty. No form of deterrence short of overt physical restraint before the deed could in any sense serve to avert such murders. The same is true of those who commit murder as a result of defective personality or highly unfortunate social environment. Nor can the death penalty be supposed to act as an effective deterrent in the case of the professional gunman. He realizes that the chances of his being apprehended at all for his crime are relatively slight; that the probability of his conviction after arrest is not more than fifty per cent; that he runs a fair chance of being released on a technicality in appeal, even if convicted; and finally, that if sentenced to death he is highly likely to have this sentence commuted to life imprisonment and may ultimately be pardoned and restored to a life of freedom. In the Chicago gang wars over seventy men have been killed since the end of the year 1924. There has not been a single conviction, and there are only four indictments pending in connection with these cases. The average gunman is no more deterred by the fear of the electric chair than is the average voluntary recruit by the remote chance that he may fall upon the battlefield. We have remaining as the only possible class of murderers who could be at all influenced by the deterrent effect of the death penalty those who commit murder under the stress of unusually adverse circumstances, mainly for the purpose of pecuniary or other material advantage. Even here the death penalty could scarcely act as a highly effective deterrent, because of the strong pressure to commit murder and the consciousness of a large probability of escaping its application.

The above facts demonstrate that the death penalty, even if applied invariably to every apprehended and convicted murderer, without any subsequent intervention of commutation or pardon, would not seriously deter many of those whose personality types permit in any sense the operation of deterrent influences. Yet the present defective police, detective, and court system brings about a situation in which much less than half of those guilty of murder are even arrested, while a large proportion of those arrested are unjustly freed through the inefficiency of the court and jury system. There can be no doubt that an individual is more seriously deterred by a sense of absolute certainty of relatively mild punishment than by the thought of the possible loss of his life through a type of punishment in which there is less than one chance in ten that it will ever be applied to him. Further, the exponents of capital punishment enormously exaggerate the degree of fear of death which exists on the part of the average individual. It is scarcely an exaggeration to say that one risks his life as much in a premature start through the traffic of Fifth Avenue at Forty-second Street, New York City, as by a reasonably discreet commission of a murder. Nevertheless, one familiar with the conduct of pedestrians in New York traffic is able to observe in a sufficiently thorough and convincing fashion the slight influence which the fear of death or maiming exercises upon the control of human behavior.

It is also quite obvious that the deterrent effect of capital punishment, even if it existed, is largely lost because of the modern methods of executing the death penalty. If one desired to make the death penalty most effective as a deterrent influence, it would be desirable to make a great public spectacle of it and carry it out under the most brutal and degrading circumstances. The painless electrocution of a few murderers, almost unobserved in the secrecy of the prison death-chamber, is about the least effective conceivable method of bringing the terrors of the death penalty before those potential murderers who are hypothetically to be deterred from their dastardly acts by fear of the consequences. If one were to take seriously the theory of the deterrent influence of capital punishment, he would inevitably be led to recommend publicly burning at the stake in the Polo Grounds all murderers from the New York district instead of electrocuting them in relative privacy in the isolation of the death-chamber at Sing Sing. We know, of course, from history that even the most severe forms of capital punishment publicly administered actually have slight or no deterrent influence. In England in the eighteenth century, the brutal hangings were public and often compulsory. Yet there was no evident decline in the crime rate. Indeed, pocket-picking became so common in the crowds assembled to witness the public hangings that the latter had to be made private. This excessive pocket-picking was observed to take place unabated at the public hangings of notorious pick-pockets.

The facts of human psychology, as applied to a discriminating analysis of the motives for murder and the types of individuals who commit murder, demonstrate, then, the complete fallacy of the theory of the deterrent influence of capital punishment. The history of criminal jurisprudence and the statistics of crime show likewise that the death penalty has never exerted the degree of deterrent influence which its exponents contend always accompanies its operation. In England in the eighteenth century there were more than two hundred capital crimes, but crime increased to an alarming degree during this very period. History reveals the most varied and numerous proofs that there is no close correlation between the severity of the criminal code and the infrequency of crime. Likewise, as Warden L. E. Lawes and others have definitely proved, the statistics in regard to the frequency of murders where the death penalty exists and where it does not exist fail to support the thesis that the death penalty actually exerts a deterrent influence. The statistics which we have available show that there is no ground whatever for holding that the murder rate increases when the death penalty is abolished. E. R. Calvert, who is perhaps the foremost authority in the world on the death penalty, gives it as his final conclusion that: "In no single instance is there evidence of a permanent increase in homicidal crime as the result of aboli-

tion; in many there has been a decided decrease." The following table is taken from Warden Lewis E. Lawes' book, *Man's
Judgment of Death*. It gives the homicide rate in highly
comparable abolition and capital punishment states and shows
that in the abolition states the homicide rate is decisively
lower than in the capital punishment states.

COMPARISON OF HOMICIDE RATES
(per million of population)
IN COMPARABLE GROUPS OF STATES

YEAR	ABOLITION STATES Maine Rhode Island Michigan Kansas Minnesota	CAPITAL PUNISHMENT STATES New Hampshire Connecticut Ohio Missouri Indiana
1914	39.4	56.0
1915	37.2	52.4
1916	39.8	54.4
1917	41.0	69.6
1918	31.0	54.8
1919	38.2	55.6
1920	33.0	50.4
1921	44.0	58.8
Average	37.9	56.5

It is often held that the low murder rate in England is
due to the fact that the death penalty is inevitably carried out
with promptness and uniformity in that country. Mr. Lawes
made a study of the infliction of the death penalty in England and Wales, as compared with its execution in twelve
representative American states having a combined population

about equal to that of England and Wales. He discovered that in England and Wales only fifty-three per cent of the death sentences were actually carried out, whereas in the American states seventy-one per cent of those condemned were actually executed. It is obvious that the lower murder rate in Great Britain is due to the greater assurance of arrest and conviction in England and not to terror in the face of the certain and immediate application of the death penalty.

Any possible deterrent influence of the death penalty would, furthermore, be nullified by the fact of the relatively few persons put to death for homicide in the United States. The figures in this regard are certainly startling. For example, in California in 1924 there were three hundred and seventy-four homicides, but in 1925 there were only thirteen legal executions; in Indiana in 1924 there were two hundred and twenty-three homicides, and in 1925 two legal executions; in Louisiana in 1924 there were three hundred and fifty-eight homicides, and three legal executions in 1925; in Maryland there were one hundred and nineteen homicides in 1924, and but one legal execution in 1925; in New York State there were five hundred and ninety-six homicides in 1924 and only fifteen legal executions in 1925; in Ohio there were four hundred and twenty-two homicides in 1924 and but thirteen legal executions in 1925; there were five hundred and seventy-one homicides in Pennsylvania in 1924 and only twenty legal executions in 1925; in Tennessee in 1924 there were four hundred and forty-five homicides with two legal executions in 1925. In general, we may conclude that Warden Lawes is correct in the following generalizations about the death penalty:*

From the foregoing data I believe that at this point we may safely draw a few general conclusions regarding the application of the death penalty.

First. The death sentence is spasmodic and uncertain in its application. No other punishment lacks to so marked a

---

*L. E. Lawes, *Man's Judgment of Death*, pp. 55-56.

degree that most important of all elements, certainty of execution.

Second. In states where any choice is permitted juries and even courts are loath to impose the extreme penalty of death. While it remains on the statute books, it becomes in practice what has so been aptly termed a vestigial remnant.

Third. Life imprisonment is not so uncertain as it has been or is popularly supposed to be, nor is it so difficult of application. It presents the opportunity for individualization of treatment which is a very necessary element in any system of punishment.

Fourth. There is a somewhat greater facility in obtaining convictions for homicide in abolition states and in those which permit a choice between life imprisonment and the death penalty, than in the states which arbitrarily impose death.

Even if we were to admit that some form of punishment could act as a deterrent to the commission of the majority of murders, it might well be argued that life imprisonment would be a more effective deterrent than the exaction of the death penalty. It is certain that the prospect of a life in prison under present conditions is far more terrible to contemplate than death itself. Exponents of the death penalty frequently admit this fact, but contend that life imprisonment is purely a theory, not a practical reality. They insist that in the case of a sentence to life imprisonment there is a high probability of ultimate pardon which enormously reduces the deterrent influence of the prospect of a life sentence. This objection may be answered in two ways. In the first place, if the sentence to life imprisonment cannot be actually executed in practice, this is a defect in our present system of criminal jurisprudence and in the exercise of the pardoning power, and should be attacked from this point of view. The argument is not against life imprisonment as such. But equally important is the fact that if the prospect of pardon reduces the alleged deterrent influence of life imprisonment, so does the prospect of complete acquittal lessen the deterrent influence of the hypothetical death penalty for premeditated murder. The mitigation of life imprisonment by pardon is thoroughly matched by the admittedly greater reluctance of a jury to convict a man when the inevitable sentence which would follow conviction must be the death penalty. Many juries would unquestionably return a verdict of guilty in many cases if the penalty were life imprisonment. Yet they often hesitate to bring a verdict of guilty on the basis of the evidence when they know that such a verdict means the exaction of the life of the accused.

As an actual matter of fact, however, available statistics completely undermine the traditional argument against life imprisonment as a deterrent, namely, that prisoners are much more likely to escape the execution of life imprisonment than they are the carrying out of the death penalty. Warden Lawes made a careful study of those who received death sentences and those who were condemned to life imprisonment between 1912 and 1919. He showed that twenty-nine per cent of those sentenced to death were later pardoned or had their sentences commuted, whereas only twenty-three per cent of the life prisoners had their sentences modified during this period. To be sure, some of the lifers might later be paroled and pardoned, but these figures indicate the complete lack of foundation for the conventional view that the death sentence is almost invariably executed while life imprisonment generally ends in a speedy pardon. Another argument in favor of life imprisonment is, of course, the fact that this penalty enables one to rectify errors, whereas the death penalty makes it quite impossible to reconsider a case where it becomes obvious that an innocent party has been punished.

It is further evident that the exponents of capital punishment assume that murderers are invariably the worst of the criminal classes and that they all represent essentially one unified type, for which a single form of punishment should be prescribed as the most effective remedy available in the premises. Anyone at all familiar with the facts of modern criminal science or anybody possessing any extensive experience in penal administration knows that the first of these assumptions is in no sense borne out by the facts. Modern criminal science has proved beyond any possibility of doubt that, except on relatively rare occasions, the crime itself is no adequate criterion of the nature of the personality lying behind the crime. Hence, scientific criminology entirely repudiates the basic assumption of conventional criminal jurisprudence: namely, that it is possible to fit a punishment to a crime with propriety and precision. It is the almost universal testimony of many experienced and capable prison administrators that the majority of their most trusted and best behaved convicts are those who have been imprisoned for life for the commission of murder.

It is even more absurd to contend that murderers are all of a single type requiring the same form of treatment. It would be difficult to imagine a greater diversity of personality types than such famous murderers as Chester Gillette, Harry Thaw, Jean Gianini, J. P. Watson, Russell Scott, Odell, Loeb, Leopold, Judd Gray, Ruth Snyder, Hickman and Remus. Some of these individuals were of a personality type which would make them always dangerous in society, however treated, while others of the group could have been quickly restored as safe members of society by proper medical treatment and social reëducation. The case of Loeb and Leopold, considered alone, indicates the absurdities of the older criminal jurisprudence. Both of these men were accomplices in the same crime, and it has been assumed that they were equally dangerous to society and should be treated alike. The psychological examination of these two individuals quickly demonstrated the absurdity of such an assumption. Leopold was shown to be a person of almost unique and unrivaled intellectual power, suffering from a homosexual neurosis which probably would have yielded to an intensive course of psychoanalytic treatment. Scientifically and intelligently treated, Leopold would have been less dangerous to society than any one of the thousands of bootleggers allowed to wander freely about certain sections of the city of Chicago. Loeb, on the other hand, was a person of only average mentality, in the initial stages of an incurable psychosis, which carried with it the criminal compulsions that lay at the basis of the varied and hideous crimes committed by these two individuals. No form of medical treatment known to modern science would have rendered Loeb safe for society, and extermination by a painless method would have been the most economical and humane mode of disposing of him.

The writer of this chapter has not brought forward any of the so-called sentimental objections to capital punishment: namely, that it is against the spirit of humanity, that it brutalizes the human intellect, or that we have no right to take human life. Such arguments appear to the present writer to be intellectually on a par with the barbarous or anachronistic assumptions of the exponents of capital punishment, such as the theory of the free moral agent and the justifiability of social revenge. The writer would agree that there are very logical arguments for the extension of the practice of exterminating useless, defective, and dangerous human types. The objections were considered in much detail and answered by Dr. McKim nearly a generation ago in his famous book on *Heredity and Human Progress*.

But the argument for extending painless extermination of dangerous types is in no sense an argument for capital punishment. The adoption of the extermination program would mean a rational defense against the vast army of degenerates, of whom the defective and non-reformable murderers constitute but the most infinitesimal fraction. Further, the extermination of dangerous and hopeless types represents a thoroughgoing acceptance of the modern scientific view of the causation of criminal conduct. It rests upon the adoption of the theory of determinism and assumes that there are specific hereditary defects in certain individuals which will make it forever impossible for them to act in a safe or normal fashion. These assumptions repudiate for all time and in their entirety the doctrine of a free moral agent and the notion of social revenge, which form the very keystone of the arch of conventional jurisprudence. The writer doubts if the adoption of a scheme for exterminating hopeless types would necessarily brutalize humanity, particularly a humanity and a civilization which today, in a careless and nonchalant fashion, deprives many thousands of individuals of their lives each year by careless manipulation of motor vehicles, and complacently observes the death or maiming of tens of thousands through the absence of safety devices in mines and factories and of millions in needless wars.

The final answer of the scientific criminologist to the exponent of capital punishment is that if we desire to get rid of crime we must adopt the same scientific attitude that society has taken with respect to the elimination of physical disease. We must eliminate those biological defects which lie at the basis of many criminal types. We must reduce as far as possible the unhealthy social environments which generate the bad habits which emerge in criminal conduct. In the actual repression of existing criminals, we must so improve our police and detective systems that we will actually apprehend the majority of those who commit crimes. We must then introduce a system of providing and examining evidence which will lead to the conviction of the guilty who are arrested. This will involve a thoroughgoing reorganization of the present court and jury system, if not the complete elimination of the jury. We must put the task of the conviction for crime in the hands of a permanent body of paid and competent experts who will be actually interested in the facts in the case. Having assured the arrest and conviction of the guilty, we must so treat the convict classes as to secure the permanent segregation of the non-reformable types and the introduction of a broad scheme of reformative and corrective treatment which will rehabilitate the majority of those temporarily incarcerated. The problem of capital punishment, then, appears rather insignificant and unimportant in relation to the much broader and more fundamental problem of the reconstruction of criminal jurisprudence and penal administration.

It will be evident from the foregoing that the writer is thoroughly opposed to the continuation of capital punishment. Indeed, he does not concede that a person of any reasonable cultivation and possessed of even rudimentary knowledge of criminology can defend the perpetuation of this relic of human savagery. At the same time, it is necessary to view the problem in proper perspective. The writer regards it as highly undesirable to picture capital punishment as the chief evil of contemporary jurisprudence and criminal procedure. The number put to death in the United States through capital punishment, about one hundred and twenty-five yearly, is utterly insignificant compared to those who meet death in some other violent form. For example in 1927 no less than twenty-one thousand one hundred and sixty persons were killed as an incident of automobile traffic alone. While the author has never been willing to concede the existence of convincing evidence connecting Sacco and Vanzetti with the murder of Parmenter, it is obvious to anyone that scores of perhaps more estimable Italians have died unheralded under the wheels of automobiles and motor trucks in the Boston area in the interval since 1920.

As against this petty number of one hundred and twenty-five annual executions, there are nearly two hundred thousand convicts rotting away in state prisons, reformatories, reform schools and jails. The inhuman treatment accorded to most of these constitutes a situation infinitely more deplorable than the infliction of the death penalty upon a hundred individuals whose premature removal from society one must honestly admit, in the majority of cases, may be a benefit both to themselves and to society. Therefore, anyone who attempts to represent the abolition of capital punishment as the core of the reform program is rendering a distinct disservice to the cause of enlightened criminology. The abolition of the death penalty is certainly a worthy objective for any philanthropist or reformer, but it must be viewed in proper relationship to infinitely more serious and far-reaching aspects of the crime problem today.

In addition to its inherent merits, the agitation for the abolition of the death penalty may, of course, serve a valuable purpose in another way, namely, in constituting an opening wedge in the effort to secure a more rational attitude toward the crime problem in general. Much of the educational propaganda which is most helpful in promoting the abolition of the death penalty is incidentally highly relevant to the production of a more sane and better informed attitude toward the general problem of crime and its repression.

SELECTED REFERENCES

Bedau, Hugo A., ed. *The Death Penalty in America.* Chicago, 1964.

Bye, Raymond T. *Capital Punishment in the United States.* Philadelphia, 1919.

Calvert, E. Roy. *Capital Punishment in the Twentieth Century.* 5th ed. 1936; Reprinted Montclair, N. J., 1972.

Capote, Truman. *In Cold Blood.* New York, 1966.

Child, Richard W. *Battling the Criminal.* New York, 1925.

Duff, Charles. *A Handbook on Hanging.* London, 1928.

Elliott, Robert, and Beatty, Albert R. *Agent of Death.* New York, 1940.

Hall, John W. *Capital Punishment on Trial.* London, 1927.

Hoffman, Frederick L. *The Homicide Problem; Murder and the Death Penalty.* Newark, 1925.

Johnsen, Julia E., comp. *Capital Punishment.* New York, 1939.

Joyce, James A. *Capital Punishment.* New York, 1961.

Kavanagh, Marcus A. *The Criminal and His Allies.* Indianapolis, 1928.

Kirkpatrick, Clifford. *Capital Punishment.* Philadelphia, 1925.

Koestler, Arthur. *Reflections on Hanging.* New York, 1956.

Lawes, Lewis E. *Man's Judgment of Death.* 1924; Reprinted Montclair, N. J., 1969.

Lawes, Lewis E. *Meet the Murderer.* New York, 1940.

Mencken, August, ed. *By the Neck: A Handbook of Hangings.* New York, 1942.

Scott, George R. *The History of Corporal Punishment.* London, 1938.

Teeters, Negley K. *Hang by the Neck.* Springfield, Ill., 1967.

Teeters, Negley K. *Scaffold and Chair.* Philadelphia, 1963.

White, Walter F. *Rope and Faggot: A Biography of Judge Lynch.* New York, 1929.

CHAPTER X

Treatment Versus Punishment

I. THE NEW ORIENTATION

OUR entire system of criminal jurisprudence is wrong-headed and unscientific because, in the first place, it rests upon the fundamental assumption of the primary importance of detecting guilt and adjusting the punishment to the crime. Modern criminology insists, on the contrary, that guilt with respect to a particular crime is often far from the most important point at issue. The commission of the specific crime charged is relevant in the case only insofar as it helps to throw light upon the nature of the personality of the accused person. The real question is whether or not the individual accused is a fit person to be at large before or after adequate treatment.

Even more important, modern criminology entirely repudiates the objective of making the punishment fit the crime. In the first place, our modern knowledge of the nature of criminal conduct renders the whole conception of punishment archaic. It is as futile and foolish to punish a criminal as it is to punish a person suffering from a physical or mental disease. In the second place, it is not the crime which needs to be dealt with, but the criminal. Hence, modern criminology supplants the old slogan of making the punishment fit the crime by the new objective of making the treatment fit the criminal. If we accept this view of the matter, it becomes clear that the treatment must be carried out by those competent in the premises: obviously, physiologists, physicians, psychiatrists and sociologists, but not lawyers, except in so far as they are, like Dr. Kirchwey or Mr. Darrow, criminologists. The diagnosis and treatment of the criminal is a highly technical medical and sociological problem for which the lawyer is rarely any better fitted than a real estate agent or a plumber. We shall ultimately come to admit that society has been as unfortunate in handing over criminals to lawyers and judges in the past as it once was in entrusting medicine to shamans and astrologers, and surgery to barbers. A hundred years ago we allowed lawyers and judges to have the same control of the insane classes as they still exert over the criminal groups, but we now recognize that insanity is a highly diversified and complex medical problem which we entrust to properly trained experts in the field of neurology and psychiatry. We may hope that in another hundred years the treatment of the criminal will be equally thoroughly and willingly submitted to medical and sociological experts.

II. A SCIENTIFIC PLAN FOR THE REPRESSION OF CRIME

Some who accept the validity of our indictment of the modern prison system might ask what we have to substitute. The answer is easy in theory, but the possibility of introducing a rational system of treating the criminal in the face of public ignorance and bias is highly remote. Since crime is a socio-medical problem, we should as in general medicine, lay primary stress upon preventative therapy. As far as possible, we should prevent the procreation of types likely to be unusually predisposed toward anti-social conduct. Here we have the field of negative eugenics and sterilization. Juvenile courts and child guidance clinics, thoroughly linked up with the public-school system, will enable us to discover sufficiently early those types which, through an unfavorable environment, with resulting bad habits, or through various nervous or mental difficulties, seem headed toward a criminal career. By careful attention to these cases we may certainly save many from disaster and fit them for constructive and law-abiding social existence. Highly unfortunate living conditions, which generate those bad habits that lead to crime, should be rapidly and thoroughly eliminated. This would require not only better housing conditions, better facilities for recreation, and better educational methods, but also such a fundamental reorganization of economic life and motives as would lead to the possibility for every able-bodied individual to earn a decent livelihood.

In the case of those convicted of crime, all who have been guilty of the less serious types of crimes, or who, upon examination, do not reveal highly defective, abnormal, or dangerous personalities, should not be incarcerated in any type of institution, but should be released on probation under a suspended sentence. In this situation they should have the most careful and sympathetic assistance of psychiatric clinics and well trained social workers, from whom both practical guidance and encouragement to reform may be secured. Thoroughgoing examination of those who seem to require incarceration should be provided. Such obviously non-reformable types as low-grade feeble-minded prisoners, and paretic and other types of insane convicts suffering from incurable psychoses, should be remanded to the proper institutions for permanent segregation, irrespective of the crime committed.

We would then have remaining the group which could not be safely entrusted at the outset of probation and apparently does not require permanent segregation. This group should be classified and subjected to the desirable form of medical treatment and social reëducation. Physical health should be restored and maintained at the highest possible level. Neuroses and psychoses should be treated through psycho-analysis and other psychiatric methods. Social reëducation along such lines as Mr. Osborne's *Mutual Welfare League* should be introduced in order to create the proper social habits of trust and responsibility. The possibility of maintaining one's self through lawful modes of activity should be assured by the teaching of a trade or profession to those not already thus equipped. After such a course of treatment the individual convict would then be in a position to be subjected to experimental release. There should be as thorough after-care for the discharged criminal as now accompanies the release of the inmate of a psychopathic hospital. Every effort should be made to secure employment for the discharged convict and to bring about adequate readjustment to normal social existence. In the case of a relapse, as demonstrated by the repetition of criminal conduct, the individual should be taken back for further treatment. If repeated experiments in this respect prove unsuccessful, then the individual should be permanently segregated.

Such a scheme as we have outlined above would really secure the reformation and social protection which the present prison system assumes to produce but fails to achieve to any significant degree whatever. In the case of those on probation it would provide guidance and encouragement toward reformation and would avert the degrading influence of jail or prison life. By bringing about the permanent segregation of non-reformable types, irrespective of the seriousness of the crime, we should protect society permanently from the potentially dangerous group who are today released to prey upon society. With respect to the third group, those subjected to treatment in institutions set aside for the handling of the criminal classes, every expedient and device to bring about reformation would be actually applied. The failure of such efforts would be adequate indication of the necessity for that permanent segregation which would give complete protection from the recidivist criminal who now carries on his depredations as long as his life goes on.

In the place of the contemporary prison, which does nothing to reform the convict and does everything to degrade and destroy his personality, we should have institutions presided over by socially-minded experts who would do everything possible to promote reformation and nothing to produce mental, moral, and physical disintegration. The present system neither protects nor reforms, while the method proposed would achieve both to the highest possible degree consistent with the defects inherent in any scheme devised by man or applied to human material.

If it be objected that this plan would be so pleasant that penal institutions would be swamped with voluntary applicants, one might ask the relevant question as to whether any great mobs have yet been observed clamoring for admission to state hospitals for the insane or to colonies for the feeble-minded? The prison of the future, whether called a prison or not, would bear a close resemblance in its objectives and methods to the better state hospitals for the insane which now exist. Certainty of apprehension and treatment according to scientific methods would act as a deterrent to a far greater degree than the present slight prospect of subjection to contemporary prison savagery, and it would possess the enormous advantage of bringing the resources of modern science to bear upon the task of protecting society from the anti-social classes.

Those who advocate a continuation and increase of the savage contemporary system of repression as the best method of eliminating crime, point to the Baumes Laws in New York State and to the allegation—possibly true—that these laws have notably diminished crime. In the first place, we cannot be sure that they have actually diminished anti-social action, as many may have been driven into borderline activity not yet branded as overtly criminal and many have simply left New York. The one great lesson of criminological history is that severity of punishment is not an adequate deterrent, as proved by such facts as that the public hangings of pick-pockets had to be discontinued in England because of the great increase of pocket-picking at such occasions. There is no doubt that severe punishments have some effect. The prevalence of pneumonia could probably be reduced by making its contraction a crime punishable by imprisonment for five years, but one would not contend on that account that this would be the best possible preventive therapy for this particular disorder.

Let us see what actually happens under the dispensation of the Baumes Laws. In order to receive the life sentence, which is the core of the Baumes Laws, the offender must have been convicted four times of a felony. Under average circumstances this would mean that such a person had committed from ten to one hundred crimes. Hence his depredations upon society would be enormous before the protection—expensive to maintain—is secured at all.

Under the system which we have outlined as the program of scientific criminology the protection would have been secured much earlier and at less expense. In the first place, most of the fourth offenders would, under a scientifically guided system, never become criminals but would be detected in childhood and either cured by clinics or segregated in the proper institutions. In the case of those committing crime we should not wait until the fourth offence, but would take the individual in hand at approximately his first offence and either treat or segregate him so as to render him no longer a menace to society. We cannot expect one hundred per cent success with such a scheme, but we should escape the near hundred per cent failure of the present system.

III. The Psychiatric Approach to the Treatment of Crime

Having presented briefly the position of the newer criminology to the effect that vindictive punishment must be supplanted by enlightened treatment, we may now turn to a consideration of the most promising method of treating crime in the light of modern knowledge, namely, the application of psychiatry to the diagnosis of the criminal personality and the reconstruction of the criminal.

Critics of psychiatry have often extended reference to a brisk and airy article on psychiatry by one Ralph Coghlan in the *American Mercury* for May, 1928. The weakness of the *Mercury* article was nowhere more apparent than in the analysis of psychiatry in the courtroom. Special capital was made out of the fact that Dr. Healy stated in the Loeb-Leopold trial that something which Dr. White had written fifteen years ago should be scrapped today. This, however, means nothing more than that psychiatry, like other phases of medicine, is in a state of development. What have we done with manuals on surgical diagnosis, anaesthesia, serums and vaccines, syphilology and diabetes written a decade ago? The psychiatrists for the defense and prosecution in the Loeb-Leopold case are represented as in every way opposed and in diametrical disagreement as to the mental state of the accused. As an actual matter of fact, they were in essential agreement, with the exception of Dr. Krohn, and desired to hand in a joint and unanimous report. To this request Mr. Crowe refused to give his assent for obvious political reasons.

No doubt many fakirs have posed as psychiatrists, and many psychiatrists have injured the reputation of their professions by such excursions outside their professional bounds as Freud's adventures into ethnology, but the core of psychiatry and mental hygiene is certainly sound and is something of which medicine and social science may alike be proud. No other socio-medical movement of our generation holds as much of promise for the relief of human suffering and a curative grip upon social ills.

The value of psychiatry to criminology and penology promises to be as great as the services which it has already rendered to medicine. It was recently the privilege of the writer to re-read Cesare Beccaria's classic essay on *Crimes and Punishments*. It seems that nearly all of the progress which criminology and penology has made since 1764 we owe to the psychiatrists, or certainly to the psychiatrists and mental testers taken altogether. With the exception of the psychiatric analysis of the genesis of the personality, there is little in contemporary criminology and penology which was not stated or foreshadowed by the Italian publicist in his influential brochure.

It should be made clear that the partial disrepute into which psychiatry has fallen in connection with criminology has been due to the handicaps which have been imposed upon it by courtroom procedure and the conventional rules of evidence. Science can function respectably only when devoted to the cause of establishing the truth, whereas criminal lawyers in the courtroom are frequently unable to win their case unless they obscure the truth. The psychiatrist in the courtroom can present his material only in the form of answers to questions put by the attorneys involved, which often means that he has no chance whatever of presenting his report in a complete or coherent manner. What can be done in this way by a lawyer to distort the reality is well illustrated by the aforementioned Loeb-Leopold case in which Mr. Crowe made his alienists on the stand appear to be in violent disagreement with Mr. Darrow's alienists, whereas two weeks before they had all desired to give official and public testimony to their fundamental agreement.

The psychiatrist, eager to put his scientific knowledge at the service of criminology, has been faced with a perplexing dilemma. As a scientist he could scarcely expect to escape from the procedure of the courtroom without humiliating lesions on his professional honor and technical standing. The only way he could report on the mental state of an accused person as a self-respecting scientist would be to submit a unified and complete statement, in the same manner as he would if called in hospital consultation. But any such procedure has been impossible in the courtroom, where the psychiatrist has been limited to answering carefully-selected questions put to him by lawyers who are as frequently interested in distorting the truth as they are in adducing and clarifying it. Scientifically speaking, then, the psychiatrist should have resolutely refused to defile himself through personal contact with the intellectual debasement inherent in conventional courtroom procedure. Yet, if he did this the possible educational influence which he might have on the community would be greatly reduced, and the value of psychiatry in revealing the multifarious causes of crime would be more or less permanently obscured. Therefore, we have had the unedifying spectacle of psychiatrists entering the courtroom and, through no intentional fault of their own, leaving the impression that there is no general agreement among them on any fundamental aspect of medical psychology and suggesting by implication that the most expert psychiatric opinion is as freely marketed as the services of a professional criminal lawyer. Thereupon, these very lawyers who have by their methods discredited psychiatry in the public mind denounce the psychiatrists for their vagueness, professional differences and vain pretensions.

The writer differs sharply from those who hold that psychiatry has no quarrel with the criminal law. To be sure, it has no quarrel with a rational and modernized brand of criminal law, such as might be drafted by men like Dean Roscoe Pound or Dr. George W. Kirchwey. Yet there is certainly a quarrel to the death between psychiatry and the conventional criminal law, which is based upon the theory of the criminal as a free moral agent and attempts awkwardly to allot a certain measure of punishment to a definite crime. The case of psychiatry and law is like that of science and religion; there is less quarrel if one defines law and religion in the right manner. Yet there is the same basic and fundamental divergence in assumptions and objectives between psychiatry and conventional criminal law as exists between the science of Einstein and the religion of John Roach Straton.

There would seem to be little possibility that psychiatry can be adapted to the conventional jury trial. In the first place, the legal definition of insanity, by which the court is guided, is an intellectual and moral conception which has today no medical significance whatever. The M'Naghten insanity test—the power to differentiate between right and wrong in an absolute and metaphysical sense—is foreign to the conceptions of the genesis and nature of the human personality held by dynamic psychology and psychiatry. There are a large number of insanities with different symptomatology. Many of these are emotional disorders with little or no impairment of intellectual faculties. The *reductio ad absurdum* of the legal conception of insanity appeared in the recent Remus case in Ohio. Here the examining psychiatrists informed the court that by legal test Remus was sane and should be freed by the court, whereas by medical tests he was obviously insane and a highly dangerous person to the community, and should be permanently segregated for the social good. Fortunately, the judge took the medical rather than the legal point of view, only to have his wise action reversed by the Superior Court. Hence, the testimony of psychiatrists in the courtroom, even if it could be given freely and fully, would be in large part invalidated by the fact that the court and the psychiatrist are moving in quite different realms of thought and definition. The court is proceeding on the theological-metaphysical basis of the criminal law, while a reputable psychiatrist is talking in terms of dynamic psychology and contemporary psychiatry.

In the second place, as we have already pointed out, the psychiatrist is prevented by conventional courtroom procedure from making a complete report on the case, so that his scientific knowledge is nullified by the limitations imposed upon its dissemination. Finally, even if the psychiatrist were able to present his material in a satisfactory form, and even if the court were guided by medical conceptions of "insanity," the effect of psychiatric testimony would be rendered futile in most cases because it deals with a technical subject far beyond the mental grasp of the average jury. Imagine the typical jury listening to diagnoses of a disorder set forth by a dozen eminent surgeons and then deciding as to which procedure should be followed in this treatment of a particular patient! And yet surgery is a very simple affair as compared to psychiatry. Therefore, psychiatry in the conventional courtroom: (1) represents the imperfect and misleading testimony of eminent experts which is nullified and perverted by the technicalities of the procedure under which it is divulged; (2) would be of little significance even if completely expounded, because it must be interpreted by incompetent and ignorant men; and

(3) has little or no relevance because the psychiatrist is dealing with medical considerations while the court is governed by theologico-metaphysical concepts derived from antiquity and the Middle Ages that have no more scientific standing and validity than witchcraft, astrology and alchemy. There is little prospect of exploiting psychiatry successfully in the courtroom until the criminal law squares itself with the scientific notion of human behavior, accepts medical conceptions of insanity, adopts the slogan of making the treatment fit the criminal, abolishes jury trial and hands the defendant over to a group of permanent paid experts solely interested in questions of medical fact and social protection.

The Briggs Law of 1921 in Massachusetts marked an enormous step in advance when it took the psychiatrist out of the humiliating and obstructing atmosphere of the courtroom and ordered him to make his examination of the defendant in a calm scientific manner and to submit his report in a complete form prior to the trial. Yet the results of a truly medical examination and report are likely to be nullified in large part as long as they are submitted to the ultimate decision of incompetent and uninformed juries and are governed by legal criteria of insanity which have little or no relation to medical facts.

Nevertheless, what can be done when we have an intelligent judge and no objection from interested counsel is well illustrated by the disposition of the case of Dr. Thierry in the spring of 1925 under the operation of the Briggs law. Here an insane murderer was brought before the court and jury, the report of the examining psychiatrists was read, the judge ordered a verdict of "not guilty by reason of insanity," and within two hours from his appearance in the courtroom Dr. Thierry was on his way to the State Hospital for the Criminal Insane at Bridgewater. Contrast this with the weeks devoted to the Loeb-Leopold case, in which the psychiatrists were as fully agreed as to the mental state of the defendants as they were in the case of Dr. Thierry but were prevented from functioning honestly by the conventional savagery of State's Attorney Crowe. In any event, the Briggs Law represents the first essential step in putting psychiatry at the service of the courts in any effective manner. What we need next is a legal conception of insanity which squares with the medical attitude and the substitution of a permanent body of examining criminologists for the archaic jury system.

Until the day comes when criminal procedure in the courts dealing with adult criminals is based upon science rather than tradition and superstition, the humanitarian and reformer in the field of criminology and penology must concentrate his attention upon introducing as much psychiatry as he is able in those aspects of our criminal procedure which are most accessible to scientific procedure. Here, obviously, the greatest promise lies in the juvenile courts. There is no scientific reason why the causation of criminal conduct in the juvenile should be regarded as in any way different in principle of procedure from criminality in the adult, but humanitarian considerations have, fortunately, opened up a field for constructive work here which is still blocked in the courts dealing with adults. Society is willing to permit, on the basis of sentimental sympathy, a procedure with juveniles which it still illogically denies to most adults. We often have in the same courthouse the strange spectacle of a juvenile court judge, operating without a jury and taking the advice of psychiatrists and social workers as to the nature of the defendant and the best mode of handling his case, while in an adjoining room the conventional criminal session for adults is grinding away on the basis of conceptions and procedure compatible with the civilization of Hammurabi, Pericles, Pontius Pilate, Charlemagne or Philip Augustus.

Hence, the scientific criminologists should concentrate with especial vigor upon the campaign to create an adequate system of juvenile courts where psychiatry can come into its own with no restrictions imposed by the dead-hand of archaic juristic conceptions and procedure. To make the operation of the juvenile courts most effective, they should not be limited to the treatment of youth already detected in flagrant commission of crimes. They should be linked up with child-guidance clinics and the public school systems, so as to enable psychiatrists and social workers to detect and treat problem children before they enter actively upon a career of crime. We are happy to be able to report that far more notable progress exists in this respect today than in regard to putting courts for adult criminals upon a scientific foundation.

The juvenile courts represent almost the only place where psychiatry can function freely with respect to the handling of the accused in the courtroom, but much may be expected from greater emphasis upon the introduction of psychiatry into the treatment of the criminal, once he is out of the clutches of the judges and lawyers. In other words, ever greater effort should be made to introduce psychiatry effectively into the prisons, reformatories and houses of correction. This would require a complete reconstruction of the personnel of penitentiary and reformatory administration. The conventional warden, with his brutal subordinates, is an admirable and appropriate adjunct to the conventional judge who administers the traditional barbarities in accordance with the notion of making the punishment fit the crime.

If psychiatry is to dominate penology, then the officers of penitentiaries and reformatories must be medical men, to no less a degree than the staffs of state hospitals for the insane are today. The keepers and guards of the present dispensation would, under such a régime, be reduced to the status of the humble attendants in state hospitals, with no ultimate authority except discipline. To be operated with any degree of success such a system would have to rest upon the support of an adequate indeterminate sentence law, so that the ultimate freedom of the convict could be determined by the medical officials of the penitentiary, in the same way that the superintendent of a state hospital for the insane now decides the liberation of his patients. And the parole system of penitentiaries would come to resemble the system of after-care now employed by state hospitals.

A third field where the outlook for the psychiatric approach is especially promising is that of probation. As we come to understand that institutional treatment, particularly in the modern prison, is disastrous to most of the participants, we shall endeavor to treat as many criminals as possible outside of prison walls. For certain types, which may be safely dealt with in a non-institutional setting, probation presents many advantages. As it is the function of the probation officers to promote social readjustment, they will necessarily depend greatly upon psychiatry which is veritably the science of social and individual readjustment. No probation officer can be regarded as well trained who has not been grounded in the essentials of the psychiatric approach to social work and criminology. Moreover, probation officers should work hand in hand with trained psychiatrists in dealing with all cases which need special and technical care. In many ways probation work offers more of a scope to the psychiatric technique than courts or institutions, because it is less hampered by legal and physical limitations. The probation officer has wide independence in action and can make use of the large variety of psychiatric agencies that may deal with individuals not confined in institutions or subject to court rules. In particular can the probation officer exploit the resources of the child guidance bureaus and the psychiatric clinics. A wider use of probation under the direction of more adequate and better trained probation officers may be the first significant step which we can take to offset the disastrous effects of our prisons and reformatories in their bungling efforts to repress crime.

It is frequently alleged by hard-boiled critics of scientific criminology that courts and institutions manned by psychiatrists will have no deterrent influence whatever; that our courtrooms will be packed by those curious to be examined by expert boards and that our penitentiaries or hospitals for criminals will be crowded to the doors by eager applicants for residential facilities therein. Actual observation affords little ground for such apprehension. In the few places where delinquents have been offered the alternative of going before the conventional courtroom or before a psychiatric examining board they and their lawyers have tended overwhelmingly to prefer to take their chances before a judge and jury. The record of state hospitals affords no evidence that such institutions have been mobbed by eager and curious petitioners for housing accommodations. Such pronouncements are on an intellectual level with the frequent assertions of learned New York City justices that the archaic and obsolete state penitentiary at Ossining is the best appointed country club in the Hudson River highlands. That medical superintendents of such reconstructed institutions for delinquents would prove over-sentimental and release dangerous criminals before there was any evidence of reformation is belied by our whole experience with state hospitals for the insane, where superintendents have usually been criticized, if at all, for their extreme care and conservatism in releasing patients. Indeed, we may refer the sceptical to the February, 1928, issue of *Plain Talk* in which Mr. P. H. Skinner, with what justice the writer cannot say, severely criticized the eminent superintendent of the St. Elizabeth's Hospital, Dr. William A. White, for his failure to release patients with sufficient alacrity.

While we are emphasizing the necessity of stressing the introduction of psychiatry into the juvenile courts and the institutions for the treatment of delinquents as the most promising avenue of immediate application of science to the repression of crime and reformation of the criminals, it is necessary to pursue a parallel campaign for the gradual but certain projection of psychiatry into the procedure as regards the adult criminal. The most essential thing here is to educate the public as to the socio-medical nature of the problem of crime. We are now willing to allow medical men to care for the mental defectives and the insane, but the fact that we are complacent in doing so today is a result of a century or more

of education emphasizing the medical nature of these problems and disorders. As soon as the public comes to regard
crime as a socio-medical problem, we shall have little trouble
in getting general consent to hand over its treatment to psychiatrists and sociologists.

The greatest obstacle to successful public education on this
point resides in the popular theologico-metaphysical conception of man as a free moral agent, capable of arbitrary self-
determination of conduct irrespective of physical ancestry or
social experience. We must educate the public to accept the
scientific view of the socio-biological determination of conduct, which at once undermines the whole basis of the conventional theory of punishment and opens the way for the
socio-medical treatment of the person who commits an anti-
social act. We must not, however, underestimate the difficulty
which we shall meet in uprooting the archaic free-moral-agent
conception. One of Mr. Mencken's sound contributions to
criminology is to be found in his *Prejudices Sixth Series* (pp.
227 ff.) where he maintains, quite correctly, that the greatest
popular opposition to scientific criminology will be found to
reside in the persistence and determination with which the
average man will attempt to retain the free moral agent doctrine of conduct. The writer, in the course of a wide lecturing
experience on criminology, fully corroborates Mr. Mencken's
contention. Everywhere, except among scientific groups, the
chief opposition to scientific criminology arises from its fundamental and inevitable espousal of the psychological conception of determinism in conduct. Yet, if we have separated the
populace from the belief that insane persons are victims of
diabolical possession, it is not likely to prove a hopeless task to
convince them that the criminal is the victim of his heredity,
his social surroundings, or both.

While discoursing thus about psychiatry and criminals, it
is necessary to call attention to the fact that thus far psychiatry has been applied to convicts, namely, those criminals
who have been apprehended and convicted. In the United

States we know, from the comparative statistics of crimes committed and criminals convicted, that the convicts number less than one-fourth of the criminals. Therefore, with our present system for the arrest and conviction of criminals, psychiatry, even if unhampered, could not well be applied to more than a fraction of the total number of criminals. How we shall be able to get at the large majority of the criminals who are never arrested opens up interesting problems. A first step would be the improvement of our police system, so that we might apprehend an ever larger number of offenders. No method of examination and treatment, however modern and advanced, can well be of much effect in repressing crime unless we are able to apprehend the offenders and turn them over to experts. As to whether we shall ever be able to tolerate or approve a psychiatric census of the population is a subject for speculation alone at the present time. Certainly it will follow by a long period that distant date when we shall give psychiatry free-rein in dealing with apprehended and convicted criminals. Perhaps the nearest thing to a psychiatric census practically attainable, and something which would serve the purpose of crime repression nearly as well, would be the above-mentioned linking up of the juvenile court and the child-guidance clinic with the public-school system.

IV. The Outlook

In conclusion, we may consider the question as to whether there is any hope of introducing a scientific mode of coping with the crime problem. It may be answered at the outset that there is not the slightest possibility of any comprehensive and thoroughgoing plan being adopted as a whole. The best that can be hoped for is piecemeal progress. Occasionally, we shall get the invaluable exact statistical information as to the extent of crime and the modes of dealing with it in certain important metropolitan areas. Examples of such progress are the recent survey of the crime situation in Cleveland, carried out under the direction of the Harvard Law School faculty, the Missouri Crime Survey, the Illinois Crime Survey and the proposed investigation of the crime situation in Boston under the auspices of the group of progressive lawyers in the Harvard Law School. Negative eugenics and sterilization may slowly and gradually be introduced for application to the lowest grades of human derelicts. Rather extensive progress may be hoped for with respect to child guidance clinics and the growing reliance of judges in juvenile courts upon the expert advice of psychiatrists and sociologists. From time to time a progressive judge in a criminal court may be induced to stretch the law and practice sufficiently to take into consideration the advice of medical and psychological experts, with respect to both the conduct of the trial and the determination of sentence. Probation may be extended and its service become more competent. A few progressive states, following the lead of Massachusetts, may provide for the mental and physical examination of criminals and ultimately make some practical use of the information thus obtained. A few intelligent and independent prison wardens may in the future be converted to some such scheme of inmate self-government as that devised at the George Junior Republic and applied for the first time in a penal institution for adults by Mr. Osborne. The progress of education in the field of criminology may slowly but surely bring society to a point where it will be as willing to hand over the control of the criminal to experts as it has become in the last century to entrust the treatment of the insane to those technically competent in the premises. We may gradually increase the number of wardens who are, like Dr. W. N. Thayer, trained psychiatrists specially fitted to deal with delinquents.

To the writer the whole matter seems primarily to be the issue as to whether this piecemeal progress in applying the essentials of criminal science will be able to outrun the increasing incitement to crime inevitable in the growing complexities and temptations of contemporary social organization. If we can introduce science into the repression of crime more rapidly than contemporary civilization increases the crime rate, we may look forward with optimism to the future. If the ignorance of the public and the bigotry, intolerance and stupidity of lawyers and judges so obstructs the progress of intelligence and science in the field of the repression of crime that the increase of crime comes to be markedly greater than the advance of science in this field, we may well expect the ultimate extinction of the social order and the gradual disappearance of human society. Hence, the worst enemies of society would appear to the modern criminologist to be, not so much the degraded felon as the conventional jurist and lawyer who, consciously or unconsciously, is doing his level best, through defending archaic methods, to increase the number and permanence of the delinquent class in contemporary society.

SELECTED REFERENCES

Barnes, Harry Elmer. *The Repression of Crime.* 1926; Reprinted Montclair, N. J., 1969.

Beckhart, I., and Brown, W. *The Violators.* New York, 1954.

Brasol, Boris L. *The Elements of Crime.* 2d ed. 1931; Reprinted Montclair, N. J., 1969.

Burr, C. W. "Crime from a Psychiatrist's Point of View." *Journal of Criminal Law and Criminology,* February 1926.

Burt, Cyril L. *The Young Delinquent.* New York, 1933.

Chute, Charles L., and Bell, Marjorie. *Crime, Courts, and Probation.* New York, 1956.

Darrow, Clarence S. *Crime: Its Causes and Treatment.* 1922; Reprinted Montclair, N. J., 1972.

Eliot, Thomas D. *The Juvenile Court and the Community.* New York, 1914.

Ellington, John R. *Protecting Our Children from Criminal Careers.* New York, 1948.

Glueck, Bernard. "Psychiatric Aims in the Field of Criminology." *Mental Hygiene,* October 1918.

Glueck, Sheldon S. *Mental Disorder and the Criminal Law.* Boston, 1925.

Glueck, Sheldon S., and Glueck, Eleanor T. *500 Criminal Careers.* New York, 1930.

Glueck, Sheldon S., and Glueck, Eleanor T., eds. *Preventing Crime.* New York, 1936.

Healy, William. *The Individual Delinquent.* 1915; Reprinted Montclair, N. J., 1969.

Healy, William, and Bronner, Augusta F. *Delinquents and Criminals: Their Making and Unmaking.* 1926; Reprinted Montclair, N. J., 1969.

Healy, William, and Bronner, Augusta F. *Reconstructing Behavior in Youth.* New York, 1929.

Hoag, Ernest B., and Williams, Edward Huntington. *Crime, Abnormal Minds and the Law.* Indianapolis, 1923.

Lindner, Robert M., and Seliger, Robert V. *Handbook of Correctional Psychology.* New York, 1947.

Osborne, Thomas M. *Prisons and Common Sense.* Philadelphia, 1924.

Overholser, W. "Psychiatric Service in Penal and Reformatory Institutions and Criminal Courts in the United States." *Mental Hygiene,* October 1928.

Parsons, Philip A. *Crime and the Criminal.* New York, 1926.

Platt, Charles. *The Riddle of Society.* New York, 1926.

Schlapp, Max G., and Smith, Edward H. *The New Criminology.* New York, 1928.

Smith, M. Hamblin. *The Psychology of the Criminal.* London, 1922.

Stromberg, E. T. *Crimes of Violence.* Boulder, Colo., 1949.

Stutsman, Jesse. *Curing the Criminal.* New York, 1926.

Tannenbaum, Frank. *Wall Shadows.* New York, 1922.

Tappan, Paul W., ed. *Contemporary Correction.* New York, 1951.

Teeters, Negley K. *Penology from Panama to Cape Horn.* Philadelphia, 1946.

Teeters, Negley K. *World Penal Systems.* Philadelphia, 1944.

Thomas, William I., and Thomas, D. S. *The Child in America.* New York, 1928.

Van Waters, Miriam. *Youth in Conflict.* New York, 1925.

Index

Adventures of an Outlaw, 80

Allen, Stephen, 135

America, 105, 111, 121; torture in, 16

American Inst. Criminal Law and Criminology, 212

American Mercury, 34, 270

Andrews, W., classic works of, i, 235

Apostles, Twelve, 27

Architecture, in jails, 194

Ashe, Stanley, one of best wardens, 175

Assize of Clarendon, 26

Auburn prison, discipline at, 136; erection of state prison at, 133; rioting in, 216; Roosevelt's investigation of, 216; Warden Osborne's plan, 214

Australia, first English penal colony, 74, 76

Automobile, number of casualties, 263

Background, intellectual, of the reform movement, 93

Barlow, Sheriff, J. C., 23

Bates, Sanford, 175

Baumes Law, 170, 190, 269

Beach, John H., 133

Beaumont, Gustave Auguste de, 142, 202

Beccaria, and his work, 95-99, 104, 107, 120, 128, 271

Beevor, Sir Thomas, 103

Beheading, 234

Bentham, 95, 100, 104, 121, 128

Bethea, Jack, 229

Biology, rise of modern, 1

Biological defects, elimination of, 262

Birkenhead, Lord, 84

Blackmar, F. W., 221

Blood-feud, 45; mitigation of the principle of, 48

Blouet, Guillaume, 144

Boddy, Luther, 23

Boiling, 241

Boldrewood, Rolf, 80

Bolingbroke, Henry St. John, 94

Books, corrupt, 120

Booth, E., 229

Bootleggers, 260

Bradford, William, 104, 107, 120

Brandeis, Justice, 19, 188

Branding, 62

Bridgewater, state hospital at, 275

Briggs, Dr. Vernon, 206

Briggs Law, 275

Brissot, Girondist leader, 122

Britten, William, 134, 135

Brockway, Z. R., 146, 210

Brunner, H., 25

Brutality, police, 16-24; in prison, 184

Bryan, William J., 246

Burke, Frederick, 252

Burr, Prof. George Lincoln, iii

Burying alive, 241

Buxton, Sir Thomas Foxwell, 101, 102

Bygone punishments, 6, 10, 235

Calvert, E. R., 255

Camp, lime-burners' convict, 82; tent, 161

Campanella, John, 21

Canute, age of, 231

Capital punishment, 108, 231-264; abolition of, 263; historic methods in administering, 231; in the light of scientific criminology, 248; obligatory in six states, 246

Capitalists, and convict labor, 219

Carthaginians, 232

Census, psychiatric, 281
Chain gang, 160
Charcot, J. M., 205
Charles II, 29
Charlemagne, 276
Chicago, 260
Children, 119, 152; on prison hulks, 119
Christian view of man, 94
Christians, in Middle Ages, 8
Chubb, Thomas, 94
Clarke, Marcus, 80, 90
Clarkson, Matthew, 133
Clement, Pope XI, 122
Clinics, psychiatric, 216, 223, 266, 267
Clinton, De Witt, 132, 141
Code, abolition of criminal, 6
Coghlan, Ralph, 270
College extension, for prisoners, 214
Colony, Australia, first English penal, 74, 76; Devil's Island, 90; French Guiana penal, 88-91; Siberia, 91
Combe, George, 143, 145, 211
Commutation of sentence, 145, 209, 210, 259
Comparison, of convicts sent to America and Australia, 77
Comparison of homicide rates, 256
Compurgation, method of, 8
Condemned to Devil's Island, 90
Condorcet, 95, 121
Contagious diseases, 166-168
Control, public, of private wrongs, 51; of crime, 52.
Convict labor, 159, 213
Convict hulks, 115
Convict Life, 59, 80
Convict personality, how prisons demoralize, 170
Convicts, 71, 74, 80, 115, 223; mental life of, 108; number in prisons, 263; personalities, 170
Copernicus, 93
Corporal punishment, 56-66; barbarous methods abolished in

America, 111; methods of inflicting, 56, 57; persistence of in conjunction with imprisonment, 150
County jail, nuisance of, 191
Court of law, establishing of, 9
Crawford, William, 103, 143
Cray, John, 135
Crime, confession of, 10; detection, 7, 36; diabolical possession in, 4; identified with sin, 5; problem of coping with, 281; psychiatric approach to the treatment of, 270; public control of, 10; and punishment in early society, 38, 40; punished, 225; theories of, 1; waves of, 3
Crime and the Criminal, 208
Crimes and Punishments, 271
Criminal, physical stigmata, 2; conduct of, 2; scientific treatment of, 7; trials, 188
Criminal code, transformation in America, 104
Criminal law, 93; abuses attacked, 95; reform of 93; reform of, in England, 99; reform of, in America, 120
Criminal pedagogy, 172
Criminals, 280
Criminality, not reduced by severe punishments, 6
Criminology, 3
Criminologists, 35
Crofton, Sir Walter, 76, 143, 145, 210, 211
Crowe, Attorney, 276
Crucibles of Crime, 190, 193
Custom, 38

Dannemora, 229
Darrow, Clarence, 249, 265
Davenport, Circuit Judge, W. D., 23
Degenerates, 261
Deists, British, 94, 204
Delinquents, non-institutional care of, 223
Dementia-praecox, 4

Demetz, Frédéric Auguste, 144, 202
Democracy in America, 142
Detective service, 35
Deterrence, 5
Detroit News, 155
Development, cultural, 1
Diderot, 95, 104
Discipline, prison, 136, 155, 163, 168; at Norfolk Island, 209
Dix, Dorothea Lynde, 141, 205
Dostoyevsky, Feodor, 91
Drowning, 232
Ducking-stool, 65
Dugan, Mrs. Eva, 237
Dugdale, R. L., 221
Dumont, Pierre, E. L., 101
Duncomb's Trials (1665), 27
Duroix, M., 59
Dwight, Louis, 139, 204
Dwight, Theodore, 210

Eastern penitentiary, 229
Eddy, Thomas, 132
Edmunds, Sterling, E., 34
Education, program of, 101
Electrocution, 243; adopted by 15 states, 247
Elmira reformatory, 76; system, origin and development of, 141, 144, 212; now archaic, 148
Emerton, Prof. Ephraim, 49
England, criminal population (1830), 6; (1885), 6; jails in, 100; reform of criminal law in, 99
Environment, 38, 251
Essay on Crimes and Punishments, 96
Eugenics, negative, 282
Exile, 43
Explanations, psychological, 2

Farms, county, 199
Feeble-minded, 205
First offenders, 146, 203
Fishman, Joseph F., 193, 195
Five Hundred Criminal Careers, 171

Flogging, 56, 150, 155
Folk, J. W., 188
For the Term of His Natural Life, 80, 90
Foulke, William Parker, 141
Foxley, 85-88
Franck, Harry A., 89
Franks murder case, 22
Franklin, Benjamin, 121, 126
Freud, Dr. Sigmund, 205, 271
Friends, Society of, 66, 104, 125
Frye, Elizabeth, 102
Fundamentalism, 249

Gaertner, Dr. Frederic, 235
Galen, 250
Galley-slaves, 68, 115
Gang wars, 253
Geoffry Hamlin, 80
George Junior Republic, 203, 214, 282
Ghent, prison in Belgium, 122
Gianini, Jean, 260
Gillespie, Prof. James E., 73
Gillette, Chester, 260
Glover, James, 133
Glueck, Bernard, 148, 205
Glueck, Eleanor, 171
Glueck, S. S., 171
Gods, placating the, 4
Goddard, H. H., 205, 221
Gray, Judd, 243, 260
Grimhaven, 229
Griscom, Prof. John, 132, 202
Guillotine, 25
Guilt, historic methods of ascertaining, 1; in early society, 7
Gunmen, 252

Hanging, 236, 237
Harvard Law School, 281
Haynes, Gideon, 141
Healy, W., 208, 270
Helvetius, 95, 96
Henry II, 26
Henry, VIII, 236
Herbert, Lord, of Cherbury, 94
Heredity and Human Progress, 261
Hickman, 260
Hill, Frederick, 145, 211

Hill, Matthew D., 145, 211
Hippocrates, 250
Hippolyte Vilain XIII, 122
History of Penal Methods, i, 71,
    75, 103
Historical Essay Concerning Witch-
    craft, 249
Hobhouse, L. T., 8, 10
Homosexuality, 77, 179
Hopkins, Senator, 133, 135
Hospitals, in prison, 185; for crim-
    inal insane, 205; for insane, 205
House of Refuge, first in U. S.,
    202; New York, 210; Phila-
    delphia, 210
House of the Dead, The, 91
Houses of Refuge, 201, 202
Howard, John, 99, 120; and Euro-
    pean origins of prison reform,
    122; letter to, 124
Hubbell, Gaylord, 146, 210
Huggins, 85
Hughes, C. E., 188
Hughes, Dr. Llewellyn, 233
Humanity and its Problems, 233
Hume, David, 94, 96, 121
Huntingdon reformatory, 213
Hulburt, Harry L., warden, 155
Hutchinson, Francis, 249

Idleness, in prison, 221
Imprisonment, effect of, 6, 174; ef-
    fect on mind of prisoner, 172;
    for debt, 193; for life, 258;
    nature and evils of, 150
Incarceration, 5
In Prison, 190
Inmate self-government, 213
Innocent III, 26
Inquisitio, beginning of the, 25
Insanity, 275
Insanities, 273
Introduction to the Middle Ages,
    49
Ives, George, 1, 52, 63, 103, 116

Jail, 195; county, in Albany, N.
    Y., 196; in Maryland Free State,

197; in South Carolina, 198;
    women in, in U. S., 198
James I, 29
Janet, P., 205
Jay, John, 132
Jefferson, Thomas, 122
Johnston, Governor, 168
Julius, Dr. Nicolaus Henrich, 144
Jurata, 26
Jurists, 212
Jurisprudence, 38, 121, 141;
    American reaction against crimi-
    nal, 105; changes in criminal,
    225; criminal, 53, 95, 104,
    107, 131, 258, 265; English,
    105; French interested in
    criminal, 141; Roman, 25
Jurisdiction, criminal, 190
Jury, trial by, 9, 25; English,
    26-28; elimination of, 262
Justice, distribution of, 9
Juvenile courts, 277, 279
Juvenile delinquents, 201
Juvenile probation laws, 224

"Kangaroo Court," 178
King, power of, 54
Kingsley, Henry, 80
Kirchwey, Dr. George W., 217,
    218, 265, 273
Krohn, W. O., 271
Ku Klux Klan, 30, 233

Labor, prison, 146; development
    of, 219
Labor organizations, 220
Lateran Council (1215), 9
Lavoisier, A. L., 93
Law, custom and religion in primi-
    tive society, 38
Lawes, L. E., Warden, 255
Leopold, N., 4, 22, 188, 260
Lethal gas, 245
Lieber, Francis, 141
Livingston, Edward, 141
Locke, John, 94
Loeb, R., 4, 22, 188, 260
Lombroso, Cesare, theory of, 1
London Daily Mail, 243

London Review, 209
London Society for Improvement of Prison Discipline, 143
Lowie, Prof. Robert H., 47
Lownes, C., 120
Lucas, J. M. Charles, 142, 145
Lynds, Capt. Elam, 135

Mackintosh, Sir James, 101, 102
Maconochie, Capt. Alexander, 76, 143, 145, 209
Maitland, F. W., 25
Manley, George, 238
Man's Judgment of Death, 256
Marett, R. R., Prof., 39
de Marsangy, Bonneville, 145, 211
Martin, E. D., 186
Matthews, T. S., 32
McAllister, James, 23
McCann, A. W., 66
McCoy, 85-88
McCulloch, 221
McGregor, Dr. Robert, 156
McKim, Dr. C., 261
Mencken, H. L., 188, 249, 280
Mental Hygiene, 206
Metaphysics, 1
Middle Ages, 25, 47, 68, 116, 154, 233, 234, 242.
Middleton, Conyers, 94
Miller, Elijah, 133
Missouri State Prison, 152
Mithridates, 232
Montesinos, 146
Montesquieu, 95,122
Moral Philosophy, 211
More, Sir Thomas, 69
Murder, 109; first degree, 109; manslaughter, 109; second degree, 109
Mutilation, 150, 246; a type of punishment, 60
Mutual Welfare League, 214; built up by Warden Thomas Mott Osborne, 214, 267; discipline of convicts, 215; employment bureau, 215; rules of discipline, 215

Neuroses, 267

Neurosis, compulsion, 4
Newcastle, 81
Newgate prison, 137
New Jersey state prison, 151
Newton, 93
New Republic, 19
New York Nation, 18
New York Times, 22
New York World, 20, 89, 217, 229, 243
Niles, Blair, 90
Norfolk Island, 76-80, 145
Normans, 26

Obermaier, 146
Oglethorpe, J., 203
O'Hare, Kate, 165; brutality exposed by, 185; description of conditions in Missouri state penitentiary, 165-168; description of conditions in women's department of a state penitentiary, 179-181
Oppenheimer, Dr., 39, 47
Orient, death penalty in, 232
Orientation, the new, 265
Osborne, Thomas Mott, 2, 214; built up Mutual Welfare League at Auburn, 214
O'Toole, Father, 66
Overholser, Dr. Winfred, 206; conclusions of, 206-208

Paine, Tom, 94, 104, 121
Panopticon, 125
Pardoning, 133
Parks, G., New Jersey, 20
Parliamentary committee, report of, 119, 120
Parmenter, 263
Parole system, value of first noted, 211
Parsons, P. A., 208
Peel, R., 101
Penal institutions, 113, 172; Auburn, N. Y., 113
Penitentiary Systems of America, The, 144
Penitentiaries, erection of two in New York, 133; Atlanta, 175;

at Auburn, 133; Eastern and Western Pennsylvania, 168; Jackson, 156; Missouri state, 152, 165; Pentonville, 143; report on, 142; Sing Sing, 137; Wisconsin state, 176

Penn, William, 122, 202

Pennsylvania, 105, 125, 141; reform of criminal code of (1776), 104-111; system of prison discipline model for New York, 125; model for other countries, 144

Pennsylvania system, 104-111; adopted in Belgium (1838), 144; in Denmark (1846), 144; in England (1835), 144; in France, 144; in German and Prussian states, 144; in Holland (1851), 144; in Norway (1851), 144; in Sweden (1840), 144

Penology, 113, 138, 224; American, 154, 217; progress of, 201-229; progress in last century, 204

Pericles, 271

Persian Letters, 95

Philadelphia, center of American civilization, 121; Walnut Street jail, 129-132

Philadelphia Society for Alleviating the Miseries of Public Prisons, 123, 130, 132

Philadelphia Society for Assisting Distressed Prisoners, 126; constitution of, 127; first of great modern prison reform societies, 126

Philosophes, French, 94, 204

Pike, Classic works of, i

Pillory, 63

Pillsbury, Amos, 141

Pinel, P., 204

Plaia, Frank, 247

Plain Talk, 279

Poisoning, 232

Police system, 35

Pollock, F., 25

Pontius Pilate, 276

Pope, Alexander, 94

Portsmouth naval prison, 218

Pound, Dean Roscoe, 273

Powers, Gersham, 141

Prejudices Sixth Series, 280

Prentiss, Mark O., 34

Price, Tom, 234

Primitive society, punishment of crime in, 42; improvement in, 47

Prison, 113, 122, 133; association in, 172; Atlanta, 175; Auburn, 133; employed in, 175; of the future, 269; Jackson, 156; Missouri state, 152, 165; Pentonville, 143; Sing Sing, 137; Wisconsin state, 176

Prisons, 113-148, 159; in colonial period, 114, 144; education in, 213; in England, 123; in Ireland, 210; in New York, 133; papal, 122; their rise and development, 113-148; in the South, 160-168; trade institutions in, 213; in United States, 155-165

Prison discipline and officers, 181

Prison Discipline Society of Boston, 139

Prison farms, 162

Prison hulks, 117

Prison labor, 159, 175, 213

Prison officials, improve personnel of, 212

Prison reform, 122; beginnings of in New York state, 131; in Philadelphia, 123

Prison system, origins of in America, 120; modern, 173; modern in Europe, 122

Prisoners, 71, 80, 108, 170, 263; pardoned, 133

Probation, 223

Progress, cultural, 93

Psychiatrist, 3, 206

Psychiatry, 3, 4, 270-272, 274; and crime, 204; progress in, 222

Psychiatric examination, most pro-

gressive step, 206
Psychology, 251; medical, 3
Psychosis, paranoid, 4
Punishment, 5, 163, 166, 183;
corporal, 47; impressive example, 5; through imprisonment, 6; and the public mind,
186; other sundry, 64; transportation, as a method, 68

Quakers, 66, 104, 146, 150
Questionnaires, to panel of jurymen, 30, 31

Rahway reformatory, 213
Rashleigh, Ralph, 81, 85-88
Ratigan, John E., iii
Rationale of Punishment, The, 47
Rationalists, 94, 96
Reform, prison, 104-111, 123,
125; societies, 141
Reformers, 76, 120, 123, 141,
144, 146
Repression of crime, a scientific plan
for, 266
Retaliation, 48
Revenge, social, 4, 41, 228
Revolution, American, 73
Riots, in prison, 169, 170; cause
of, 170
Robbery Under Arms, 80
Robinson, Prof. James Harvey, ii,
249
Rochefoucauld-Liancourt, Duke of,
141
Romilly, Sir Samuel, 101
Roosevelt, Governor F., 216, 218
Rota, Prof. L. G., 243
Rush, B., 120, 126

Sacco, 23, 263
Sadism, 187
Salmon, Dr. Thomas W., 148
Salsedo, Andrea, 23
Sanborn, Frank, 141, 210
Sanitation, lack of, 161-163, 165,
166
San Michele, papal prison of, 122

Savagery, juristic, 190
Schools for convicts, 213; for illiterates, 213
Schuyler, Philip John, 132
Science, remarkable development of,
93
Scientific differentiation, 201
Scott, Russell, 260
Searle, Sherman W., 16
Sedgwick, A. C., 18
Segregation, 221
Sentence and parole, the indeterminate, 210
Seward, William H., 141
Sex situation, 165, 176, 179, 180
Sexual problems, 180
Shaftesbury, Earl of, 94
Shaw, Bernard, 186, 189, 227
Sheriff, a political officer, 194
Sighele, E., 186
Sing Sing, 137, 214, 218, 255
Skinner, P. H., 279
Sleighton Farms, 203
Smith, Adam, 121
Snook, Jacob, 151
Snyder, Ruth, 243, 260
Society, 40; developed tribal, 44
Socrates, 233
Solitary confinement, 129, 134,
135, 139
Sorcerer, 43
Spencer, Ambrose, 132
Spirit of Laws, 96
Springfield Republican, 247
Stealing Through Life, 229
Sterilization, of feeble-minded and
habitual criminals, 221
Sterilization laws, in 13 states, 222ꞏ
St. Louis, in France (1260), 9
Stocks and Pillory, 62
Stoning, 232
St. Pierre, Abbé de, 95
Strangeways, Major, 240
Strangulation, 239
Straton, Dr. John Roach, 246, 273
Stutsman, J. O., 214
Suffocation, 241
Sullivan, 133

Sweat boxes, 164
System, reformatory, 143; new American penitentiary, 144
System, Auburn, 135, 142, 201; Dwight, 140; Elmira, 141; French report on, in America, 142; inhuman, 181; New Jersey, 138; Pennsylvania, 138, 140, 142, 201
Systems, struggle between Auburn and Pennsylvania, 138

Taboo, 41
Tannenbaum, Frank, prison investigator, 155; quoted from *Wall Shadows*, 183; report of investigations in U. S., 155-165
Territion, stage of, 11
Tesla, Nicola, 243
Thaw, Harry, 260
Thayer, J. B., 25
Thayer, Judge Webster, 33
Thayer, Dr. W. N., 282
Theory of Imprisonment, The, 145
Theory, biological, 1, 5; free moral agent, 1
Thierry, Dr., 275
Third degree, 16, 21, 22, 24; fear of, 23; forbidden in England, 24; persistence of torture in modern times, 15
Tibbits, George, 135
de Tocqueville, Alexis, 142, 202
Torture, early, 11; long history of, 11; as a method of ascertaining guilt, 10, 15; mental, 12; modes of, 12-15; physical, 12
Torture room, 11
Transportation, as a method of punishment, 68; British experience with, 68, 71, 73, 74, 81; other experiments with, 88; French, 88-91; Russian, 91

Treason, 43
Treatment versus punishment, 265
Trial, jury, 33
"Trusties," 177

United States, third degree in, 24
Utopia, 69

Vanderkemp, Dr., 75
Vanzetti, 23, 263
Vaux, Richard, 127
Vaux, Robert, 127, 132, 141, 192
Vengeance, group, 5, 47
Veredictum, 26
Vermin, 165
Vigilantes, 236
Villard, O. G., 22
Vollmer, Chief August, 35
Voltaire, 95

Wall Shadows, 183, 190
Watson, J. P., 260
Wardens, 228
Welfare Magazine, 16
Wergeld, 49
Western penitentiary, 175
Whately, Archbishop, 145, 209
Whippings, convict, 60, 150, 164
White, Bishop, 127
White, Charles, 59
White, Dr. William, 124, 205, 279
William the Conqueror, 26, 61
Wines, E. C., 141
Wines, F. H., 232
Wisconsin state prison, 176
Wistar, Richard, 125
Witchcraft, 43
Woods, Arthur, 35
Work, for convicts, 175
Wymondham, prison of, 123

Yates, Governor, 135

Ziang, Sun Wan, 18

PATTERSON SMITH REPRINT SERIES IN
CRIMINOLOGY, LAW ENFORCEMENT, AND SOCIAL PROBLEMS

1. Lewis: *The Development of American Prisons and Prison Customs, 1776-1845*
2. Carpenter: *Reformatory Prison Discipline*
3. Brace: *The Dangerous Classes of New York*
4. Dix: *Remarks on Prisons and Prison Discipline in the United States*
5. Bruce *et al: The Workings of the Indeterminate-Sentence Law and the Parole System in Illinois*
6. Wickersham Commission: *Complete Reports, Including the Mooney-Billings Report.* 14 Vols.
7. Livingston: *Complete Works on Criminal Jurisprudence.* 2 Vols.
8. Cleveland Foundation: *Criminal Justice in Cleveland*
9. Illinois Association for Criminal Justice: *The Illinois Crime Survey*
10. Missouri Association for Criminal Justice: *The Missouri Crime Survey*
11. Aschaffenburg: *Crime and Its Repression*
12. Garofalo: *Criminology*
13. Gross: *Criminal Psychology*
14. Lombroso: *Crime, Its Causes and Remedies*
15. Saleilles: *The Individualization of Punishment*
16. Tarde: *Penal Philosophy*
17. McKelvey: *American Prisons*
18. Sanders: *Negro Child Welfare in North Carolina*
19. Pike: *A History of Crime in England.* 2 Vols.
20. Herring: *Welfare Work in Mill Villages*
21. Barnes: *The Evolution of Penology in Pennsylvania*
22. Puckett: *Folk Beliefs of the Southern Negro*
23. Fernald *et al: A Study of Women Delinquents in New York State*
24. Wines: *The State of the Prisons and of Child-Saving Institutions*
25. Raper: *The Tragedy of Lynching*
26. Thomas: *The Unadjusted Girl*
27. Jorns: *The Quakers as Pioneers in Social Work*
28. Owings: *Women Police*
29. Woolston: *Prostitution in the United States*
30. Flexner: *Prostitution in Europe*
31. Kelso: *The History of Public Poor Relief in Massachusetts: 1820-1920*
32. Spivak: *Georgia Nigger*
33. Earle: *Curious Punishments of Bygone Days*
34. Bonger: *Race and Crime*
35. Fishman: *Crucibles of Crime*
36. Brearley: *Homicide in the United States*
37. Graper: *American Police Administration*
38. Hichborn: *"The System"*
39. Steiner & Brown: *The North Carolina Chain Gang*
40. Cherrington: *The Evolution of Prohibition in the United States of America*
41. Colquhoun: *A Treatise on the Commerce and Police of the River Thames*
42. Colquhoun: *A Treatise on the Police of the Metropolis*
43. Abrahamsen: *Crime and the Human Mind*
44. Schneider: *The History of Public Welfare in New York State: 1609-1866*
45. Schneider & Deutsch: *The History of Public Welfare in New York State: 1867-1940*
46. Crapsey: *The Nether Side of New York*
47. Young: *Social Treatment in Probation and Delinquency*
48. Quinn: *Gambling and Gambling Devices*
49. McCord & McCord: *Origins of Crime*
50. Worthington & Topping: *Specialized Courts Dealing with Sex Delinquency*

51. Asbury: *Sucker's Progress*
52. Kneeland: *Commercialized Prostitution in New York City*
53. Fosdick: *American Police Systems*
54. Fosdick: *European Police Systems*
55. Shay: *Judge Lynch: His First Hundred Years*
56. Barnes: *The Repression of Crime*
57. Cable: *The Silent South*
58. Kammerer: *The Unmarried Mother*
59. Doshay: *The Boy Sex Offender and His Later Career*
60. Spaulding: *An Experimental Study of Psychopathic Delinquent Women*
61. Brockway: *Fifty Years of Prison Service*
62. Lawes: *Man's Judgment of Death*
63. Healy & Healy: *Pathological Lying, Accusation, and Swindling*
64. Smith: *The State Police*
65. Adams: *Interracial Marriage in Hawaii*
66. Halpern: *A Decade of Probation*
67. Tappan: *Delinquent Girls in Court*
68. Alexander & Healy: *Roots of Crime*
69. Healy & Bronner: *Delinquents and Criminals*
70. Cutler: *Lynch-Law*
71. Gillin: *Taming the Criminal*
72. Osborne: *Within Prison Walls*
73. Ashton: *The History of Gambling in England*
74. Whitlock: *On the Enforcement of Law in Cities*
75. Goldberg: *Child Offenders*
76. Cressey: *The Taxi-Dance Hall*
77. Riis: *The Battle with the Slum*
78. Larson *et al*: *Lying and Its Detection*
79. Comstock: *Frauds Exposed*
80. Carpenter: *Our Convicts*. 2 Vols. in 1
81. Horn: *Invisible Empire: The Story of the Ku Klux Klan, 1866-1871*
82. Faris *et al*: *Intelligent Philanthropy*
83. Robinson: *History and Organization of Criminal Statistics in the United States*
84. Reckless: *Vice in Chicago*
85. Healy: *The Individual Delinquent*
86. Bogen: *Jewish Philanthropy*
87. Clinard: *The Black Market: A Study of White Collar Crime*
88. Healy: *Mental Conflicts and Misconduct*
89. Citizens' Police Committee: *Chicago Police Problems*
90. Clay: *The Prison Chaplain*
91. Peirce: *A Half Century with Juvenile Delinquents*
92. Richmond: *Friendly Visiting Among the Poor*
93. Brasol: *Elements of Crime*
94. Strong: *Public Welfare Administration in Canada*
95. Beard: *Juvenile Probation*
96. Steinmetz: *The Gaming Table*. 2 Vols.
97. Crawford: *Report on the Penitentiaries of the United States*
98. Kuhlman: *A Guide to Material on Crime and Criminal Justice*
99. Culver: *Bibliography of Crime and Criminal Justice: 1927-1931*
100. Culver: *Bibliography of Crime and Criminal Justice: 1932-1937*

PATTERSON SMITH REPRINT SERIES IN CRIMINOLOGY, LAW ENFORCEMENT, AND SOCIAL PROBLEMS

101. Tompkins: *Administration of Criminal Justice, 1938-1948*
102. Tompkins: *Administration of Criminal Justice, 1949-1956*
103. Cumming: *Bibliography Dealing with Crime and Cognate Subjects*
104. Addams *et al: Philanthropy and Social Progress*
105. Powell: *The American Siberia*
106. Carpenter: *Reformatory Schools*
107. Carpenter: *Juvenile Delinquents*
108. Montague: *Sixty Years in Waifdom*
109. Mannheim: *Juvenile Delinquency in an English Middletown*
110. Semmes: *Crime and Punishment in Early Maryland*
111. National Conference of Charities and Correction: *History of Child Saving in the United States*
112. Barnes: *The Story of Punishment.* 2d ed.
113. Phillipson: *Three Criminal Law Reformers*
114. Drähms: *The Criminal*
115. Terry & Pellens: *The Opium Problem*
116. Ewing: *The Morality of Punishment*
117. Mannheim: *Group Problems in Crime and Punishment*
118. Michael & Adler: *Crime, Law and Social Science*
119. Lee: *A History of Police in England*
120. Schafer: *Compensation and Restitution to Victims of Crime.* 2d ed.
121. Mannheim: *Pioneers in Criminology.* 2d ed.
122. Goebel & Naughton: *Law Enforcement in Colonial New York*
123. Savage: *Police Records and Recollections*
124. Ives: *A History of Penal Methods*
125. Bernard (Ed.): *The Americanization Studies*
    Thompson: *The Schooling of the Immigrant*
    Daniels: *America via the Neighborhood*
    Thomas *et al: Old World Traits Transplanted*
    Speek: *A Stake in the Land*
    Davis: *Immigrant Health and the Community*
    Breckinridge: *New Homes for Old*
    Park: *The Immigrant Press and Its Control*
    Gavit: *Americans by Choice*
    Claghorn: *The Immigrant's Day in Court*
    Leiserson: *Adjusting Immigrant and Industry*
126. Dai: *Opium Addiction in Chicago*
127. Costello: *Our Police Protectors*
128. Wade: *A Treatise on the Police and Crimes of the Metropolis*
129. Robison: *Can Delinquency Be Measured?*
130. Augustus: *A Report of the Labors of John Augustus*
131. Vollmer: *The Police and Modern Society*
132. Jessel: *A Bibliography of Works in English on Playing Cards and Gaming.* Enlarged
133. Walling: *Recollections of a New York Chief of Police*
134. Lombroso: *Criminal Man*
135. Howard: *Prisons and Lazarettos.* 2 vols.
136. Fitzgerald: *Chronicles of Bow Street Police-Office.* 2 vols. in 1
137. Goring: *The English Convict*
138. Ribton-Turner: *A History of Vagrants and Vagrancy*
139. Smith: *Justice and the Poor*
140. Willard: *Tramping with Tramps*